Merlin

OTHER BOOKS BY THE SAME AUTHOR:

The Celts
King of the Celts
Women of the Celts

MERLIN

Priest of Nature

jean markale

Translated by Belle N. Burke

INNER TRADITIONS
ROCHESTER, VERMONT

Inner Traditions International
One Park Street
Rochester, Vermont 05767
www.InnerTraditions.com

First U.S. edition published in 1995
First published in French under the title *Merlin L'Enchanteur*
by Éditions Retz, Paris 1981

LIBRARY OF CONGRESS CATALOGING-IN-PUBLICATION DATA
Markale, Jean.
[Merlin L'Enchanteur. English]
Merlin : Priest of Nature / Jean Markale : translated
by Belle N. Burke. — 1st U.S. ed.
p.   cm.
Originally published under the title Merlin l'Enchanteur.
Paris: Editions Retz, 1981.
Includes index.
ISBN 0-89281-517-5
ISBN 978-0-89281-517-3
1. Merlin (Legendary character) in literature. 2. Wizards—Scotland—Legends.
3. Celts—Scotland—Legends. 4. Mythology, Celtic. I. Title.
PN686.M4M3713 1995
809'.93351—dc20   95-15750
CIP

Printed and bound in the United States

10 9 8 7 6 5

Text design and layout by Bonnie F. Atwater
This book was typeset in Weiss with Barbara Svelte and Thor as display faces

ONTENTS

PREFACE

Merlin the enchanter is universally known. He has had the good fortune of becoming a popular figure not only through literary texts but also by way of numerous adaptations for children, comic strips, and films in which he appeared with King Arthur and the knights of the Round Table.

But that does not mean that one really knows this exceptional figure. For the most part, the source of all the adaptations has been the English text of Thomas Malory who, drawing upon various sources, recapitulated in *Le Morte d'Arthur*, sometimes brilliantly, the great fantastic epic of the Arthurian knights. The text of the version called *Lancelot in Prose* has been equally useful, particularly in its development of the enchanter's love affair with the fairy Vivian. We know neither the real person who gave birth to the legend and in whose name we possess poems in the Welsh language, nor the original form of the legend—that of the Wild Man, the man of the forest—that contains all the recollections of an ancient mythology linked to Carnival, to Gargantua, and ultimately, to druidism.

Moreover, confusion has arisen from the different adaptations. Merlin has been considered a simple sorcerer or magician, when in fact we are dealing with a divine representation. Especially among the French public, the belief still exists that Merlin is a character from folklore whose domain is the forest of Paimpont-Brocéliande in Armorican Brittany, when in reality he is a native of the Scottish Lowlands. Having had occasion to write a dramatic text on the forest of Brocéliande for French television[1], and having myself played the role of Merlin in this

evocation, I was struck by the ignorance of our contemporaries as to the precise role and significance of this fabulous (in the proper sense of the word) figure who far surpasses the amusing profile that we are sometimes offered.

Indeed, Merlin is often considered to be an entertainer, a joker who passes his time playing tricks on others and who, one day, falls victim to female perfidy, allowing us to draw conclusions of a moral nature such as: "woman is more cunning than the devil," or "the shrewdest man always finds someone shrewder than himself." In these circumstances, it must be said, Merlin the enchanter can hardly be distinguished from those magicians of comedy who are seen hovering about in many animated cartoons. Merlin, however, represents something very different, and—no play on words intended—he is a terribly spellbinding character for those who want to know his ultimate essence.

This is why I believed it necessary to present an image of Merlin that, without being definitive, aimed to be as complete as possible. To accomplish this, it was sufficient to refer to the oldest and most characteristic texts that relate his adventures. Starting from that point, it was possible to go into greater depth and while analyzing the personage, proceed with the necessary cross-checking and comparisons.

For Merlin was not an isolated case in the great wave of legends that arose from the Middle Ages. Actually, he belongs to no particular time or era if one considers only the legendary figure. Following history closely, however, we find that he lived in the sixth century among the Britons of the north—that is, the Celtic peoples settled in the present Lowlands around Glasgow, authentic Britons who fought to preserve their independence in the presence of the Saxon invaders. How did this actual history, which later fell prey to legend and was embellished by mythological additions, cross the ocean? And how did it become localized in Armorican Brittany, halfway between Rennes and Vannes, in the last vestiges of the immense forest that once covered the entire center of the Armorican peninsula? The explanation is simple. First of all, there are political reasons. When the Plantagenets dominated Britain and a portion of present-day France and aspired to extend their empire over all of occidental Europe, they had a need for mythic support. Faced with the *chansons de geste,* the letters patent of nobility of the Capetians, they wished to develop the legend of a King Arthur, master of Great and Little Britain, glorious conqueror of the continent. And

was not Merlin the counselor of King Arthur? And second, with relations between Great Britain and Armorican Brittany as continual in the
Middle Ages as they were in ancient times, and the British language
nothing more than a variation of the Welsh or the Cornish languages
(also the inheritors of ancient Brythonic), traditions moved back and
forth across the English Channel. It is utterly logical to find identical
or analogous mythological and legendary themes in one or the other
region. The absence of such confluence would be astonishing.

It was necessary, therefore, to place Merlin in a historical context
and at the same time in the literary, cultural, and political context of
the elaboration of his legend. Thus were drawn the principal features
of the character of one of the most famous figures of tradition. Merlin
is, indeed, unique and multiple: he is the enchanter, of course, but he is
also the prophet. What is less well known is that he is also the madman
of the forest, the Wild Man, the master of animals, the sage par excellence, who succeeds in rediscovering the purity of mythical times when
humans lived in peace with the lower orders, the mythical times of the
Golden Age or of biblical Eden.

The figure of Merlin lends itself to numerous commentaries. He in-
terests us not only from an archaeological or literary point of view, or
from the point of view of a dilettante, but also and particularly from
the philosophical point of view. He represents, in fact, a certain conception of the world and of life. His behavior might be the exemplary
model for those who in the twentieth century are endeavoring to rec-
oncile man and nature. By taking refuge in the heart of the forest, or by
agreeing to go to the invisible prison of the fairy Vivian, Merlin withdraws completely. He separates himself from the society of his time
and affirms his discovery of a new reality, a new alliance. From this it is
evident that Merlin, who is taken for a madman, is in fact a sage. Furthermore, he has also acquired a knowledge of the language of animals,
a knowledge given only to rare initiates in our time, although it was
formerly common, as the popular tales of the oral tradition of our coun-
trysides confirm. When we know the language of animals we can make
a pact with them. Moreover, we are able to understand the mysterious
language of nature, to know what it is that nature expects of us. For
nature does speak to us. But in our industrial civilization, based totally
upon logic, science, and profit, and in our urban civilization completely
cut off from its essential roots, which are, however, the source of hu-

manity, we no longer know how to listen to nature, no doubt because we no longer understand her language.

Merlin knows this language. Is Merlin an ecologist? Without any doubt. He knows that the world can continue to exist only if the connections between beings and things, delicate connections in an equilibrium that is constantly being challenged, are fully respected. For this reason it is good to evoke Merlin and to have him tell us, in very simple words, which roads lead to the future. He is a prophet and can, in a certain sense, show us what our human condition can be if we are able to rid ourselves of the consequences of our pride in wanting to rule the world. Is he a magician? Without any doubt, but an authentic magician who teaches all of our contemporaries that the ways of wisdom are perilous and that often they behave like apprentice sorcerers, not to say charlatans.

Merlin is also spirit. And whether we like it or not, spirit, regardless of what we intend by the term, controls our actions and the outcome of history. It is up to us to distinguish the *real*, concealed in the depths of lakes, or in forests.

If one spends an evening in the forest of Brocéliande, one sometimes hears strange echoes among the trees. Skeptics will say that it is the wind singing in the branches. Others will say that it is, perhaps, Merlin's voice pointing out to us the great road of human adventure.

PART 1

The Literary Texts

(TWELFTH TO SIXTEENTH CENTURIES)

Chronologically, the oldest text that mentions the Latin name of Merlinus, corresponding to the French Merlin and the Welsh Myrddin, is a curious work dating from 1132: the *Vita Merlini* of Geoffrey of Monmouth, who was an erudite, latinized Welshman in the sphere of influence of the dukes of Normandy and, later, that of the Plantagenets, who had become kings of England. It is in verse form and is rather disjointed, a compilation of diverse elements probably borrowed from oral traditions concerning a bard-prophet thought to have lived in the second half of the sixth century, that is, fifty years after the famous King Arthur.

In fact, there is nothing Arthurian in this text. It deals only with those we call the Britons of the north, also known as the Britons who were established in the kingdom of Strathclyde, in present-day Scotland. They were the descendants of those British tribes that the imperial Roman government had settled in the frontier zones of the north to protect the island of Britain from the Picts, inhabitants of northern Scotland who made frequent incursions into the imperial territory and ravaged everything in their path. These British tribes had remained much more Celtic than those in the south and the west of the island, who had been slightly Romanized.[1] After the fall of the Roman empire, and even after the Roman troops had left the British Isles, the Britons of the north had been the soul of recelticization and had played a considerable role in British national awareness and in the battle against the

1

invading Saxons, Angles, Frisians, Picts, and Gaels. But this had not happened without internal rifts, and the *Vita Merlini*, like the vaguely historic traditions about the bard Myrddin, echoes the implacable wars between the Britons on the Roman side, ready to perpetuate the empire for their own reasons, and the independent Britons, ready to ally themselves with the Saxons and the Picts in order to eliminate all Roman influence.[2]

But insofar as the *Vita Merlini* is a compilation written in verse by a scholar, one finds in it both a very clear intent toward logical simplification and an abundance of details whose origin remains obscure. Are these oral traditions? Are they folktales? Are they historical fragments? We do not know. Certainly the mythological part is important in this *Life of Merlin*, and at first glance, these references have no connection with the legend that was related to us in the romances of the Round Table.

Indeed, Merlin does not possess the characteristics of magician and enchanter that are readily accorded him in the Arthurian epic. He is at once the prophet, the solitary who lives in the woods, and the bastard child who knows the first principles of the world. He seems to be much more archaic in the *Vita Merlini* than in the courtly versions for which he is more widely known. He appears as if sprung from the night of time, his essential character that of the wild man restored to the primitive condition at the dawn of humanity, when beasts and humans understood each other, when he whom the Latins called Saturn reigned as the king of the Golden Age, the king of a paradise lost through the fault of men. This is why Geoffrey of Monmouth's text is fundamental even if it upsets the general view of Merlin the enchanter. It is the image of Merlin *before his transformation*. Paradoxically, it was Geoffrey of Monmouth himself who, some years later, effected this metamorphosis.

>————————THE LIFE OF MERLIN————————<

"Merlin the Briton was celebrated in the world. He was king and prophet. He was the lawgiver for the proud people of Demetae [Dyved, in Wales] and foretold the future for their leaders. Nevertheless it came to pass that several of them quarreled over the kingdom and there was a merciless war during which numerous cities were destroyed. Peredur, the leader of the Venedotians [Gwynedd, in the

northwest of Wales], warred against Guennolus [Gwendoleu], who reigned in Scotia. Merlin came to combat Peredur and also Rodarcus [Rydderch Hael], king of Cumbria [Cymru, or Wales], both of them cruel. Three of the chief's brothers . . . fell and perished . . . having witnessed that, Merlin was filled with grief and pain and left the war party." Merlin then flees to the forest of Caledonia (Kelyddon in the south of Scotland)[3] and commences to live like a wild beast.

In the forest, Merlin laments his destitution and the rigors of winter. A traveler recognizes him and informs Merlin's sister, the young Ganieda (Gwendydd), who is the wife of King Rodarcus. Ganieda sends one of her servants to play the cithara in order to charm her brother and bring him back to the court. The servant discovers Merlin near a fountain.[4] He then captivates him with music and Merlin allows himself to be led to the court of Rodarcus. He is welcomed with kindness. But at the sight of so many people his madness takes hold of him again, and once more he escapes to the forest. Rodarcus goes to find him and begs him to return. As Merlin refuses to hear of it, the king has him put in chains and brought back forcibly.

One day Queen Ganieda comes to her husband, who removes a leaf caught in her hair. Merlin, observing the scene, begins to laugh. The king asks him the reason for his laughter, but Merlin refuses to speak. After long discussions, Rodarcus promises to set him free if he speaks. Merlin then explains to him that the leaf came from a tree under which she had just met her lover.[5] Rodarcus does not know what to think. In order to dispel suspicion, Ganieda claims that her brother is mad and suggests that his alleged gift of clairvoyance be tested. The same child is shown to him three times in succession, and each time Merlin is asked to explain how the child will die. Merlin gives three different answers: "The child will die in a fall from a rock; he will die in a tree; he will die in a river." It appears that Merlin's madness has been proven. The king is reassured and frees Merlin, who hastens back to the forest. Before leaving he even consents to allow his own wife, Guendoloena (Gwendolyn) to remarry whomever she chooses. But there are certain conditions to his consent: the new husband must never meet Merlin. He must always avoid his path. And on the day of the wedding, Merlin will come bringing gifts for Guendoloena.

Now, the child whose death Merlin had predicted in three different fashions falls on a rock in a chasm while chasing a stag, drowns in a river, and is caught and held by a tree branch. The king begins to think that Merlin is not mad and that his wife is concealing certain things from him. Merlin, however, learns by observing the stars that King Conan (Cynan) will succeed King Constantin (Cystennin)[6] and that Guendoloena is going to marry again. The next day, mounted on a stag and driving before him a herd of stags and deer, he appears in front of the house where the marriage is to take place. He calls to Guendoloena. She comes to the window and is amused to see Merlin astride a stag. But her fiancé also appears at the window, thus disobeying the interdiction. Merlin tears out an antler of the stag he is riding and hurls it at the fiancé, breaking his skull.[7] Then, still riding his strange mount, he returns to the forest.

But while crossing a torrent, Merlin loses his balance and falls into the water. Rodarcus's servants, who were following him, bring him back to the court. Ganieda has her brother watched day and night but, continually haunted by his desire to live in the forest, he falls into melancholy and ceases to eat and drink. Then one day he sees a seated beggar in front of the palace gate and begins to laugh. He also laughs upon seeing a young man buy a pair of shoes with extra pieces for mending them. Rodarcus asks him why he laughed. Once again, in exchange for his freedom, Merlin consents to reply: the beggar did not know that he was sitting on top of a treasure, nor the young man that he would die a few moments later. Merlin's assertions are examined and proven accurate. He leaves for the forest.

Ganieda, however, has made him agree to live in a certain amount of comfort. She has a group of houses built for him, for she herself intends to spend some time near her brother. Not far away and somewhat isolated will be Merlin's abode, with seventy doors and seventy windows enabling him to observe the stars. It is in this house that Merlin will live for the winter months. In the summer he will roam in the woods with a gray wolf.[8] Seventy scribes will collect his prophecies on the future of Britain.[9]

In his sister's presence, Merlin foretells future events. Then he announces that Rodarcus is dead and orders Ganieda to go deliver the elegy at her husband's funeral and afterwards to bring back to him Thelgesinus (the bard Taliesin), who should have returned from Armorica where he had been studying at the hermitage of Gildas.[10] Ganieda obeys. She does indeed return with Thelgesinus and decides to remain with her brother. Thelgesinus gives Merlin a lengthy report on what he has seen, particularly concerning the island of Avalon, here called the Insula Pomorum. "The Isle of Apple Trees, or of Apples [literally, 'of fruits'] is also called 'Blessed Isle' because all its vegetation is natural. . . . The people there live for a hundred years and more. It is ruled by nine sisters under a system of benign laws to which visitors coming from our regions are introduced. Of these nine sisters, one surpasses the others in beauty and power. Her name is Morgen [Morgan] and she teaches the uses of plants and how to cure sickness. She knows the art of changing one's appearance and of flying through the air with the aid of wings, like Daedalus.[11] . . . It is there that, after the battle of Camblan [Camlann], we took the wounded Arthur on the ship Barintho,[12] guided by the waves and the stars. . . . She had the king carried to a golden couch in her chamber and carefully laid bare his wound. She watched over him for a long time, finally saying that he could recover his health if he remained on the island with her and was willing to accept her treatments."[13]

Merlin and Thelgesinus both deplore the unhappy fate of Britain since Arthur's disappearance. Thelgesinus suggests sending a messenger to Avalon to find out if the king has recovered and if it is possible to bring him back. Merlin replies that the time has not yet arrived when King Arthur will be able to reunite Britain, Ireland, and Scotland with Armorica. Merlin is then told that a new spring has just gushed forth nearby. He tastes of the water and immediately regains his sanity.[14] After thanking his creator he asks Thelgesinus to explain to him the origin of this water. Thelgesinus answers with a long and difficult dissertation.[15] Meanwhile, the news of Merlin's recovery spreads throughout the country. He is pressured to reassume his place in society and to become king again, but refuses, saying that he is too old. He prefers to remain in the forest. One day a raving madman

*comes to Merlin, who recognizes him as an old friend named
Maeldin. One time, in the course of a hunt, he had drunk from a
fountain poisoned by a woman who was jealous of Merlin and
wanted revenge. But Merlin had not drunk the water. Now he leads
Maeldin to the fountain and has him drink the miraculous water.
Maeldin recovers his sanity; he and Taliesin decide to renounce the
world and join Merlin. Ganieda allies herself with them and is then
seized by prophetic frenzy. Merlin declares that he will never again
make prophecies, but will remain silent now that his sister has the gift
of clairvoyance, a gift more powerful than his.*

It is clear that the *Vita Merlini* is not in fact a biography of its central
character. His origins are unknown. The author limits himself to saying that he was king; and the work encompasses only a part of his life,
the part in which he becomes the "madman of the forest." This is, in
short, the same image as that of the Christian hermit, but unlike the
romances of the Round Table, the Christian context is very tenuous in
the *Vita Merlini*; on the contrary, it appears that pagan elements, those
prior to Christianity, predominate greatly, although Geoffrey of
Monmouth does not systematically emphasize them. And then, despite geographical confusion, it seems that Merlin's retreat is in the
forest of Kelyddon among the Britons of the north. The manner in
which Geoffrey, as a good Welshman, scatters references to Wales is
somewhat false.

It is completely different in Geoffrey of Monmouth's major work,
the *Historia Regum Britanniae*, written about 1135, which assured his re-
nown. The many manuscripts of this work, its numerous translations in
the Welsh language entitled *Brut y Brenhinedd* (or *Brut des Rois*, from Brutus,
the name of the mythical ancestor of the Britons) attest to its immediate success. And thanks to an adaptation in 1155 entitled *Roman de Brut*
by Robert Wace, a Norman, Geoffrey's work invaded the European
continent and became one of the basic sources for the creation of the
romances of the Round Table. For the *Historia* is the first literary—and
clerical—text to present in coherent fashion the legend of King Arthur;
without repeating the errors of judgment of scholars at the beginning
of the twentieth century, who saw in Geoffrey the only source of
Arthurian literature, one must admit that he played a decisive role in
the creation of the epic cycle sometimes called the British romances.

The *Historia Regum Brittaniae* is ambitious: it is truly a "History of the Kings of Britain" from its origins to the post-Arthurian periods corresponding to the definitive victory of the Saxons over the British. Geoffrey claims that in order to do this, he translated a manuscript dealing with this subject from the British language into Latin.[16] It had long been believed that this assertion was only a trick designed to give more credence to his text, but in view of later research based on certain allusions found in other medieval works in Great Britain and on the continent, it appears that Geoffrey is telling the truth. It is true, at least, that Geoffrey did not make use of one manuscript but of several, and of different sources, now unfortunately lost, which represented the most authentic traditions concerning the history of the Britons. The only remaining problem is the part played by Geoffrey's personal creation. When he traces the Britons to Brutus, descendant of Aeneas and therefore of the Trojans, he wants, by means of this literary trick, to give letters patent of nobility to his people, placing them on an equal footing with the Romans. But was this his idea? Was he the first to have the audacity to incorporate the legend of Merlin into the adventures of King Arthur?

In any case, at the time, the *Historia Regum Brittaniae* responded to a need. It was the fashion almost everywhere to write the national history of a people, and if documentation was lacking one invented it. It was necessary to trace the antiquity of the people in question very far back and to glorify it. Wales, last remnant of the vast British island empire, had to struggle against Anglo-Norman encroachments. To introduce deeds that proved the specificity and the value of the inhabitants was an effective means of combat. Had not the same thing been done in the same era in Ireland, where the famous *Lebor Gabala*, or "Books of Conquest," compiled in the Gaelic tongue by clerics, proposed to clarify all the obscure points of the history of the Gaels? And we must not forget the cultural policy of the Anglo-Norman sovereigns: in incessant combat with the Capetian dynasty, heir to the great figure of Charlemagne—a figure embellished by the *chansons de geste*—they needed an equivalent island tradition to justify their presence and rights, and did all they could to put forward a figure no less glorious than King Arthur. The Plantagenet Henry II would also inspire creation and diffusion of Arthurian romances, a not insignificant cause of the extraordinary spell cast upon twelfth-century Europe by the Arthurian theme.

It is in this context that the Merlin of Geoffrey of Monmouth appears in the *Historia Regum Britanniae*. He is already very different from the Merlin of the *Vita*. In fact, one does not feel that it is the same person. Here it is no longer the "madman of the forest" but the child who speaks—the soothsayer, the magician, even the demiurge. He is already the enchanter, just as he will appear in the French romances of the Round Table. Integrated into the great Arthurian ensemble, Merlin takes on a completely different dimension. Is this what Geoffrey wanted? It doesn't matter: it is a fact. Merlin the enchanter is now established and brought to life before us, the result of various symbioses born, perhaps, of heterogeneous traditions but unique and significant by reason of his mysterious aura.

>——HISTORY OF THE KINGS OF BRITAIN——<

After the death of the British chieftain King Constantine the Blessed (Cystennin Vendigeit), Vortigern (Gwrtheyrn, or "Great King," evidently a surname) usurps power and becomes king, while the two heirs, Aurelius Ambrosius (Emrys Gwledig) and Uther Pendragon, are forced to take refuge in Armorica. Vortigern allies himself with the Saxons and becomes the son-in-law of Hengist, chief of the Saxons. But the Saxons grow ever greedier, and in order to save his life Vortigern must cede more land to them each day. He escapes from a conspiracy during which the Saxons kill many British chieftains and flees to Wales, where he wishes to have an impregnable fortress built.

He chooses Mount Eriri (Snowdon) as the site, but each day the work done on the preceding day regularly crumbles to the ground. Vortigern summons his magi[17] and asks them what he must do. They reply that he must find a fatherless child and mix his blood with the mortar.[18] The foundations will then be solid. Vortigern sends his messengers to seek a child with no father. They come to Carmarthen (Kaermerddin),[19] where they witness a dispute between two children, one of whom calls the other a bastard. They make inquiries; this child, Merlin, is the son of the daughter of the king of the Demetae (the land of Dyved in the south of Wales); she is a convent nun. They bring the child and his mother to King Vortigern.

The king, most respectful of the daughter of the king of the Demetae, asks her for proof of Merlin's illegitimacy. She answers: "Upon his soul and mine, my lord king, never have I known a man who impregnated me. I know only one thing: when I was with my companions, resting in my chamber, there often appeared to me a most handsome young man. He would take me in his arms and kiss me on the mouth. After a few moments he would disappear, and I saw nothing more of him. Also, when I was alone somewhere, he often came to speak to me but I never saw him. And when he had visited me in this way for a long time, he often made love to me in the guise of a man, with the result that he made me pregnant." Vortigern then summons a wise man and inquires of him if such a thing is possible. The wise man replies: "I have read in the books of our philosophers and in numerous histories that many men were conceived in this way. As Apuleius maintained, concerning the god of Socrates, there are between the earth and the moon, certain spirits whom we call incubi.[20] They have elements of both human and angelic nature and, when it pleases them, they assume human form and have relations with women."

Vortigern then has the child brought to him. It is learned that his full name is "Merlinus Ambrosius."[21] Merlin confronts the magi and accuses them of lying. He reveals that on the site where the fortress is to be constructed there is a subterranean lake, and that in this lake two dragons are fighting, thereby knocking down the foundations that are being built. Vortigern orders the ground dug up and the dragons are found. One is white, and is at first the victor. The other is red, and forces the white one to retreat.[22] Vortigern demands that Merlin explain all this. Merlin immediately dissolves in tears, falls into a prophetic trance,[23] and speaks as follows: "Woe to the Red Dragon, for he is approaching his end. His cave will be completely occupied by the White Dragon, who represents the Saxons whom you have brought to this land. The Red Dragon represents the Britons who will be subjugated by the White Dragon, for the mountains and valleys of Britain shall be leveled, and the torrents in the valleys shall run with blood . . . "

Merlin continues prophesying in this vein, which is an inspired lyric flight in a rather remarkable style. He symbolically predicts Britain's misfortunes and the attempts it will make to cast off the yoke of the invaders. He also predicts that a wild boar will come from Cornwall to fight effectively against the enemies of the Britons. This could be an allusion to Arthur, but there are many other elements in these pages of verbal delirium that could refer to various persons and events. The whole thing ends with a grandiose sidereal eclipse in which Merlin, addressing Vortigern personally, advises him of his tragic fate and of the imminent return of Ambrosius and Uther Pendragon.[24]

Indeed, Aurelius Ambrosius, coming from Armorica, does land on the island of Britain. All the Britons rally to him. Ambrosius attacks the Saxons and pursues Vortigern, who takes refuge in a fortress that is then set on fire. The usurper perishes with his entire family.[25] Then Ambrosius, conqueror of the Saxons, reestablishes peace everywhere.[26] He wants to erect a monument to the memory of the four hundred Briton chiefs traitorously massacred by the Saxons on Salisbury Plain. Not knowing how to undertake this, he sends for Merlin, whom his messengers find living near the fountain of Galabes.[27]

When Merlin has been brought before him, Ambrosius asks him to predict the future. Merlin refuses, for in his opinion it is not the moment to reveal things of that nature. Instead, he gives his opinion of the monument planned by Ambrosius: "If you wish to honor the dead by an everlasting tomb, send messengers to the Circle of Giants on the mountain of Cillara in Ireland. In that place are stones that no one in these times can assemble, except by ingenious art. They are large stones that have no equal. Let them be arranged in a circle in that place, and they will last forever." The king is astonished that it is necessary to go so far to find stones when there are so many in the island of Britain. Merlin then adds: "They are mystical stones endowed with various curative powers. In the past the Giants brought them from the heart of Africa to Ireland where they lived. They put them in their baths and thus were all their illnesses cured. They also mixed them with poultices of plants to heal their wounds."[28]

Ambrosius sends Merlin to Ireland with an army led by his brother, Uther Pendragon. After defeating the king of Ireland, who opposed the idea of the Britons taking the stones, they attempt to move the blocks under the somewhat mocking eye of Merlin. As they are unsuccessful, in the end Merlin uses his magic[29] to transport the stones to the ships and so to Britain. There, thanks to his magic spells, they are placed in the desired site,[30] King Ambrosius commands great feasts to be given to mark the occasion.

The Saxons, however, attack again with the support of Pascen, one of the sons of Vortigern. Uther Pendragon prepares to go into battle against Pascen with the aid of Merlin's counsel. But during this time a Saxon succeeds in giving Aurelius Ambrosius a poisoned drink, and Ambrosius dies. A star then appears in the sky and Merlin declares that the king is dead but that Uther must fight his enemies, for he will be victorious. Indeed, Pascen and the Saxons are defeated. Uther has his brother buried and becomes king. He once again takes up the war against the Saxons and their allies.

One day when he is in the fortress of Tintagel,[31] held by Gorlois, duke of Cornwall, Uther Pendragon notices the duke's wife, the beautiful Ingerna (Eigyr in Welsh, Ygerne in French), with whom he falls madly in love. He attemps in vain to obtain the duchess's favors; nothing works. He is in despair. Gorlois, who has observed the situation, quarrels with Uther and declares war on him. He imprisons his wife in the citadel of Tintagel and removes himself to another castle.

King Uther is increasingly devoured by passion. He appeals for help to Merlin who, through magic, transforms Uther's appearance and gives him the countenance of Gorlois. He also transforms Ulfin, Uther's companion, into a companion of the duke, and changes himself into a certain Britaelis, a Cornishman. Thus Uther Pendragon can pass the night serenely in the castle of Tintagel with the beautiful Ingerna, who suspects nothing. "That night she conceived Arthur, the most famous of men, who later gained great fame for his bravery." Moreover, everything goes smoothly for Uther, for a short time later Gorlois dies in battle. The king can marry Ingerna, who will give him two children, Arthur and Anna. And Merlin disappears completely from the rest of the narrative.[32]

The character of Merlin the enchanter is now launched even though Geoffrey never revealed to us what became of his hero. Perhaps he thought that, after all, he had said enough about him in his *Vita Merlini*. In any case, starting with anecdotes recounted in the *Historia*, the romancers of the twelfth century would embroider a grand tapestry of this figure, no doubt utilizing historic or legendary elements different from those to which Geoffrey had access.

It is one Robert de Boron who appears to have contributed most to the expansion of the legend of Merlin. Robert de Boron was a cleric who came from the area of Montbéliard and lived in Great Britain around the year 1200. He must have frequented the court of the Plantagenets, where the Celtic legends inspired him to create a work that probably was quite grandiose but of which a large part, unfortunately for us, has been lost. All that is left to us is the romance in verse of the *Histoire du Saint-Graal*, and some fragments, also in verse, of an account of one "Merlin." But it is thought that his *Merlin* was subsequently adapted in prose, perhaps by himself, and incorporated in the Arthurian ensemble known as the *Lancelot in Prose*. Robert de Boron represents a tradition decidedly influenced by Christianity and for him the Holy Grail remains the keystone of the entire epic of the knights of the Round Table. It is equally possible that certain subsequent texts such as the Didot *Perceval* and the romance called the Huth *Merlin* are more or less faithful adaptations of Robert de Boron's primitive work, at least of his *Merlin* and his *Perceval*. In any event, neither in Geoffrey of Monmouth in 1135, his French adapter Robert Wace in 1155, nor in Robert de Boron, around 1200, do we find the slightest allusion to Merlin in the famous romances of the Round Table. Neither Chrétien de Troyes, though he launched the theme of the Grail and integrated the character of Lancelot of the Lake[33] into the Arthurian complex, nor his followers in *Perceval* mentioned Merlin's name, which after all is rather surprising in view of his subsequent success.

It is, then, in *Lancelot in Prose*,[34] that vast Arthurian epic from about 1230, that Merlin reappears. This time, the legend seems to be complete. Its diverse elements have been amalgamated and there appears to be a connection between the child who speaks, the bard-prophet, and the madman of the forest. It is obviously the best-known version of the legend and the most popularized by modern adaptations, films, and even comic strips. Nevertheless, even in its apparent clarity it poses numerous problems that cannot always be resolved, and it presents very old Celtic elements under a respectable veneer necessary in a society where Christianity cannot be debated.

❯————THE LANCELOT IN PROSE————❮
(THE STORY OF MERLIN)

Furious at the sight of Jesus come to save souls from hell, Satan decides to send to earth an Antichrist who will be born of a devil and a woman. He chooses for his scheme a most pure maiden in whom he provokes langorous dreams. An orphan, she speaks of these dreams to her confessor. The priest advises her never to go to sleep without a light near her bed, for "the devil does not willingly come where there is light." Then one night, remembering the death of her parents, she despairs, weeps, and forgets to light the lamp. "The devil was very pleased. He assumed his human form and, while she slept, he came to her and had carnal knowledge of her." Upon awakening, the young woman realizes what has happened. She goes to her confessor, who gives her absolution on condition that she "eat only once on Friday and abstain from all lust except for that which comes in sleep and which no one can guard against. She promised him. The devil understood that he had lost and was very angry."

It soon becomes obvious, however, that she is pregnant. According to the custom of the time she must be judged and condemned for not knowing the father of her child, unless she becomes a prostitute. Since she refuses to prostitute herself, she is locked up in a tower. She gives birth there to a boy "hairier than any newborn child has ever been" and whom she has baptized Merlin, the name of her maternal grandfather. One day as she is lamenting, the child begins to speak to her and console her. She is so frightened that she cries out. She is taken before the judge, who is ready to condemn her, when Merlin begins to speak, saying to the judge: "I know my father better than you know yours." The man demands an explanation and sends for his own mother. Upset by Merlin, she finally admits that the judge is the son of a priest. The judge forgives his mother and releases Merlin's mother, who will go to a convent. But first Merlin explains whose son he is:

"Know that I am the son of an enemy who deceived my mother. And know that these enemies are called incubi and live in the air. God has permitted their knowledge and their memory to be instilled in me and, like them, I know all that is done and said and has happened. But in addition, because of the goodness of my mother, because of her repentance and penitence, Our Lord has also allowed me to know the future."[35]

A little later, King Vortigern orders an impregnable tower to be built so that he can take refuge there when Uther Pendragon, whose throne he has usurped, returns. But as the tower is built, it collapses. The scholars and astronomers of his court deliberate about the phenomenon and announce that "the blood of a seven-year-old fatherless child" must be mixed with the mortar.

Messengers are sent to look for this child. They discover Merlin who, knowing all, follows them without hesitation. In Vortigern's presence he explains that there are two dragons under the tower. After an excavation ordered by Vortigern, two dragons, red and white, are found fighting. The white dragon is wounded, but before dying he burns the red dragon with his flaming breath. When the king asks him the meaning of this battle, Merlin replies: *"The red dragon represents you and the white dragon the son of King Constant (Uther), whom you robbed of his inheritance. If the two dragons fought at great length it is because you have held the kingdom for a long time. If the white one set fire to the red one it is because Uther Pendragon will have you burned."[36]* Indeed, Uther lands in Great Britain several days later. The Britons rally to his side and attack Vortigern, who is consumed by fire in his fortress.

Once he has become king, Uther Pendragon wants to meet Merlin and sends messengers to seek him. In a forest they find Merlin in the guise of a woodcutter with a very long beard, who tells them, allegedly in Merlin's name, that he will not go to see the king, who must take the trouble to come to him. Uther comes to the forest, where Merlin appears to him in the shape of a deformed shepherd. When the shepherd is urged to lead the king to Merlin, he assumes the aspect of a young man. *"The king was overjoyed and desired to take him to his* court. But he refused, for he was very wise.[37] He assured the king, however, that he would assist him with all of his power." In fact, Merlin helps Uther defeat the "very wicked pagans," that is, the Saxons, and establishes the famous monument of Stonehenge whose stones he has caused to be brought from Ireland.

One day when Uther is holding court at Carduel, in Wales, he falls in love with the beautiful Ygern, wife of the duke of Cornwall, Hoël of Tintagel. The duchess spurns Uther's advances and the duke, furious, withdraws to his lands. Uther lays siege to Tintagel, allegedly to avenge the affront inflicted upon him by the duke in abruptly taking leave of his court. As he is still madly in love, however, Merlin, by means of magic, arranges for him to spend the night with Ygern in the guise of Hoël, while he himself takes on the appearance of the knight Bretel. Shortly thereafter, Duke Hoël is slain. Uther Pendragon weds the beautiful Ygern, but as he cannot reveal to her what happened and as Merlin has made him swear to bestow a gift upon him, he gives the enchanter the infant who was conceived the night he pretended to be Hoël. This child is the future Arthur. After giving him into the care of a wise knight, Antor, who already has a son named Kay, Merlin returns to the forest.

Uther Pendragon dies sixteen years later, two years after Ygern.[38] Following Merlin's advice, the barons meet on Christmas Day to choose a new king. Leaving mass, they notice a large cut stone and on it an iron anvil in which a sword is embedded up to its hilt. Beneath it are written these words: "He who removes this sword will be the king chosen by Jesus Christ." The barons try in vain to pull out the sword. Some days later Arthur and Kay pass by the anvil. Arthur pulls out the sword, which is seized by Kay. Old Antor understands Kay's boastfulness and has the sword returned to its place by Arthur. On New Year's Day in front of all the barons Arthur removes the sword, which is called Excalibur, "which in Hebrew means cuts iron and steel."[39] Despite the reluctance of the barons regarding this unknown young man, Arthur is crowned king. However much Merlin proclaims the truth, the barons rebel against the idea that Arthur is Uther's son. Fortunately, thanks to Merlin's magic and

Arthur's valor, the recalcitrant barons make amends and ally themselves with Arthur before the Saxon menace. Merlin has King Ban
and King Bohort of Little Britain brought to Arthur, and promises
the king's aid to King Léodagan in his battles with his neighbor, King
Claudas, who has rendered homage to Julius Caesar, emperor of
Rome. And Merlin himself goes into the forest of Romany.

In Rome the emperor Julius Caesar has a very lecherous wife who
is attended by twelve pages dressed like girls. Then a young girl
named Avenable, who is disguised as a boy, arrives and becomes the
emperor's seneschal. One night the emperor has a dream which he
cannot explain. On the following day a serf comes to the city and,
kneeling before the emperor, speaks to him: "You will find no one but
the Wild Man to explain your vision." The serf disappears. The emperor then promises his daughter to the man who finds either the serf
or the Wild Man. The seneschal, who calls himself Grisandole,[40] is
lucky enough to be able to summon the Wild Man, who, when he is
before the emperor and his barons, bursts into laughter at the sight of
the empress and her make-believe young ladies, and also when he
looks at Grisandole. Then he explains the truth. All ends well; the
emperor will marry Avenable-Grisandole. Before departing the Wild
Man he writes these words "in Hebrew letters": "Know that the great
antlered stag who was hunted in Rome, as well as the Wild Man
who interpreted the emperor's dream, was Merlin, the prime councillor
of King Arthur of Britain." Meanwhile, King Arthur repulses a coalition of Gauls, Romans, and Germans.[41] He falls in love with
young Guinevere, daughter of Léodagan. On the advice of Merlin,
he returns to the island of Britain to aid the rebellious kings who are
fighting the Saxons. Then Merlin leaves for the forest of Brocéliande,
"the most pleasant in the world, high, resonant, with good hunting,
full of does, stags, and deer." By a fountain[42] there he meets young
Vivian, daughter of a nobleman.[43] He falls in love with her at once,
and appears to her in the guise of a young man. He pretends to be a
wandering manservant looking for the master who taught him his
trade. She questions him about his trade. He replies: "For example, to
lift up a castle if it were surrounded by men attacking it and full of

men defending it. Or to walk on a lake without getting one's feet wet, or to make a river run where none has ever been seen. . . ." Most interested, Vivian promises Merlin her love if he reveals some of his tricks. Merlin takes a rod and strikes the fountain with it. Immediately knights and ladies appear, going in and out of a magnificent castle. The celebration continues for a long time. In the evening, Merlin makes everything he has created disappear except, at Vivian's entreaty, a beautiful orchard called "Haven of Joy." And before leaving her, he teaches her some of his tricks.

Merlin returns to the court of Arthur, who has defeated the Saxons, and in disguise, speaks to the king as follows: "King, it is up to you to create a new knighthood. God has decided that a fellowship will be established around you." This fellowship will be symbolized by a round table "to signify that of all those who sit there no one will have precedence." Thanks to this sacred company, "great benefits and great marvels will come to this kingdom." But, "to the right of my lord the king will always remain an empty place in memory of Our Lord Jesus Christ: no one will be able to take that place without risking the fate of Moses who was swallowed up by the earth, except for the best knight in the world, who will win the Holy Grail and know its meaning and its truth." The king agrees, and at once there appears in the middle of the room a round table around which are one hundred and fifty wooden chairs. Arthur's knights swear to respect the rules of their new fellowship and Merlin, having thus established the Round Table, returns to the forest of Brocéliande.

He rejoins Vivian, to her great joy. But she says to him: "Sweet lovely friend, won't you teach me some new tricks? For example, how can I make a man sleep without awakening for as long as I wish?" Merlin is no fool. He asks the reason for this request. She replies that it is to put her father to sleep so that she can admit Merlin to her chamber. Merlin refuses, but Vivian continues to repeat her request for seven days. Finally, when they are in the Haven of Joy, Vivian, seeing that Merlin is more amorous than ever, asks him at least how to put a woman to sleep. Merlin teaches her the way "and many other things besides: three words, for example, which she wrote down,

*whose virtue was that no man could possess her carnally while she
kept those words with her. Thus she armed herself against Merlin
himself,* for woman is more cunning than the devil. *And he could
not stop himself from giving in to her always."*

Merlin leaves Vivian regretfully and returns to Arthur's realm.
Disguised as an old man he admonishes Gawain, who is hunting,
and sends the king's nephew to fight in the war against his enemies.
A great battle is being fought on Salisbury Plain. Merlin assists the
Britons and intervenes in a quarrel between one of the king's nephews
and his seneschal Kay. Then he attends the marriage of Arthur and
Guinevere and departs from the court in the company of Kings Ban
and Bohort. They pass the night in the castle of Agravadain, where
Ban falls in love with the daughter of the lord of the castle. Merlin
casts a spell that enables Ban to spend the night with Agravadain's
daughter, who conceives a son—the future Lionel. And the following
day, back in his domain of Bénoic, King Ban will conceive with his
wife Helen another son, who will be Lancelot of the Lake. Merlin
stays with Ban for eight days and then returns to Vivian in
Brocéliande.

Vivian takes advantage of this to learn more and more tricks. Always she refuses to give herself to Merlin, taking great care to place
the three magic words under her pillow when she goes to sleep. One
day he takes her to a lake where the tomb of Faunus, the friend of
Diana, is located. He relates to her how Diana, in order to get rid of
Faunus, caused his death by treachery so that she would be free to
embrace a new lover. At Vivian's request, Merlin has the most beautiful castle ever seen built for her. Vivian shows her delight. *"Merlin
was so glad to see her happy that he could not keep himself from
showing her several more of his enchantments. In short, he taught her
so much that from then on he was considered mad, and still is.*[44] *For,
having been instructed well in the seven arts, she wrote down everything."* Finally she asked him: *"How could I imprison a man without
a tower, walls, or irons in such a way that he could never escape
without my consent?"* Merlin hesitates, but as this is the only condi-

tion Vivian imposes for giving herself to him, he tells her that he will teach her how on his next visit. And he returns to Arthur's realm.

Merlin appears at the court in different guises. Then he announces that the Holy Grail has been transported to Britain, and that the adventures that will lead a pure and unblemished knight to the hiding place of the sacred vessel will soon begin. Arthur goes to fight the giant Rion. Because of Merlin's magic, the giants are overcome and Arthur kills their king. A little while later Merlin goes to the king and queen and tells them that he is leaving them forever. They try to keep him, but there is nothing to be done: Merlin takes leave of everyone and departs.

Since he does not return and no one has news of him, Arthur asks his knights to look for him. One day Gawain, the king's nephew, passes through Brocéliande where certain misadventures befall him. He sees before him "a kind of translucent vapor" and hears a voice speaking to him. He recognizes Merlin's voice and asks him to become visible. Merlin replies that he cannot, for "there is no tower in the world as strong as the prison of air" in which his lady love has confined him. And he explains to Gawain what has happened to him: "One day as I wandered in the forest with my lady, I fell asleep at the foot of a thorny bush, my head at its center. Then she arose and with her veil made a circle around the bush. When I awoke I found myself on a magnificent bed in the most beautiful and most impenetrable chamber that ever was. 'Oh, Lady,' I say to her, 'you have deceived me. What will become of me now if you do not stay here with me?' 'Sweet lovely friend, I will be here often and you will hold me in your arms, for henceforth you will find me available for your pleasure.' So there is no day or night that I do not have her company. And I am madder than ever, for I love my lady Vivian more than my freedom." And Gawain returns to Arthur's court where he reports the news of Merlin's fate. The king orders the scribes to put these accounts in writing.[45]

Here is Merlin then, definitively in the forest. That he has chosen his situation deliberately, that this situation is due to insanity or to a mad passion of love in no way changes Merlin's essential character: he is the madman of the forest, if one takes into account that the concept of madness includes the "mysterious wisdom inspired by the divine essence" as well. For Merlin's madness is sacred. He is a prophet and a magician. During the same period, at the beginning of the thirteenth century, we see him become the hero of a morality fable which takes the form of a folktale.

>———THE WICKED DONKEY-DRIVER[46]———<

Once there were two brothers who eked out a poor living selling wood that they hauled on a donkey. One day it was so cold that one of them could not cut his wood. Bemoaning his inability to feed his family, he heard a voice coming from the trees, which said: "I am Merlin, a prophet and a seer. I have taken pity on you and am going to show my friendship by making you rich forever." He made the peasant promise to show charity to the poor and to return to the same place each year to tell him what he had done. Then he showed him a hidden treasure. The wicked man, after having called his benefactor "my lord Merlin," went home with the gold. In a short time his life changed: he became the rich bourgeois owner of many lands. But at the year's end he returned to see Merlin, whom he called only "Sir Merlin," and asked him for more: he wanted to be provost of the town. Merlin granted this to him. The same thing happened each year. The peasant attained a high degree of power; one year he returned to meet Merlin, whom he now called "Merlot," to inform him that he would ask for nothing more and would henceforth no longer return to speak to his benefactor. But Merlin punished his ingratitude. The peasant lost his entire fortune and was reduced to his former poverty.

But Merlin does not necessarily remain in his forest. Moreover, it is specified in the *Lancelot in Prose* that he cannot escape from it without Vivian's consent. We see the old enchanter reappear in other versions of the Arthurian legend in which he actively participates in events that occur in Arthur's realm. If in the *Lancelot* Merlin in some way instigates the quest for the Holy Grail, in other texts he is even more involved. Thus in the Huth *Merlin*,[47] which seems to be a quite faithful adaptation of the primitive *Merlin* of Robert de Boron, the enchanter is the ambiguous witness of the "traitorous blow," or "dolorous blow" by which the Fisher King will be wounded and the kingdom of the Grail made barren and cursed until the arrival of the good knight who will restore the situation that existed before.

⟩————————THE HUTH MERLIN————————⟨

The story relates, with a great many details, the conception and birth of Merlin. Merlin's mother's confessor is a priest named Blaise, who becomes Merlin's companion. Merlin asks him to write an account of the events in which he is involved, as well as the story of the Holy Grail. Everything happens more or less as it does in the Vulgate. However, Arthur, who does not know his own origins, lies with the wife of King Loth of Orkney, already the mother of Gawain, without knowing that she is his half sister. It is Merlin who reveals to him that he is the son of Uther and so has committed incest. He predicts to the king that from this incest a child (Mordret) will be born who will destroy the kingdom. Arthur assembles all the children born at approximately the same time as his incestuous son (for he does not yet know that it is the son of the queen of Orkney) intending to have them slain. But the children are saved. Merlin, who had told Arthur that he was powerless against destiny, arranges for him to be officially recognized as the son of Uther and arranges a "reunion" with his mother Ygern. A young girl belonging to Morgan, the Lady of Avalon, arrives at the court. She carries a sword in her belt and says that only a knight with a pure heart will be able to unfasten this belt. The knight Balin[48] passes the test, but against Merlin's advice lays claim to the sword. Merlin warns him that his act will have disastrous consequences for everyone. He predicts, in fact, that Balin, because of this "sword of the strange clasps,"[49] will deliver the "dolorous blow" that will put three kingdoms in "mourning and misery" for thirty years, and will strike the holiest man in the world. Nevertheless Balin, having been obliged to cut off the young girl's head with the sword, leaves the court and finds himself battling various dangers. One involves a knight accompanied by a maiden. While they are traveling, a javelin hurled by an unknown hand kills the knight and a fragment of it remains in the wound. The maiden pulls out this fragment and takes it away with her. Balin swears that he will avenge her companion, then meets another knight who informs him that the death can be avenged only by the fragment of weapon that the maiden carries. While he is crossing a cemetery, the second knight is killed in his turn. At this moment Merlin appears in disguise and warns Balin that his adversary is a certain Garlan, brother of King Pellehan.[50] He immediately advises Balin to renounce his plan of revenge.

Balin, however, ignores Merlin's advice. Accompanied by the maiden, he comes to a castle where all the young girls must give of their blood to cure a sick lady.[51] Balin is separated from the maiden and locked in a dungeon. He manages to escape, finds the maiden, and reaches another castle where he is welcomed. He learns that the son of the lord has been wounded by means of a spell, and that once again it is Garlan who is responsible. Balin asks to be taken to Pellehan's castle. He eats a meal served by Garlan, then kills him with the javelin fragment. Pellehan rushes to pursue his brother's murderer. Balin enters a magnificent room where, on a table, a lance[52] with its point facing down appears to support itself miraculously in a gold basin. He seizes the lance and strikes Pellehan; the castle collapses. A voice announces that the lance has been touched by unworthy hands and that "the adventures will begin." Merlin then appears in the room, frees Balin, and tells him that his host and the young girl are buried under the ruins. He adds that from now on this kingdom will be called "the Waste Land." Balin dies in his turn, for Merlin can do nothing to save him.

Merlin returns to King Arthur's court. A beautiful young woman arrives at the head of a troop of hunters. She is the daughter of a king and her name is Nivieme or Vivian. She is warmly welcomed by the king, but Merlin falls hopelessly in love with her and does not leave her side. Although she is afraid of him because he is a child of the devil, she profits from the situation to learn the "tricks" known to him.

She proves to be a very good pupil but always refuses Merlin, know-
ing well "that he is only after her maidenhood." One day she decides
to return to her home in Little Britain. Merlin determines to accom-
pany her, and Vivian does not know how to rid herself of him.

    In Little Britain they enter a land called "En Val" where the Lake
of Diana is located. Merlin tells Vivian the tragic story of Diana
and Faunus. To gratify Vivian's wish, Merlin has a magnificent
castle built that he renders invisible to anyone outside it.[53] *Then*
they go to the country of King Ban of Bénoic. Merlin predicts the
magnificent destiny of the young son of Ban and Queen Helen, the
future Lancelot, and Vivian never tires of playing with the beautiful
child.[54] *They then pass through the Perilous Forest. Merlin shows*
Vivian a splendid grotto that contains the tomb of two lovers who
lived completely cloistered there. At Vivian's request, he lifts the
gravestone by means of his magic, for the slab cannot be raised by
human force. Vivian says that she wants to sleep with Merlin in
this subterranean chamber, but when Merlin is asleep she casts a spell
on him so that he can no longer react. She summons her people and
wonders how to make the old enchanter disappear. Someone suggests
killing him, but she refuses. She has Merlin lowered into the tomb
and, as she knows all of the enchanter's spells, replaces the slab so
that no one can raise it again. Then she leaves the grotto. Four days
later King Baudemagu enters the grotto and, hearing Merlin's lament,
wants to raise up the slab. But Merlin recounts what has happened
and tells him his efforts are useless. "Neither you nor I nor anyone
can lift this stone. Only she who imprisoned me here can do it."
It is the last time that Merlin speaks to a human being; his brait
(cry) is heard throughout the kingdom and gives rise to many
marvels.[55]

    It is in the text that we now know as the Didot *Perceval* that Merlin
plays an important and original role compared to previous accounts.
Here we are in the midst of the quest for the Holy Grail, and the enchanter is in no way Vivian's prisoner. The Didot *Perceval* appears to be
a prose adaptation of the lost *Perceval* of Robert de Boron, adapted by

him, perhaps, but augmented and altered by other authors. In any case it is a tradition different from the one used by Chrétien and by the unknown author of *The Quest for the Holy Grail*.

> ──────── THE DIDOT PERCEVAL ──────── ‹

Before his death, Alain, Perceval's father, is informed by the Holy Spirit that his son will become the Grail King. He advises Perceval to go to the court of King Arthur, which the young man does. He is named a knight by Arthur and participates in the renewal of the Round Table that is celebrated upon Merlin's recommendation. Perceval wants to try to sit upon the Perilous Seat. The stone then splits under him, a cry issues from the earth, and night falls upon the land.[56] A voice is heard, reproaching King Arthur for having tolerated this sacrilege. For now King Bron, or the Fisher King, Perceval's grandfather, has fallen into listlessness.[57] King Bron will not get well nor the stone be made whole until one of the knights seated at this table succeeds in reaching the castle of the Fisher King and posing some questions concerning the Holy Grail. Naturally, all the knights leave on the quest.

Perceval has many adventures and meets his sister, who tells him that his mother has died. He encounters Merlin, disguised as a woodcutter, who reminds him that he should not hesitate to ask questions about the Grail. But when Perceval finally reaches the castle of the Fisher King and is present at the celebrated procession so often described since Chrétien de Troyes, he dares not speak. When he awakens the following morning the castle is completely deserted. For seven years Perceval wanders the forests. One day, thanks to Merlin, still disguised as a woodcutter, he rediscovers the road leading to the Fisher King's castle. This time he asks the expected questions and the king is cured. Three days later, having entrusted the monarchy of the Grail to Perceval, the king dies. At the same moment, when all the knights of the quest are together at the Round Table, a terrible noise is heard and the stone of the Perilous Seat is joined again. Accompanied by his master Blaise,[58] Merlin goes to the castle of the Grail.

It is the end of enchantments but not of Arthur's troubles; he must go on an expedition to the continent. During his absence his nephew Mordret assumes power. Arthur does battle with his nephew and pursues him to Ireland. In killing Mordret Arthur is wounded himself. He is taken to the isle of Avalon by his sister Morgan in order to recover and return one day to reunite Britain. Perceval, still king of the Grail, mourns his departed friends and spends his life praying for them. As for Merlin, he builds a house in the forest near the castle of the Grail with Blaise, who writes down the adventures of the Round Table and the Grail and is the alleged author of the narrative. It is here that Merlin will prophesy all that God will ask him to reveal.

We seem to have come full circle; the Didot *Perceval* puts a kind of period not only to the adventures of the knights of the Round Table, but also to those of Merlin. Nevertheless, medieval writers elaborated on this literary theme and often inserted into their narratives episodes that they discovered in oral or written traditions unknown to us. Thus, around the year 1470, a knight by the name of Sir Thomas Malory, who was not a writer but who had distinguished himself during the Wars of the Roses, undertook to translate—or rather, to adapt—into English the huge *Lancelot in Prose*. This work, titled *Le Morte d'Arthur*, was printed in 1485.

In fact it was neither a translation nor an adaptation but a compilation. For Malory does not use only *Lancelot*. Well informed about the Arthurian legend, he takes a little from wherever he finds interesting details and anecdotes not found in the principal source. Thus he deliberately includes Tristan among the Arthurian knights even though the Tristan legend (despite some later episodes) is totally outside the Round Table cycle. It is true that Chrétien de Troyes had done the same thing by introducing Lancelot of the Lake, as did Geoffrey of Monmouth by bringing in Merlin. Also, Malory knows the tradition of Robert de Boron and uses it freely to clarify certain obscure points, especially concerning Arthur's magic sword. Finally, thanks to insular sources, he gives us an unexpected conclusion to Merlin's story. This work, dense and crowded, rich in variegated episodes and extraordinary incidents involving the most diverse characters, is an important element in our

understanding of the legends of Arthur and Merlin. Constantly repub-
lished in England, where it is a classic, it constitutes the essential basis
by which Anglo-Saxons came to know of the adventures of King Arthur
and the knights of the Round Table.

LE MORTE D'ARTHUR

*The story begins the moment Uther Pendragon falls in love with the
beautiful Ygern (Ygraine), wife of the duke of Cornwall. Merlin
promises to help Uther on the condition that Uther bestow a gift on
him.[59] When the king has sworn to do so, Merlin says to him: "You
will sire a son tonight when you lie with Ygern. You must entrust this
child to my care as soon as he is born." Everything happens as in the
other versions. The child Arthur is given to Merlin, who entrusts him
to a certain Hector (Antor), who already has a son named Kay.
Two years later Uther falls gravely ill and his enemies take advantage of the situation to attack him. Merlin has the king carried on a
stretcher to the field of combat. The Britons are victorious, but Uther
grows sicker. Then Merlin gathers the nobles around Uther and tells
him that his son will become king in four days.*

*Uther Pendragon dies. Many barons would like to become king.
Merlin asks the archbishop of Canterbury to summon them all to the
great church of London on Christmas Day. When the barons leave
the church they see the famous sword and everything happens as in
the other versions,[60] except that no one knows that Arthur is Uther's
son. In the end Arthur wins out over the recalcitrant barons and, together with Kings Bors and Ban, fights various enemies. Thanks to
Merlin, the war ends in victory for the Britons.*

*"Then Merlin took leave of Arthur and the two kings and went to
find his master Blaise, who lived in Northumberland. He rejoined his
master, who was very glad to see him. Merlin described to him how
Arthur and the two kings acted during the great battle, and how it
ended. He mentions the name of every knight worthy of praise. It is
thus that Blaise wrote the account of the battle word for word as told
to him by Merlin.[61] Afterwards, he left. . . . " King Arthur is at*

Bedegraine's castle in Sherwood Forest. Merlin goes to find him, but in disguise: "He was clad in the skins of black sheep with a pair of great shoes, a bow, arrows, a red wig, and he carried wild geese in his hand. It was the morning of Candlemas."[62]

Merlin claims his gift from the king. The king agrees. Then Merlin says: "You would do better to offer me a gift that is not in your hand rather than losing great riches. For, mark it well, where a great battle took place there is a great treasure hidden in the earth." Arthur is amazed by the rustic's story, but the knights recognize Merlin and all burst into laughter. One day the knight Pellinor fails to recognize the king, who is alone, and seizes his horse. Arthur, greatly embarrassed, is joined by Merlin—now disguised as an old man—who tells him that he is the son of King Uther Pendragon, which Arthur did not know. Naturally, the king does not want to believe it. Merlin goes away and soon returns disguised as a young man. He tells him the same thing. Finally he makes himself known and Arthur begins to believe him. But when Merlin tells him that he will perish in battle, he is distressed. Merlin replies: "It is not unusual, for it is God's will that your body be punished for your bad deeds. But I have the right to be distressed, for I must die a shameful death whereas you will have a glorious death."

A little later Merlin saves Arthur, who is fighting with Pellinor, by casting a spell on the latter. Pellinor falls asleep, and the two depart. An essential episode follows that is found only in Malory's version.

"Arthur says, 'But I have no sword. . . .' 'It doesn't matter,' says Merlin, 'there is a sword here that will be yours.' They come to a large, beautiful lake, in the middle of which Arthur sees an arm clothed in very fine white silk. The hand that emerged from the sleeve held a beautiful sword. 'There,' Merlin says, 'is the sword of which I spoke.' Then they see a maiden coming toward the lake. 'Who is this maiden?' Arthur asks. 'She is the Lady of the Lake,' Merlin says, and in this lake is a rock and in this rock there is a place like no other on earth, nor is there any richer;[63] but this maiden will come to

you. Speak nicely to her so that she will give you the sword.' The
maiden comes up to Arthur and greets him. He replies to her greeting.
'Maiden,' Arthur says, 'what is this sword that an arm is holding
above the water? I would like it to be mine, for I have none.' 'My lord
King Arthur,' the maiden says, 'that sword is mine, and if you will
grant me a gift upon my request, it is yours.' 'By my faith,' Arthur
says, 'I will grant you the gift that you will ask of me.' 'Good,' the
maiden replies, 'take this boat and row yourself to the sword. Take it,
along with the scabbard, and I will ask you for a gift in my own
time.' Arthur and Merlin tied their horses to a tree and embarked in
the boat. They came to the sword held by the hand. Arthur grasped
it by the hilt and pulled it out. The hand and arm then disappeared
beneath the water."[64]

A little later Merlin asks Arthur: "'Which do you prefer, the
sword or the scabbard?' 'I prefer the sword,' Arthur says. 'Then you
are not a wise man,' Merlin says, 'for the scabbard is worth ten
swords: as long as you carry this scabbard with you, you will never
bleed if, by misfortune, you are wounded.'"[65]

One day when Arthur is in his castle a maiden comes to him. She
is wearing a sword as if she were a man. She asks for a brave knight
above reproach to remove the sword from its scabbard. Arthur tries
unsuccessfully. Other barons try also but are no more fortunate.
Then a poor knight named Balin succeeds in removing the sword from
the scabbard. He claims it for himself, but the maiden tells him that he
was wrong to do so, since with it he will slay his best friend, and this
very sword will be the cause of his own destruction.[66] Several days
later the Lady of the Lake arrives and asks Arthur for the promised
gift: "Balin's head, or the head of the maiden who brought the sword."
Arthur refuses. Balin, informed of what is going on, beheads the
Lady of the Lake.[67] Furious, Arthur drives him away. He flees but is
pursued by the knight Lanceor, whom he kills. He meets his brother
Balan[68] and they both go to the court of King Mark, where they are
joined by Merlin in disguise; he prophesies that the two best knights
of the world will be Lancelot and Tristan. He also tells Balin that he
will wound the most genuine of knights and the most respectable of

men and that, because of this grievous blow, three kingdoms will fall into deep poverty, misery, and distress for twelve years. Indeed, Balin slays Garlon, the brother of Pellam the Fisher King, who pursues him into the castle. Balin seizes the wonderful lance and wounds Pellam; the castle collapses and Balin is buried under the ruins. After Merlin frees him, Balin wanders off again. He and his brother meet without recognition and kill each other. Merlin buries them both in the same grave and puts Balin's precious sword in a safe place.[69] However, Merlin has fallen madly in love with Nimue, one of the Ladies of the Lake. "Merlin gave her no rest; he wanted to be with her constantly. At first she was kind to him, until she had learned from him all sorts of things that she wanted to know. And Merlin was so besotted with her that he could not live without seeing her. One day Merlin takes his leave of the king and queen, saying that he is going away forever." The maiden of the Lake had departed, and he followed her wherever she went. In other times he would have obtained her favors by subtle spells, but she had made him swear that he would never cast a spell over her and he had given his word. So she and Merlin traveled by sea to the kingdom of Benwick where King Ban reigned and was waging a great war against King Claudas. "Merlin speaks at length with King Ban and Queen Elaine. He can see the child who will grow to be Lancelot of the Lake, and foretells the exploits of the future best knight in the world. "Soon thereafter the Lady and Merlin left. Merlin showed her wonders as they traveled. They arrived in Cornwall. And always Merlin slept by her side in order to have her maidenhood, but he never succeeded. And the Lady grew less and less tolerant of this. She would have liked to get rid of him, for she was afraid of the fact that he was the son of the devil. . . ."[70]

"Now, one time it happened that Merlin showed her a rock that was a great wonder. Indeed, it was possible, by enchantment, to slide underneath the large stone. Then Nimue, by means of subtle words, convinced Merlin to go under the stone to show her the marvel. He did so, but she was able to make sure that he would never emerge from under it despite all of his spells. Then she left, abandoning Merlin."

This is a most tragic and "shameful" end for Merlin, the wise enchanter victimized by his insane love for a woman who fears and scorns
him after having obtained his secrets. There is, however, a distinct difference between this Nimue, selfish and calculating, and the Vivian of
the French romances. Vivian was selfish, perhaps, and no doubt anx-
ious for knowledge, but she redeems herself by the single-minded love
that leads her to confine Merlin in order to keep him for herself. If
Nimue is a cold woman, Vivian is a woman in love. Thomas Malory is
the only one to report this conclusion to the love affair between Merlin
and the Lady of the Lake. Where does this version come from? Is it
Malory's invention? Is it one of the versions of the legend that was
current in Great Britain during this period? We will never know. What
should be noted, nonetheless, is the clearly antifeminist spirit that animates Malory's work. We are surely no longer in the courtly era when
the Lady simultaneously represented sovereignty and material, spiritual, and moral perfection. One has the impression, in reading *Le Morte
d'Arthur*, that all women, especially fairies, are frightful bitches: indeed,
Nimue is not the only one to behave in this way. Arthur's sister Morgan, who is said to be the wife of Uryen and the mother of Yvain
(Chrétien de Troyes' Knight of the Lion), several times attempts to kill
her brother in order to seize power. She has a lover named Accolon,
and for his sake she also tries to kill her husband. And Arthur must
struggle amid the worst difficulties because of a false Guinevere who is
seeking to diminish his power. Women, who in the early Arthurian
romances were initiators, following the Celtic model, have become
castrators. It is a sign of the times.

Merlin, however, continues to haunt the imagination, especially in
Great Britain. He is taken over both by the English (who make him an
English seer) and by the Welsh, who regard him as a symbol of their
resistance to Anglo-Saxon might. And the prophecies attributed to him
are studied and copiously annotated. It is in this spirit that one Elis
Gruffud, who is known to have been one of the participants in the
Camp of the Cloth of Gold at Calais in 1520, writes a curious text in
Welsh, *Myrddin Wyllt* (Merlin the Wild Man), in which he revives the
prophet of the *Vita Merlini* in the company of his sister Gwendydd.[71]
This little-known text deserves to be studied, for it explains the state of
mind with which the Welsh intellectuals of the sixteenth century regarded the heroes of their national legend.

> ──────── MERLIN THE WILD MAN ──────── ‹

In the land of Nanconwy a man by the name of Morvryn has two children: Gwendydd, a girl, and Myrddin, a boy. The latter is of unstable mind; he has periods of total madness and periods when his sanity returns. When he is reasonable, he gives voice to prophecies, but only before his sister Gwendydd. He does not live in a house but frequents the woods, where he lives in caves or in shelters he builds out of foliage. It is Gwendydd who brings him food and drink. One day Gwendydd, who has just had several dreams, wants Myrddin to explain them. She begins by placing food and drink near Myrddin's hut. He eats and drinks, and comments upon the nourishment he has just consumed. In addition, he delivers a violent diatribe against wine and mead, which are harmful and deprive the wise man of his reason. Only milk and water find favor in Myrddin's eyes, and one has the impression of listening to a lecture during a meeting of the temperance league. Then Gwendydd asks him to interpret her dreams. Since they are all symbols of the misfortunes of a Britain invaded by the Saxons, we rediscover here the favorite themes of the prophecies dealt with by Geoffrey. One of the dreams, moreover, is characteristic: it is about a field with piles of pebbles. People take the stones from the small piles to place them on the large piles. Myrddin interprets the dream as proof that commoners (the small piles) are exploited for the profit of the nobles and the bourgeoisie (the large piles). In another dream men with axes are cutting a magnificent grove of alders. But from the felled alders spring yew trees. Myrddin interprets the woodcutters as invaders, the grove of alders as the island of Britain, the yew trees as the new generation that will restore its country's power. Finally, these prophecies are songs of hope for a new, free Britain.

In Wales the revival of the theme of Merlin could only be political. In France it emerged from a very different state of mind. It must not be forgotten that the sixteenth century never disowned the old traditions of its rural origins. Rabelais, who embellished his work with multiple anecdotes or reflections borrowed from everything he had heard recounted in his travels throughout France, particularly in Touraine and Poitou, is a striking example of this. And we know that Gargantua is a folkloric figure, the image of an ancient Celtic giant god, in the same way that Pantagruel is a traditional devil of the medieval popular theater. The writer simply revived very old characters and themes to recast them according to the taste of the day and to express his own ideas about the world and life.

Specifically, what made Rabelais decide to write his *Pantagruel* was the publication in 1532 of an anonymous work about the giant Gargantua. This work offers the oldest literary version of the legend and, curiously, it is closely linked to the theme of Merlin. For just as Merlin participates in the quest for the Grail at least in some way in certain Arthurian romances of the twelfth and thirteenth centuries, in this minor epic he is at once involved with the adventures of Gargantua, whom he has, in fact, truly created, and with those of King Arthur.

THE REAL GARGANTUA

"In the time of King Arthur there was a great philosopher named Merlin, who was more learned in the art of necromancy than anyone else in the world, and who never ceased to be of help to the nobility, from whom he earned for his feats the right to be called prince of the necromancers. This Merlin accomplished great marvels difficult to believe in by those who had not seen them. Merlin was an important adviser to King Arthur, and all the requests he made in the court of that king were granted, whether they were for him or for others. He kept the king and several of his barons and gentlemen safe from great perils and dangers. . . ." Now one day Merlin tells the king: *"Beloved and magnanimous prince, be advised that you will have many troubles with your enemies. I wish to remedy this, if you please, since I am at your service and will not always be able to be so because I will be deceived and detained by women. But be assured that so long as I remain free I will protect you from the hand of your enemies."*

Then Merlin, who *"knew all things, meaning that he knew the past through his arts and the future by the will of God,"* takes leave of the king. He goes to the top of a high mountain. *"He carried a phial of Lancelot's blood that he had collected from his wounds after he had jousted with a knight, and also the fingernail clippings of the beautiful Guinevere, King Arthur's wife."* Merlin causes an anvil of

steel as big as a tower to be built, along with three enormous hammers. Then "he had the bones of a male whale[72] brought to him,
sprinkled them with blood from the aforementioned phial, and placed
them on the anvil. These bones were rapidly crushed and reduced to
powder. And so, from the heat of the sun, the anvil and the hammers,
the father of Gargantua was begotten. Afterward Merlin had the
bones of a female whale brought and he mingled them with the queen's
nail clippings." Thus is Gargantua's mother created. Finally, Merlin
creates an enormous mare from a carcass he found on the mountain.

Merlin wakes the two giants and sends them to look for the mare.
Grandgousier and Gargamelle[73] obey, but since they are naked, they
are overcome with desire and copulate. When they return, Merlin
says to them: "You have conceived a son who will perform great feats
of arms and will aid King Arthur against his enemies." He then says
that he is going to leave them and advises them to bring their son,
when he has reached the age of seven, to the court of King Arthur in
Great Britain. So Gargamelle gives birth to a son and Grandgousier
names him Gargantua, "which is a Greek verb, meaning you have a
beautiful son."[74]

When Gargantua is seven years old his parents take him to Great
Britain. They go by way of Beauce, where the mare knocks down all
the trees of the forest situated there,[75] and by way of Mont Saint-
Michel. In fact, Grandgousier and Gargamelle have each brought
a large rock: this is the origin of the Mont and of Tombelaine.[76]
But Grandgousier and Gargamelle die as the result of a purge. Gargantua
does not know what to do. Merlin arrives, buries the parents, and
asks Gargantua to fetch the mare. But when the animal sees the
ocean, she takes fright and flees. Merlin then summons a cloud that
takes both of them to Great Britain. He announces to King Arthur
that he has brought him a person powerful enough to "put to death
all of his enemies if they were assembled in an army." Arthur and his
companions approach Gargantua on the shore where Merlin has left
him and Arthur asks Gargantua if he is willing to fight for him.
Gargantua accepts and requests that an iron club sixty feet in length
be made for him. The club is made according to Merlin's instructions.

*Then they all go to the enemy camp of the armies of Gog and
Magog, who combat them by hurling rough-hewn stones.
Gargantua destroys them all. After the celebrations and rejoicings,
Arthur orders Gargantua to lead an army against the Dutch. Merlin
dispatches him with two thousand men in a magic cloud. The battle
is terrible, but of course Gargantua is the victor. He leads his army
back to the shore where they are awaited by Merlin, who returns
them all to Great Britain by the same means.*

And so, through the imagination of a sixteenth-century author, the
theme of Merlin is linked with that of Gargantua. Basically, it is a simple
return to the source, since Merlin and Gargantua both belong to Celtic
mythology. But afterward the magician-seer will have a long sleep. It is
as if Vivian had confined him for good in the forest of Brocéliande. For
the days of Celtic magic are gone. If in the nineteenth century Merlin's
face reappears in historical or literary studies like a kind of dusty ghost,
it is only the better to bury him in his leafy tomb. He has truly become
Apollinaire's "decaying enchanter."

Even the popular oral tradition will lose its track and its name. In his
Barzaz-Breiz Hersart de la Villemarqué will introduce in vain poetic fragments about Merlin that he claims to have heard sung by peasants, for
the book will quickly be revealed as a fraud.[77] And if the name of Merlin sometimes appears in a folktale it is completely by chance, because
Merlin's name still means something.[78] The inhabitants of Brocéliande,
that is, the forest of Paimpont in Brittany, know Merlin only through
what they hear about him from tourists, and if his gravesite is pointed
out in the middle of this forest[79] it is because one day a scholar decided
where it was on his own authority. But therein lies Merlin's charm: to
make us forget that he exists when he is present in each of us.

PART 2

The Sources

The genesis of any legendary figure is necessarily complex, so much do the most diverse elements interfere with the primitive outline. But, curiously, this primitive outline survives despite all the transformations, all the camouflages, and all the heterogeneous contributions, to the point where it is always recognizable if one takes the trouble to submit a narrative to the most rigorous analysis. And generally this primitive outline has a historical core. It is productive to recall that the Trojan War, presented as a consequence of Helen's abduction by Paris, conceals in reality an economic rivalry between European Greeks (the Achaeans) and Asian Greeks (the Trojans); as for Helen, if she is the symbol of beauty, love, and even of sensuality, she is even more symbolic of the economic prosperity that was first the prerogative of the Achaeans, passed into the hands of the Trojans, and was subsequently regained in battle by the Achaeans. It is the same in the Celtic domain. The legendary story of Taliesin, tossed into a hide sack at birth and found by Elffin, son of King Gwyddno, according to a scenario inherited from the story of Moses, overlays a tangible reality: Taliesin, when a child, had been captured by Irish pirates and, having escaped in a frail vessel, had in fact been found by a king's son.

Within this framework, and without prejudging the psychological or metaphysical meanings that can be drawn from them, all legends contain a historical reality. In Cornwall, not far from the fortress of Tintagel, the funerary column of a certain Tristan, here called "son of

Cunoworus," has been found, and this Cunoworus (Konomor) is no less than the surname of King Mark. We know that Arthur really existed, but was not a king; he was only a simple *dux bellorum* (battle chieftain) in the service of the British kings he and his band of knights protected from the Saxon invaders.[1] So, why should not Merlin, too, be a historical figure?

1

MERLIN IN HISTORY

The sole historical reference we have to Merlin is linked to a battle recorded by historians and annalists—that of Arderyd (now Arthuret) near the Gulf of Solway, about ten miles north of Carlisle on the border between Scotland and England. It was said by some to have taken place in 573, by others in 533. In any case, it took place in the sixth century, but remains very vague.[1] All one can say is that to a great extent Merlin's life seems to have unfolded around the present frontier of England and Scotland in the region inhabited in that era by those whom the Welsh called Gwyr y Gogled, the "men of the north" (literally, "men of the left," the Celts looking always to the east and orienting themselves accordingly), whom we prefer to call the Britons of the north, or the Britons of the kingdom of Strathclyde.

Moreover, all of the old poetic literature found in these Welsh manuscripts refers to this region, including the poems attributed to Merlin, those attributed to Taliesin (at least the most ancient, those believed to be authentic), those attributed to Llywarch-Hen, and those definitely written by Aneurin. It indicates the importance that these Britons of the north must have had. They were the descendants of those British tribes that had been settled by the central Roman authority at the frontiers of the Picts to protect the territory against invasions by these formidable highlanders, of whom we know little. When the Roman empire was dismembered, these Britons of the north represented a considerable force. Having remained closest to their original Celtic civilization, they contributed greatly to the receltization of Roman Britain. And above all, thanks to their warrior traditions, they long resisted not only assaults by the Saxons, the new conquerors of the island, but also the incessant raids of the Picts and the Scots. These were the Gaels who had come from Ireland to settle in Scotland, to which they gave their generic name (Scots), their language (Gaelic), and their religion (Christianity). In this second half of the sixth century the regions between Wales and the mountains of Scotland were divided among different peoples. In the extreme north were the Picts, apparently a very powerful kingdom, but of whose internal affairs we know nothing. There is no doubt that the name Picts comprises peoples of diverse origins among whom can be distinguished the northern Picts and the southern Picts, according to the testimony of the Saxon priest Bede, author of an *Histoire ecclésiastique*. The celticity of the northern Picts is rather doubtful. Were they Scandinavians? It is not impossible. But the indigenous name of the Picts (for the word *Picte* is a latinized form) is interesting: *Cruthni* is Celtic, belonging to the Gaelic branch. This name *Cruthni* appears to be the origin of *Britanni* by way of *Pretani*. Accordingly, the name of Britain would derive from the Pict, which is quite plausible when one realizes that *Britain* is *Prydein* in Welsh.[2] For a long time the Picts were not affected by the changes taking place in the British Isles. They had never been part of the Roman Empire and had remained pagan for a very long time. Only the Picts of the south had been touched, at the beginning of the fifth century, by the Christianity preached by Saint Ninian. The Christianization of all the Pict lands came about because of the Irish and because of the spreading of the Gospel by the monastery of Iona, founded by Saint Columcill. And finally, the Picts were never conquered by the Britons, the Romans, or the Anglo-Saxons, but only by the Gaels of Ireland.

Specifically, as the result of an Irish migration under the leadership of Fergus Mac Erca at the end of the fifth century, these Gaels had established kingdom of Dal Riata on the west coast of Scotland. The kingdom expanded under the influence of Saint Columcill after the founding of the monastery of Iona in the second half of the sixth century, and the new kingdom of Argyll was created. In this way all of Scotland would become Gaelic. But it constituted no less of a danger to the Britons of the north.

They were divided into two small kingdoms, the two chief ones being Gododdin on the eastern front, on the site of the territories of the ancient tribe of the Votadini (whose name they kept) and Arcluyd, now Strathclyde, in the region of Glasgow in the west. Here there is a famous fortress, Dunbarton (literally, fortress of the Britons). Farther south, there was also Rheged, around Carlisle, and Cumbria to the west, adjoining Wales. But little by little the Saxons, coming up from the south, gained land; they ended by cutting off the British kingdoms of North Wales, consisting of the northern Anglian kingdom of Humber (Northumbria, later Northumberland) together with Mercia and Bernicia.

It was in this environment that the battle of Arderyd took place. But it was not a battle against strangers. On the contrary, it appears that the different British kingdoms of the north were incapable of agreement, and in fact made war upon one another continually, weakening themselves until they fell victim to the Saxon invaders. If they had been able to get along together, a kingdom as durable as Scotland would probably have been created; the British tongue might have survived in the northwest of England as it did in Wales.

It is from Welsh manuscripts, heirs to the tradition of the Britons of the north, that we have information about the battle of Arderyd. According to the *Annals of Cambria*, it took place in 573 between a British king, Gwenddoleu, and a coalition of other kings that included his cousins Gwrgi and Peredur. During this battle Gwenddoleu was killed and Merlin, who was present at the combat and had been given a gold torque as a mark of his valor, saw the sky fall on him, went mad, and fled to a forest. From the context, it appears that Merlin is Gwenddoleu's friend, but we do not know on whose side he fought. On the other hand, his legend according to the *Vita Merlini*, identifies him as the brother-in-law of King Rydderch of Strathclyde, who is a contemporary but who does not seem to have participated in the battle of Arderyd. In any case, it is attested that Gwenddoleu is the prince of the Britons of the North; we find him again in the name of a Roman fortress not far from Arthuret, at Carwinley, in fact, a word that derives from Kaer Gwendoleu (Gwenddoleu's fortress).

It was said that the battle of Arderyd had been fought between Christian Britons and pagan Britons. Merlin would have been on the side of the pagans. Actually, this hypothesis rests only on Merlin's reputation as a seer and magician. Yet the poems attributed to him are not as pagan in character as they should be if this were the case. This battle of

Arderyd was more likely one of the many incidents by which the Britons of the isle of Britain became easy prey for foreign invaders by quarreling endlessly among themselves.

One example is typical: we know from the *Historia Brittonum* that during Merlin's lifetime King Uryen of Rheged and his son Owein (Yvain of the Round Table romances) mounted an offensive against the Angles of Bernicia accompanied by Rydderch Hen, king of Strathclyde, and the chieftains Gwallawc and Morcant. It was around 590. The coalition was about to triumph when Morcant betrayed Uryen, killing him out of jealousy because he was the greatest war leader of them all. We have some very beautiful death songs on this subject, most probably authentic, attributed to Taliesin, as well as other poems attributed to one Llywarch-Hen, Uryen's cousin, clearly of a later date. At about the same time, the Britons of Manaw Gododdin under the leadership of Mynyddawg, king of Kaer Eddin (Edinburgh), made an expedition to the south to reconquer the territories occupied by the Anglo-Saxons. The battle took place at Cattraeth, probably Catterick, and resulted in a bloody defeat, no doubt as a consequence of internal dissensions in the British army. This expedition is the subject of one of the oldest texts of Welsh literature, the poem "Gododdin" by the bard Aneurin, one of the few to escape the massacre.

Basically, the British communities of the north had too much of the Celtic mentality of former times to be able to unite. Celtic societies are of the horizontal type in which there can be no supreme authority. Each group governs itself in a kind of autarchy that is on the one hand, a mark of freedom and independence, a rejection of centralization, but which, on the other, is weaker than societies organized along different lines. Certainly the kingdom of Strathclyde was powerful; it commanded the entire valley of the Clyde, a rich region open to the sea. The kingdom of Gododdin on the eastern front extended from Antoninus's Wall to Hadrian's Wall and also represented an important position. Facing more toward the west, Cumbria was the link with Wales. But these kingdoms were in reality only confederations of tribes living turned in on themselves, their little kings ever ready to take arms to broaden their influence or repulse the ambitions of others. These minor kings were surrounded by warriors who constituted a *teulu* (warrior band). In times of peace they all lived together, sharing the evening banquet as they listened to music and songs relating the high deeds of the heroes of their tribe. In times of war they marched as one man under the command of the *penteulu* (the chief of the warrior band). They returned victorious or did not return at all. In short, it was a life of adventures. And household bards, that is, poets charged with singing the praises of the chieftain, with celebrating the memory of fallen heroes, with rallying the warriors in combat, also participated in this life.

Hence there was no state, only interpersonal relations based on a kind of oath of fealty. Though these tribes accepted Roman domination, though they faithfully served the Roman Empire, though they tried, for a while, municipal organization of the Roman kind, they had not forgotten the way of life that was theirs before the conquest. As soon as the empire was dismembered, they rediscovered their past intact. It was the same even in the south of Britain, particularly in the Severn Valley, most romanized of all regions and the spiritual and political center of Britain.

Merlin's environment was thus a strange one. It is difficult to understand it without taking into account the particular background of the Round Table romances. Written in the twelfth and thirteenth centuries, these carry the stamp of a courtly and refined society based on the feudal system. King Arthur of the French romances is more a Capetian king (or a Plantagenet king) than a British tribal chieftain. Merlin is more a sage and a skilled illusionist than a domestic bard in the exclusive service of a man whose praises he is charged with singing. Nevertheless, the reality is there: if we wish to replace Merlin in the historical context that presided over the birth of his legend, we must completely revise our judgment and abandon the somewhat too-soothing images to which we are accustomed. Merlin is not a romantic. At heart he is a barbarian, with all that that implies in terms of originality and power.

So we can posit, as the first element of a properly historical research on Merlin, that he was present at the battle of Arderyd in 533 or 573; that he went mad; and that he fled to a forest. His entire legend can be understood from this.

If the person existed, we may still doubt that his name is authentic. Indeed, the *Life of Saint Kentigern* (evangelist of the kingdom of Strathclyde, then founder of the monastery of Saint-Asaph in Wales) a work probably written in the eleventh century by the monk Josselin, gives us surprising details about a certain Lailoken who lived in the middle of

the forest in a state of extreme madness and passed his time in prophecy. The coincidence is too unequivocal for us to reject it. Moreover,
the tradition of a relationship between Kentigern and Lailoken has been
verified.[3] It must be the selfsame person, especially as certain Welsh
poems make mention of one Llallawc or Llallogan with the surname
Vyrdin. Obviously this proves nothing, but an ingenious explanation
has been suggested for this name change.[4]

First of all let us remember that Merlinus (Merlin) is the Latin form
of the Welsh Myrddin.[5] Llallogan is incontestably the Welsh form of
Lailoken if we assume an intermediate Lailocen. The surname of Vyrdin
coupled with Llallogan shows the identity of two people. But this surname must come from a faulty analysis of the name of the city of
Carmarthen (Caerfyrddin), formerly Kaermyrddin. It would have been
understood as City (Kaer) of Merlin (Myrddin) when in reality its name
of the city comes from Castrum (Kaer) Moridunum, the second word
meaning "maritime fortress," reinforced by *caer*. Obviously this faulty
analysis can be ascribed only to a medieval scholar desirous of making
eponymous reconciliations, perhaps even Geoffrey of Monmouth, or
at least one of his predecessors. It should be noted that in the *Historia
Regum Britanniae*, it is precisely at Carmarthen that the envoys of King
Vortigern find the young Merlinus Ambrosius. So, where does it stand?

This hypothesis is in no way impossible, especially as there are many
other cases of this sort. But what is most disturbing is not the discovery
that Merlin's name was not Merlin, but the doubt systematically cast
on the *Vita Merlini* and the tradition of Geoffrey, as well as the *Annals of
Cambria*, which use the name Merlin, and the absolute belief in what is
related in the *Life of Saint Kentigern*. Who is wrong and who is right? The
name Myrddin-Merlin is perhaps the oldest, and for one reason or another, was later changed to Llallogan-Lailoken. After all, in many
folktales one discovers typical heroes of ancient epics but with different names. The name has nothing to do with it; it is the person who
matters. Lacking a truly conclusive document it is better to refer to the
existence of a certain Myrddin-Merlin.

And really, what would it change? This way we are assured of the
presence in the second half of the sixth century of a person named
Merlin, or Lailoken, in the kingdom of Strathclyde, under King
Rydderch (Rodarcus), then under King Melred, who was a contemporary of Saint Kentigern. We are also sure that this person participated

in 533, or more probably in 573, in the battle of Arderyd, a battle waged among various British chieftains; that he there acquired a golden torque, symbol of victory and valor; that suddenly he went mad; and that he took refuge in the heart of a forest to lead a solitary life and make predictions. Was he a bard, that is, a poet? Most certainly, and he could only have been the personal bard of Gwenddoleu, as Taliesin, his contemporary, was the bard of Uryen Rheged, or Aneurin of King Gododdin. If he had not been a bard, there would be no poems at all attributed to Myrddin. And these poems exist, even if they are apocryphal in the form in which they have come down to us.

2

POEMS ATTRIBUTED TO MERLIN

 Apart from the prophecies in Latin that were disseminated almost everywhere in France and Great Britain during the Middle Ages, there are seven poems written in Welsh attributed to Myrddin-Merlin. One of them exists only in a late (end of the eighteenth century) anthology known as the *Myvirian Archaeology of Wales*, a kind of corpus of everything that could be collected at the time in the way of Welsh manuscripts; the poem is "Gorddodau," that is, the "Fouissements" [excavations]. The others are reproduced in ancient manuscripts. The "Dialogue between Merlin and Taliesin," "The Birches," "The Apple Trees," "The Song of the Swine," and "The Song of Yscolan" are to be found in *The Black Book of Carmarthen* (Peniarth collection, no. 1), the oldest of all Welsh manuscripts, dating from the end of the twelfth century. The "Dialogue between Merlin and his sister Gwendydd" appears in *The Red Book of Hergest*, a precious manuscript from the fourteenth century (Jesus College manuscript no. 1) that contains the Welsh *Mabinogion* in its entirety and some verses of the "Fouissements."

These manuscripts are in Middle Welsh, the language of the time of their transcription. But very often one has the impression of looking at texts whose language has been updated, an impression justified by the fact that certain verses are incomprehensible, while others have preserved archaisms[1] that can be explained only by an awkward copy of a lost original in Old Welsh. It goes without saying that it is almost impossible to assign an accurate date to the composition of these poems. Some of them have been altered from a plainer primitive text, as can be seen from the contemporary allusions (for example, the Anglo-Norman penetration in Wales at the time of the Plantagenets) and others were invented to back up the case according to the *Vita Merlini* and the *Prophecies* disseminated by Geoffrey.

The poems included in these manuscripts[2] are all native to the land of the Britons of the north, whose mark and spirit they bear. But not one of these original poems has come down to us. It is probable that, following the Celtic custom, writing was not recommended; bardic poems were retold orally. And after the Anglo-Saxon advances when the Britons of the north had to fall back on one hand to the area around Dumbarton until the eleventh century and on the other hand toward Wales, they took their oral tradition with them. When Rhodri Mawr (Rhodri the Great) effected a spectacular recovery of the Britons of Wales in the ninth century, he made a point of preserving the cultural patrimony of his ancestors. He himself was descended from a family of Britons of the north—the line of Cunedda of Gododdin—and he encouraged the writing down of all the poems and narratives that were still hawked by bards from generation to generation. Because of this we possess some fragments of the great literary monuments of the heroic British era.

Taking into account then the various interpolations and alterations resulting from successive copies, we can judge the putative state of mind of the historical Merlin. There is obviously no question of his love for Vivian, or Nimue; there is no question of King Arthur (fifty years had passed since the Arthurian happenings); but there is some question about his sister Gwendydd, with whom he maintains privileged relations which lend themselves to detailed commentaries. There is also some question about the kings of that era—Rydderch, Gwenndoleu, Peredur, and Morcant—and of a king of Gwynedd (North Wales) whom he makes a participant in the battle of Arderyd.

And then, in one of his poems, the curious "Dialogue between Myrddin and Taliesin," he introduces this fantastic character, at one historic and legendary: the household bard of Uryen of Rheged, according to tradition a kind of twice-born prophet gifted with all druidic lore. The subject of the poem is the battle of Arderydd. Each of the two poets recounts the heroic deeds they have witnessed. It should be noted that Gwenddoleu is absent from this warrior hymn. The text ends like this:

Seven score noble warriors went toward the shadows.
In the forest of Kelyddon they have found death.
Since I, Myrddin, am first after Taliesin,
let my prophecy be shared by us both.

The poem, then, is signed by Merlin. Note that according to the rules of courtesy he calls himself "first after Taliesin." But that may also be an allusion to the fact that in the Welsh tradition Taliesin is considered the *pennbardd* (chief bard) par excellence, and that he is often called *pennbeirdd* (chief of the bards) in medieval texts. Moreover, the *Historia Brittonum* mentions him alongside Aneurin, Talhearn Tatagwen, and Cian, other celebrated bards of the time of Maelgwn Gwynedd and Uryen Rheged. We know that in the *Vita Merlini* Geoffrey has Taliesin come to Merlin's retreat. There is nothing extraordinary about the relationship between the two men as they were contemporaries, and colleagues, as well. We will see later on how the legend of Taliesin entwines with that of Merlin.

The poem "The Birches" is more naturalistic. The poet, finding himself alone in the forest, speaks to the trees and the animals to foretell Britain's misfortunes. This is the traditional image of Merlin as a man of the woods. But the general tone is that of the prophecies recounted by Geoffrey, with historical allusions so precise that the creation of the poem in a relatively recent age is certain:

Blessed be the silver birch of the valley of the Gwy
whose branches fall one against the other.
It will be there at the battle of Arderyd,
when the herds will bellow at the Mochwy ford,
when lances and cries will burst forth at Dyganwg,
when Edwin[3] will spread his dominion over Mon[4],
when pale and agile young men,
dressed in red, will come to meet the troops . . .

The poem "The Apple Trees," which is very long, is composed of very diverse elements: it seems to contain an outline of Merlin's madness and of the circumstances in which he led his solitary life in the heart of the forest. Apart from that, numerous alterations were made to justify Merlin's state of prophetic ecstasy by allusions to events that would take place in future ages. But the general tone of the poem is naturalistic, with the poet addressing the trees and beasts of the forest, integrated as he is in a universe beyond time and space, the paradisiacal universe that shamans attempt to recreate in their trances.

> Sweet apple tree, you of the lovely branches
> putting forth vigorous buds on all sides,
> I will predict in the presence of the master of Marcho
> that one Wednesday, in the valley of Machway [?]
> there will be blood
> and joy for the men of Lloegr[5] whose tears will be red.

Merlin turns toward a familiar animal who lives in the forest, a young wild boar who keeps him company. He needs to speak with a living being:

> Listen, little pig: on Thursday joy will come
> to the Kymry[6] and their powerful troops
> who will defend Kymmynawd with great strokes of the sword
> They will make a great massacre of Saxons with their lances of ash.
> They will use their heads to play at bowls.
> I predict the truth without disguising it:
> I predict that a child will grow up who today is hidden in the south.[7]

But the poet does not forget that the Saxons are not the only enemies to be feared. The prophecy seems to pass in review all the invasions of the Isle of Britain:

> Sweet apple tree with yellow reflections,
> you who grow on a hill above the moor,
> I will predict a war in Britain
> to defend our borders against the men of Ywerddon.[8]
> Seven ships will come by the great water,
> and seven hundred men by sea to fight us.
> Of them, none will return to his home
> for seven, empty-handed after defeat.[9]

Then, brusquely, the poem returns to Merlin's situation. He laments his fate:

Sweet apple tree of lush foliage,
I have fought beneath you to please a maiden,
shield on shoulder and sword on hip.
I have slept alone in the forest of Kelyddon.[10]
Listen, little pig, why do you think of sleep?
Lend your ear to the sweet song of birds.
Kings will come across the sea on Monday
and the Kymry will be blessed.
Sweet apple tree that grows in the clearing,
the nobles of Rydderch's court do not see you[11]
though they trample the earth at your feet.
To their eyes the faces of heroes are terrible.
Gwendydd no longer loves me and comes no more to see me.[12]
I am hateful to Gwassawg, one of Rydderch's faithful,
for I have slain his son and his daughter[13]
May merciless death come to me. . . .
Since Gwenddoleu, no prince does me honor.
I have neither joy nor a woman's company.
At the battle of Arderyd I received a gold torque,
and now she who is white as a swan scorns me.

This part of the poem is extremely interesting. First, it contains no prophecy other than a vague allusion to the kings who will come, and is therefore more likely to be authentic, or so at least we may suppose. Furthermore, it contains elements that can shed light on the complete legend, and especially its conclusion, in the French romances.

In fact, it refers to a girl for whom Merlin supposedly fought. It is not about Arderyd nor any other war, for in his capacity as a personal bard Merlin would have been obliged to accompany the chieftain into battle. It is specified, moreover, that this battle took place under the tree. Is it an allusion to a lost episode of Merlin's life or legend in which he fought for the love of a girl? Perhaps, but if so, what girl? It can only be Gwendydd, who is named later and whom he reproaches for no longer coming to visit him. Likewise, "she who is as white as a swan" can designate only Gwendydd. Therefore one can deduce that the relationship between Merlin and his sister Gwendydd is more than ambiguous. It is clear. It is a case of fraternal incest about which we will

speak again. For Ganieda's role in the *Vita Merlini*, in which Merlin prefers her to his own wife; the care and attention toward her brother with
which the Welsh tradition credits Gwendydd; the complex character
of the Vivian of the French romances, who is also the Lady of the Lake;
all this exists within the framework of a kind of sacred union. But because of the Christian morality of the environment in which the legend is expressed, this incestuous aspect is veiled. No doubt that is why
the character of Gwendydd disappears from the courtly French versions and is replaced by Vivian, who has no kinship with the hero.

In the "Song of the Swine" the bucolic and naturalistic aspect is even
more marked than in the preceding poems. Aside from one small prophecy which seems to be inserted in a primitive text, the essence of the
poem is Merlin's lamentation upon his fate:

> Listen, little pig: I have trouble sleeping
> so shaken am I by my sorrows.
> For fourteen years I have suffered so much
> that now my appearance is wretched.
> What does it matter to Rydderch, celebrating tonight,
> that I spent last night without sleeping,
> snow up to my knees
> and needles of ice in my hair, sad fate. . . .
> Listen, little pig: is the mountain not green?
> My coat is thin. There is no rest for me.
> My face is pale. Gwendydd comes no more to see me.
> When the men of Brynych[14] come to these shores with their armies,
> the Kymry will conquer and the day will shine.
> Listen, little pig: it is not my design
> to listen to the water birds make a great din.
> My hair is sparse, my clothing not warm,
> the vale is my loft, but I have no grain.
> My summer harvest gives small satisfaction.
> Since the battle of Arderyd I can feel nothing,
> not if the sky fell and the sea overflowed.

The dominant sentiment in this song is one of abandonment. Merlin
complains of his loneliness and of the scorn in which his contemporar-

ies hold him. The general tone recalls that of the poems attributed to Llywarch Hen, particularly those in which the self-styled poet bemoans his old age.[15] This appears to be a commonplace of Welsh poetry. But if we think about it, the situation is the same. After the death of his protector Kyndylan, Llywarch the Elder retreated to a forest. There he spent his time wailing and deploring the sad events he had witnessed. And always, in this melancholy and somewhat romantic complaint, the shadow of battles rises from the contemplation of nature.

But even here Vivian's confinement of Merlin is not contradicted. Gwendydd appears to have deserted her brother. Alone in the heart of the forest, unable to leave it, he wails like someone who had not chosen of his own volition to live in this solitude. One would think that something prevented him from leaving and rejoining the society of men. Is this obstacle an enchantment or a curse? Another poem attributed to Merlin inclines to the second opinion. It is the song of Yscolan. But the problem posed by this poem is insoluble:

> Black is your horse, black your cloak,
> black your face, black yourself,
> yes, all black. Is it you, Yscolan?
> I am Yscolan the scholar.[16]
> My weak reason is clouded over.
> Is it irreparable, to have offended the master?
> I have burned a church, slain a school's cows,
> hurled the Book in the waves.
> My penance is heavy indeed. . . .

According to this text then a certain Yscolan or Scolan committed grievous misdeeds for which he is punished. Among other things, he threw a book into the waves. This story has been compared to what actually happened to Saint Columcill (Columba), who "borrowed" a missal of great value and was exiled from Ireland, not for that, but for political reasons. He settled on the isle of Iona on the Scottish coast, where he founded his famous monastery, center of Celtic Christianity. So the mysterious Scolan could be Columcill, "the Dove of the Church," whom the continentals prefer to call Colomba to distinguish him from Saint Colomban, founder of Luxeuil and of Bobbio. But it seems difficult to believe.

Furthermore, there is a popular song in Armorican Brittany about a certain Yann Skolan; in his *Barzaz-Breiz* Hersart de la Villemarqué did not fail to find a place for it, augmenting it with fragments of other songs that have nothing to do with the subject.[17] But even if La Villemarqué must be considered suspect and the miraculously discovered songs false, the song of Yann Skolan certainly exists, and during the nineteenth century different versions were collected in several places.

It is possible that the poem about Yscolan belongs to an insular and Armoricain British tradition. But on which historical fact is it based, if indeed there was one? For if the theme developed in this poem attributed to Merlin is identical in the two principal regions of the Brittonic domain, it exists also in the Gaelic domain; it plainly refers to an event of 837, namely the battle of Moira in Ireland, during which a certain Suibhné (Sweeney), the king of Dal n'Araide, went mad and fled to the woods. Now, according to the Irish account by which his story has been handed down to us, Suibhné, having learned that Saint Ronan wanted to build a church in his country, *had thrown the saint's psalter into a lake.* The precious book was brought back by an otter, but Ronan cursed Suibhné, which explains why he lost his mind in battle. It is difficult to tell if the anecdote of Suibhné is historical, for his legend resembles the *Vita Merlini* too closely. But one may ask whether Suibhné's legend did not become Merlin's, or if on the contrary, it was Merlin's legend that gave rise to that of Suibhné.[18] This is much more likely because of the chronological precedence of the historical Merlin. In any case, too many coincidences exist for it to be pure chance. And the problem posed by the song of Yscolan remains unsolved.

The "Dialogue between Merlin and Gwendydd" is also curious. Though it seems not to have any authentic elements, it reveals the state of mind of those who spread Merlin's legend. Merlin and his sister evoke departed loved ones and bemoan the fate of human beings. One understands that Merlin is dying and that his sister is with him at the end. Merlin, "decaying enchanter," is quite violent as an old man. His sister says to him:

> *My only brother, do not be angry with me.*
> *Since the battle of Arderyd I have been sick.*
> *I seek only to know*
> *and I commend you to God.*

I too, I commend you
to the lord of all creatures,
white Gwendydd, refuge of poetry. . . .

Then Gwendydd asks her brother to receive communion before dying. Merlin refuses:

I will not receive communion
from excommunicated monks
whose cloaks fall to their hips.
Let God himself give it to me.

I shall commend my blameless brother
to the high City.
May God look after Myrddin.

I shall commend my sister
who is above reproach to the high City.
May God look after Gwendydd.

This poem displays a certain amount of anticlericalism, or at the very least the desire to restrict Merlin to a marginal position. After all, he lived his life outside of society and its laws. He returned to the natural world, where he rediscovered the ways and ideas of the ancient druids who had communed with nature and always refused to build temples,[19] claiming that divinity was accessible only in the midst of forests, in the *nemeton*,[20] or in deserted places away from tumult. It is certain that the poem makes of Merlin not a pagan (he requests communion of God himself), but a sort of heretic, result of the synthesis of Christianity and the old religion of the Celts. This was the state of mind of the neo-bards of the twelfth and thirteenth centuries who developed the legend of Taliesin, attributing to him metaphysical poems that show a rather astonishing syncretism. And they used Merlin as they used the equally strange figure of Taliesin.

Moreover, the "antiquarians" of the twelfth and thirteeth centuries did not yield so soon. They produced a "posthumous" poem of Merlin's, the famous "Fouissements." Here the prophecies follow one after another, and as Merlin is supposed to be speaking from his grave, the verbal delirium knows no limits. Nevertheless, there are interesting verses in this poem:

To the man who speaks from his tomb,
it has been told that within seven years
the horse of Eurdein, the Man of the north, will die.

I have drunk wine in a shining goblet
with the chieftains of the cruel war.
My name is Myrddin, son of Morvryn.

I have drunk wine in a cup
with the chieftains of devouring war.
Myrddin is my glorious name. . . .

Merlin's warlike aspect is thus emphasized, reminding us that in the Arthurian romances Merlin is always Arthur's military counselor. He is the one who dictates to the king the course of action to follow, and whom Arthur obeys blindly. It is also curious to note that in this poem from beyond the grave Merlin reveals his father's name: it is Morvryn, whom we have already encountered in the text of *Merlin the Wild Man.* This differs greatly from the courtly French texts and Geoffrey of Monmouth, who make of Merlin a "fatherless child" or call him the son of the devil.

So Merlin has entered literature not only by way of his legend, but also through the poems attributed to him. An old Welsh text dating from the tenth century, or at any rate from before the Viking incursions, which is known by the name of *Armes Prydein* (the Prophecies of Britain) and included in the *Book of Taliesin*, also mentions Merlin. The poem is attributed to Taliesin, but everything unfolds as if the presumed author was passing on Myrddin's words. Beginning in the tenth century, prophecies that one wanted judged authentic at all costs were credited to Merlin. This indicates the importance the figure of Myrddin-Merlin had assumed in the oral traditions of the northern Britons and, later, the Welsh.

Finally, mention should be made not of a poem but of the simple summary of a legend about Merlin as it was to a certain extent codified by one of the *Triads of the Isle of Britain.* It is known that these famous *Triads,* composed in Welsh in very different eras up until the sixteenth century, claim to sum up in three precise examples the principal events, traditions, and beliefs of the island Britons. Now, one of the *Triads* says this: "Three complete disappearances from the isle of Britain . . . one by

Myrddin, the bard of Emrys Gwledig, and his nine *cylveirdd*[21] who sailed by sea toward Ty Gwydrin.[22] It was never said where they had gone."[23] In its concision, this text echoes a tradition according to which Merlin vanished during a maritime expedition. There is no mention of this story anywhere else.[24]

What are we to think? The lost legend of Merlin disappearing while he searched for the glass house in no way contradicts the enchanter's confinement in the forest of Brocéliande. There is an obvious connection between this house and the invisible air castle in which Vivian confined her lover. And with this anecdote added to the rest of his legend, we understand that Merlin is truly a mythological figure whose significance is far greater than the dimension of his actual historical existence.

We come upon Merlin's fame throughout Wales all during the Middle Ages. There were many adaptations of the "Prophecies" in Latin and Welsh and in English. Continental literature was largely inspired by it. It could probably be argued that Merlin was the most prolific of all medieval poets; the number of poems or predictions attributed to him defies any attempt at nomenclature. It is not unusual to discover, even now, in a little-known or forgotten manuscript, a page signed by the enchanter-bard.[25]

Myrddin's name is on everyone's lips. If it results from a misreading of Kermerddin, no matter. That the original name had been Lailoken-Llallogan does not seem to have been taken into account. One of the *Triads of the Isle of Britain*, those digests so representative of the state of mind of the Welsh cultured classes in the Middle Ages, goes so far as to assert that the island of Britain was once called by Merlin's name: "The first name of this island before it was occupied and inhabited was *Clas Myrddin*. After it had been occupied and inhabited it was called *Ynes Mel*.[26] After its conquest by Prydein ab Aedd Mawr, it was called the isle of Prydein."[27] Of course, all this was based only on the imagination of the "antiquarians" who sought to affirm by any and all means a quasi-divine or quasi-magical origin for the British people. Eponymous heroes were required, and they were found. Since the city of Kaermerddin was very old, it had to be linked with an ancient event. And so this story of Clas Myrddin, *clas* (from the Latin *classis*) meaning "community, sanctuary," then "tribe, country," was invented. In the beginning, then, Britain was actually the Country of the Community of Merlin, from which sprang the importance accorded to the bard-prophet.

Such a success made it easy to double or even multiply Merlin. Another of the *Triads of the Isle of Britain* reveals this: "Three principal bards of the island of Britain, Merddin Emrys, Merddin son of Morvryn, Taliesin chief of the bards."[28] So there would have been two Merlins: the Merlinus Ambrosius (Merddin Emrys) of the *Historia Regum Britanniae*, and the mad poet of the forest of Kelyddon, considered the son of Morvryn. This is evidently logical, since the Merlin of Geoffrey of Monmouth is a child with no father. In any case, it proves the complexity of the character and the various contributions from which the final image benefited. It is even said in a passage of the *Iolo Manuscripts*, that collection of texts and traditions compiled by the scholar Iolo Morganawc at the end of the eighteenth century,[29] that Myrddin was the son of a certain Morydd and the great-grandson of Coel Godebawg, and that he was a monk in the monastery founded by Saint Illtud. The monk, the hermit, and the poet are compatible: they are all inspired, therefore they are prophets. After all, when Merlin decides to live secluded in the forest, accepting only his sister's company, he does nothing that was not done by the great saints of Celtic Christianity in Ireland, in Great Britain, or in Armorican Brittany.

3

P THE ARALLEL TEXTS

The earliest reference to the character who would become Merlin the enchanter is found in the *Historia Britonnum*, a small historical compilation attributed to one Nennius, who simply revised it subsequently.[1] In its essentials this text appears to be very old and relatively trustworthy. It was probably written around 630 by one of the sons of Uryen Rheged, possibly Rhun, brother of Owein, the hero immortalized by Chrétien de Troyes in his *Chevalier au Lion* under the name Yvain. In any case, the manuscripts of the *Historia Brittonum* are many and the oldest, if not the most complete, called the *Manuscript of Chartres*, came from Britain and dates from the ninth century.[2]

It springs, in all events, from a tradition of the northern Britons, and is about King Vortigern, who wishes to build an impregnable tower where he can be safe from his enemies. The tower crumbles each time its construction is attempted. Then Vortigern takes counsel with his magi, who announce that the blood of a fatherless child must be mixed with the mortar used for the foundation. Vortigern orders a search for an appropriate child. The messengers, having discovered a child with no father, bring him to Vortigern. The scene is supposed to take place in Gwynedd, that is, in northwestern Wales on the flanks of Mount Eryri, or Snowdon, in a place known in local tradition as Dinas Emrys (Fortress of Ambrosius). The king asks the child why the tower collapses. He replies that it is because of two dragons who are fighting in the subterranean cavern. Digging down reveals, in fact, two dragons in mortal combat. The child interprets the battle.

"In a while our people will rise up and bravely repel the nation of Angles from beyond the sea. You, however, must leave this citadel because you will never be able to build anything here. Travel through many provinces to find a fortress that can protect you. As for me, I shall stay here." The king asks the child, "What is your name?" He answers, "I am Ambrosius," that is, it seems, Embreis Guletic (Emrys Gwledig, also called "Ambrosius the Chief"). Then the king asks, "Of what race are you?" He replies: "My only father comes of the race of Roman consuls." The king gives him the citadel, along with all the regions of the northern coast of Britain.

This passage from the *Historia Brittonum* must leave us perplexed. Is there anything historical in it? No doubt Vortigern's meeting with a child—or young man—who is or pretends to be something of a seer, has a historical basis. This child professes to be a Roman patrician: he is, then, from a romanized British family and so claims to continue the imperial tradition. Theoretically there is no connection between this child and Merlin save for the name of Ambrosius. Then why did Geoffrey of Monmouth, taking up this passage, deliberately decide to overcome this obstacle and turn Ambrosius into Merlin the enchanter? At any rate, there are inconsistencies in this passage of the *Historia Brittonum*: it is hardly explained how a fatherless child could maintain that his only father is of the race of Roman consuls. Nor is it made clear why the child wishes to remain in that place, nor why the king gives it ·to him along with the regions of Britain's northern coasts. Perhaps we must make a connection here with the fact that, in the *Vita Merlini*, the mad bard is described as a king himself. From the context, moreover, the messengers had discovered the child *"in regione quae vocatur Gleguissing,"* that is, in the Glewissing, a small region in southwestern Wales between the Teivi and the Usk, rather distant from Kaermerddin, which is in the Dyved and where the meeting takes place, according to Geoffrey. Many of these problems may long remain unresolved, unless we agree with the opinion of Ferdinand Lot, who claimed that the editor of the primitive *Historia Brittonum* had distorted a folktale of Irish origin in his preoccupation with local etymology, that is, the name given to the ruins of the fortress of Dinas Emrys.[3] But here too one might ask why it would be an Irish tale that had been so adapted and distorted.[4]

What we must bear in mind here is that a myth of a fatherless child who has the gift of prophecy is linked to King Vortigern and to Ambrosius Aurelianus. In the text of the *Historium Britonnum*, that child is

Ambrosius himself. In the *Historia Regum Britanniae*, it is Merlin, the bard of Ambrosius, or, going back to the Welsh formulation of the tradition, *Myrddin Emrys*.

The problem of a possible rapprochement with Ireland should not be rejected—on the contrary. It must not be forgotten that the Irish (Scots) established in what is now the county of Argyll were neighbors of the northern Britons, especially of those who formed the kingdom of Strathclyde, where Merlin was supposed to have lived in the forest of Kelyddon. And it is in Ireland, or rather in the traditions of the Irish established on the western coast of Scotland, that we find an account absolutely parallel to that given us by Geoffrey of Monmouth in his *Vita Merlini*: the account of the legend of Suibhné (Sweeney), a king who went mad after a battle and took refuge in the woods. It cannot be a coincidence, especially as this legend, also, is articulated around a historic battle—that of Moira in 837.

> ———————— SUIBHNÉ'S MADNESS ————————

Suibhné, son of Colman, is king of Dal n'Araide (or Dalriada, the present counties of Antrim and Down in Ulster and Argyll in Scotland). One day he learns that Saint Ronan is building a church on his territory without his authorization. In a transport of rage, he takes Saint Ronan's psalter and throws it into a lake. Then he rejoins his troop of warriors to take part in a battle. The saint, however, is informed of Suibhné's gesture. He goes to the lake into which the psalter has been thrown; although an otter brings the book back to Ronan, it does not prevent him from cursing Suibhné. He tries to halt the battle in which Suibhné is fighting but the combatants do not want to hear his words of peace, and Suibhné, more and more furious with Ronan, kills one of the clerics accompanying the saint with a javelin thrust. Finally, he seizes another javelin and hurls it at Ronan himself. But the javelin shatters only the little bell that the saint always carries with him. Then Ronan casts a solemn curse upon the king.[5] He tells him that he will fly through the air like the javelin that slew his cleric and will die from a blow of the same weapon. Indeed, Suibhné flies through the air to everyone's stupefaction. He is gripped by panic, sees the sky open over his head, lets go of his weapons, and flies away like a bird, barely touching the ground. Suibhné arrives in Glenn Bolcain in Ireland. As his madness has calmed down a little, he settles in this green and pleasant valley. Then he wanders through Ireland for seven years and meets his foster brother Loingsechan, who is searching for him and wants to help him. Suibhné hears him coming and, as he possesses a certain visionary gift, begins to describe in verses of intense poetry his life as a man of the woods. He learns that his wife is sharing the bed of one of the pretenders to the kingdom.[6] He asks her to come to see him. When she comes to Suibhné the mad king recites poems about their past life— poems that in their melancholy and their intensity are among the most beautiful in ancient Irish literature. He also complains of the wandering life he leads, but allows his wife to live with the one she has chosen.[7]

Suibhné then goes to Ros Ercain and takes up residence in a yew tree.[8] Despite his son-in-law's invitations, he refuses to return and take his place in the kingdom. Nevertheless, his son-in-law eventually succeeds in curing his madness, and Suibhné resumes his kingship. But one day someone alludes in his presence to his former life and sickness. Madness claims him again; he climbs a tree and begins to recall his life in the forest, as well as the trees and hinds of Ireland. He then runs away to the forest and begins living once more as a man of the woods, though he is nostalgic for society. He tries to return, but Saint Ronan prays to God that he not be pardoned in this world; and Suibhné, preparing to return home, is the victim of a maleficent vision. He sees headless bodies and bodiless heads converging upon him. He is seized by terror and flees in panic, arriving at last at the hermitage of Saint Moling, who welcomes him with kindness. The monastery cook[9] prepares a bowl of milk to give him strength and comfort. But the cook's husband, who is the monastery swineherd, is jealous of his wife's intentions toward the vagabond. As Suibhné is drinking the milk, he kills him with a javelin thrust, thus vindicating Ronan's prediction.[10]

This legend of Suibhné Gellt (Sweeney the Mad) is obviously essential in attempting to understand Merlin's legend, at least the part of the legend that deals with Merlin as the "madman of the forest." The value of the Irish account relative to the different accounts of British origin remains to be seen. At one time it was the fashion to look for the source and origin of all Celtic traditions in Ireland, since Ireland, which was never occupied by the Romans, long maintained its specifically Celtic characteristics, and also because Gaelic documents are numerous and generally ancient. Today we are more cautious. It is true that certain legends, like that of Tristan, have an indisputable Irish archetype. But we may take the legend of Suibhné to be an imitation of Merlin's for a very simple reason: the date of reference for Suibhné is 837—the date of the battle of Moira, waged by the troops of the supreme king of Ireland on Irish territory against the troops of the kingdom of Kal n'Araide, Scots who had come to attempt the conquest of the island. But the date of reference for Merlin is 573, the date of the battle of Arderyd. Even considering that the legend of Merlin was not written down until the twelfth century by Geoffrey in the *Vita Merlini*, we cannot prove that the theme of Suibhné developed earlier in Ireland, since the manuscript that gives us this tale came later in time. We can only concede that there were influences in both directions, facilitated by the proximity of the Britons of Strathclyde and the Gaels of Dal n'Araide. Nevertheless, there are important analogies between *The Madness of Suibhné* and the *Vita Merlini*. The theme is the same, that of the king who goes mad in the course of a battle and becomes "man of the woods," prophet and poet.[11]

For it appears that the legend of Merlin the enchanter, as we now know it, is in fact composed of two themes that were very different in the beginning, corresponding to two distinct persons. One is the "madman of the forest," the other the child who is prophet and magician. This corresponds to the distinction made by Triad 101 concerning Myrddin, son of Morvryn—who must be the "madman of the forest" whose story Geoffrey tells us in the *Vita Merlini*—and Myrddin Emrys, the prophetic child whose story is also told by Geoffrey, but this time in the *Historia Regum Britanniae*. It is not Geoffrey who merged them, but his successors, probably Robert de Boron and his revisers. In any case, in *The Madness of Suibhné* the hero is not an enchanter. This is also true in the clerical tradition of the famous Lailoken, that Llallogan who must be the primitive Merlin.

Lailoken appears in the *Life of Saint Kentigern* by the monk Jocelyn, a monk of Furness (county of Lancaster) of uncertain origin, but British on the basis of his name. The text is from the twelfth century but presents with some fidelity certain events concerning the northern Britons in the sixth century, especially Kentigern's disputes with the kings of Strathclyde. In about 650 he had, in fact, founded a bishopric on the present site of Glasgow. The king of Strathclyde encouraged him, but his successor Morcant, of Saxon descent, harassed and abused him so much that Kentigern had to take refuge with Saint David in Menevia. It was after this that Kentigern founded in northern Wales the monastery of Llanelway, today Saint-Asaph. A certain Rydderch reigned then over Strathclyde and recalled Kentigern, who returned to settle in the area of Glasgow. It is during this time that Kentigern would have been in contact with a poor wandering madman called Lailoken. This *Life of Saint Kentigern* is completed by other documents, among which two are fundamental: they date from the twelfth century and were written in Latin in the country of the Britons of the north. They connect us closely to the life of Merlin as seen by Geoffrey of Monmouth.

LAILOKEN AND KING MELDRED

A man called Lailoken is the prisoner of King Meldred in his castle of Dunmeller. The king wants Lailoken to teach him something new. For three days Lailoken does not eat or drink, but when, on the third day, he sees the king remove a leaf from his wife's hair, he bursts into laughter. When the king asks why he laughed, Lailoken does not want to speak. Then the king promises him freedom if he agrees to answer. Lailoken says: "From venom comes sweetness and from honey comes bitterness. But neither of the two is true although both of them are. Iniquity has produced good instead of evil, and justice has done the opposite; but neither is true although both of them are." The king does not understand these riddles and insists that his prisoner clarify them. Lailoken says: "If I speak clearly you will experience grief and I a mortal affliction." The king begs him to explain. So Lailoken asks him, "He who heaps honors upon his enemy and condemns his friend to torture, what does he deserve?" "The same treatment," replies the king. "Then," continues Lailoken, "your wife deserves a crown and you deserve death, but neither of the two is true although both of them

*are." The king is not at all satisfied by this second answer. Lailoken
consents to explain if the king promises not only to free him but also,
after his death, to bury him east of the town, close to the hillock
where the Pansal flows into the Tweed. He tells the king that his wife
has deceived him with a lover and that the leaf has betrayed her.
Then he runs away. The queen seeks to reassure the king by telling
him that Lailoken is mad, she argues that Lailoken predicted he would
die in three different ways. But one day it becomes known that
Lailoken has died as he foretold.* [12]

> ——— LAILOKEN AND KENTIGERN ——— <

*In the time of Kentigern a half-mad wild man called Lailoken comes
to the holy hermit. The saint learns that Kentigern is atoning
through destitution and solitude for the sins that he has committed: he
is held responsible for the blood spilled during a battle waged between
the Lidel and Corwannock rivers. In the tumult he saw the sky open
amid an immense din and heard a voice tell him that he would be
punished and live among the beasts of the woods till his death. Afterwards, Lailoken vanishes into the woods, where he remains on top of
a rock* [13] *overlooking the torrent of Mellodonor (Molendinar) near
Glasgow. He complains bitterly and prophesies, but no one pays attention to his obscure remarks. One day, however, Lailoken goes to
find Saint Kentigern and asks him for communion, claiming that he
will die that very day from the blows of sticks and stones. Kentigern
questions him further and Lailoken replies that he will die pierced by
a wooden skewer. Kentigern goes on with his interrogation and
Lailoken tells him that he will die by drowning. Although the saint
considers these incoherent remarks, at the entreaty of his clerics he
gives absolution and communion to the unfortunate vagabond. That
same day Lailoken is pursued by King Meldred's herdsmen, who
strike him with sticks and stones. He tumbles down the steep banks of
the Traved (county of Peeble) and dies in the water, transfixed by a
sharp stake placed there by fishermen.* [14]

Obviously Geoffrey of Monmouth was completely aware of the tradition concerning Lailoken. Details like the leaf that betrayed the un-faithful queen and that of the triple death are reproduced in their en-tirety in the *Vita Merlini*. There can be no doubt, therefore, as to the identification of Lailoken and the Merlin of the *Vita Merlini* and the Welsh poems attributed to Myrddin. Moreover, there is a definite con-nection between Lailoken and Suibhné. The hero is a man of the woods, a madman of the forest. He is transported by a prophetic frenzy, speaks in riddles, and above all has been struck by madness during a battle for which he, to a certain extent, is held responsible. Finally, the location is unmistakable: the territory of Strathclyde, at the heart of the power-ful and most durable kingdom of the Britons of the north.

But this is really about Myrddin ab Morvryn, Merlin man of the woods. The second Merlin, Myrddin Emrys of the *Historia Regum Britanniae*, is essentially different and is related to the child who speaks and is endowed with certain powers. This theme pertains as well to another historical figure, Merlin's contemporary, often associated with him if only in the *Vita Merlini* and in a poem attributed to Myrddin. It is Taliesin, an important figure in Celtic history and mythology, an am-biguous character whose mystery is not easily penetrated. The Taliesin legend appears to have developed at the same time as Merlin's, around the twelfth century, when the enigmatic poems which fill the *Book of Taliesin* were composed under his name. It seems that he became, at this time, the symbol of the lost druidic tradition just as efforts were being made to retrieve it from any fragments of oral tradition that might have survived. This legend is transcribed in part in a later manuscript[15] which, however, takes into account a formulation dating from about the twelfth century.

> ————— THE STORY OF TALIESIN —————

A certain Keridwen asks Gwyon Bach to tend a cauldron whose contents are intended for her son; it consists of a magic potion of wis-dom, knowledge, and inspiration. Three drops of the liquid are ab-sorbed by Gwyon, who is endowed instantaneously with perfect knowledge of the past and the future.[16] The enraged Keridwen pur-sues Gwyon, who flees, changing himself into various animals. As Keridwen chases him, she also metamorphoses herself.[17] In the end,

*Gwyon takes the form of a grain of corn and Keridwen the form of a
hen: she swallows the grain of corn.*[18] *But she becomes pregnant and
gives birth to a boy just before the first of May,*[19] *puts him in a
leather sack and casts him into the sea.*[20] *The sack is retrieved by
Elffin, son of King Gwyddno, a young man for whom nothing turns
out well. He discovers the child and names him Taliesin. The child
begins to speak, comforts him, tells him who he is, and promises Elffin
that all will go well with him. Elffin takes Taliesin to Gwyddno, who
is amazed: "You are able to speak even though you are so small?" "I
am more capable of speaking," replies Taliesin, "than you are of ques-
tioning me." "Then I want to hear what you have to say," concludes
Gwyddno. And Taliesin sings strange and prophetic songs. Afterwards he helps Elffin and becomes his household bard, also display-
ing undeniable magic powers.*[21]

There are definite connections between this fantastic story and
Merlin's childhood as recounted by Geoffrey or by Robert de Boron.
The conception of the child is not natural. If Merlin has been conceived of a devil and a pious young girl, Taliesin *conceives himself* in the
body of Keridwen, image of the mother goddess, she who initiates and
dispenses. In any case, Taliesin and Merlin share a common ground:
they are fatherless children. Stress is placed on the irregular birth of
one to whom a great destiny is promised. There is nothing new in that:
the shadows of Moses and of Remus and Romulus hover over Merlin
and Taliesin, and the shadow of Christ as well. For when all is said and
done, being conceived by the Holy Spirit is not much different from
what happens to these extraordinary people. And the theme of oral
fecundation, so frequent in the Celtic realm, is precisely the same as
that of the virgin who gives birth: it corresponds to ancient beliefs
from the time when woman was the object of veneration and dread
because no one could really explain why she alone was able to bring
forth life.

A second point in common between Merlin and Taliesin is that they
are children gifted at a very early age with speech and knowledge. In
Robert de Boron's *Merlin*, the child immediately comforts his unhappy
mother, as Taliesin comforts Elffin. Both of them amaze judges and
kings with their words marked by wisdom and mystery. Merlin en-

lightens Vortigern's wise men, that is, the druids. Taliesin ridicules King Maelgwn Gwynedd's bards for not knowing as much as they should. Finally, it is curious that although both Merlin and Taliesin belong historically to the second half of the sixth century, their legends place them in an earlier time so that they are Arthur's contemporaries. They who are Britons of the north are given as companions to a man who bears the marks of southern Wales and Cornwall.

A poem exists in which Taliesin is in direct contact with Arthur: the famous thirtieth poem of the *Book of Taliesin* entitled "Preiddieu Annwfn," or "The Remains of the Abyss" (or of the otherworld); its references and allusions render the text extremely obscure and, due to the lack of context, it is beyond our comprehension. It must be the altered remainder of an ancient episode of the Arthurian legend, now lost and difficult to reconstruct. A single mention of Arthur's expedition, the subject of this poem, occurs in the Welsh account of "Culhwch and Olwen," but we learn nothing more. Should we turn, perhaps, to the second branch of the Welsh *Mabinogi*, in which the hero Bran Vendigeit is seen leaving on a similar mission, also accompanied by Taliesin? In that case Arthur would have replaced the more ancient figure of Bran. For good measure, we must refer to an Irish poem, whose hero is Cuchulainn, that offers an analogous story of an expedition to the otherworld in search of a miraculous cauldron. And who knows if this Celtic cauldron is not the archetype of the Christian Grail?

> ─────── "THE REMAINS OF THE ABYSS" ───────

A certain Gwair,[22] as a result of the vengeance of Pwyll and Pryderi,[23] is a prisoner in the mysterious city of Kaer Sidhi.[24] Arthur and his companions organize an expedition to free him. This city is also Kaer Perdryvan, the "city of four walls." Within it is a cauldron "that does not cook food for the faint-hearted" and is heated by the breath of nine maidens.[25] There appear to be strange processions in this city described by the poet as inaccessible and having various names. But finally, "when we went with Arthur in his noble enterprises, only seven returned."[26]

As Arthur's companion on his expeditions, his bard and confidant, prophet and magician, Taliesin can be considered identical to Merlin, who plays the same role with the king. The two legends must have developed at the same time among the Britons of the north and been completed by the Welsh, who established correlations between them that profited the authors of the romances of the Round Table. In any case, even if Merlin does not appear in "Culhwch and Olwen," the archaic Welsh version of the Arthurian legend, the king is surrounded by those whose magical or supernatural powers are evident. Of particular note are the peculiarities of Kay, who will be in the French romances Arthur's foster brother and seneschal, a boastful and grotesque personage: "Kay had a special strength that enabled him to breathe under water for nine nights and nine days. He could go without sleep for nine nights and nine days. No doctor could heal a blow from his sword. Kay was a man of rare gifts: when it pleased him, he became as tall as the tallest tree in the forest. Another talent: no matter how hard it rained within a hand's breadth of him, everything that he held in his hand remained completely dry, so great was the heat of his body. It could even light a fire for his companions when they suffered from cold." His other faithful companion, Bedwyr,[27] the Béduier of the French romances, has only one arm, but "his lance caused one wound as it entered but nine when it was withdrawn." He has an interpreter, Gwrhyr Gawlstawt Leithoedd, who "knew all languages," even those of animals. He can also change form and appear as a bird. As to his other companion, Menw, when faced with their enemies, he can "cast spells and enchantments so that they cannot be seen by anyone while they can see everyone." He can also ensorcel savage beasts to render them harmless. This accords well with the "wild man" aspect of Merlin, and also with the methods used by the enchanter to enable Uther Pendragon, and then Arthur, to defeat their enemies.

But Welsh tradition includes another person often associated with Taliesin, and who could very well be comparable to Merlin in his role of enchanter-magician: Gwyddyon, son of the goddess Don, nephew of King Math, master of magic, and incestuous brother of the goddess Arianrod. Here we are in the heart of Celtic mythology, for there does not seem to be a historical person to begin with, despite numerous references to the story of Gwynedd in northwestern Wales. In fact, Gwyddyon is the hero of an immense saga of Gwynedd, a saga heavily influenced by the Gaelic tradition of Ireland extended to Gwynedd through frequent raids by the Irish. Gwyddyon is mentioned very often in the poems attributed to Taliesin and he is the hero of the fourth branch of the *Mabinogi*.

⟩——— THE STORY OF GWYDDYON ———⟨

Gwyddyon, son of Don and the nephew of Math, king of Gwynedd, owns an all-powerful magic wand and has learned magic from his uncle. His brother Gilvaethwy [28] loves young Goewin, but she must remain a virgin for she has a very important function. In times of peace Math can live only with his feet in the lap of a virgin, and this virgin is Goewin. Gwyddyon wishes to help his brother. To do so he must create a situation of war, for then Math will be able to leave Goewin and go into battle. First he excites his uncle's greed by telling him about the marvelous pigs owned by Pryderi, king of Dyved, and suggests going to Gwyned in disguise to obtain them. So it comes to pass. Gwyddyon offers to give Pryderi even more marvelous animals in exchange for the pigs. And at night he goes to work: "Using his artifices, he began to display his magic power. He caused to appear twelve stallions and twelve black hunting dogs, each of whom had a white breast, with twelve collars and twelve leashes that everyone would take for gold, the bridles matched the saddles." [29] The next morning he offers them all to Pryderi, as well as twelve gold shields that are merely transmuted mushrooms. Pryderi accepts Gwyddyon's gifts in exchange for the famous pigs whom Gwyddyon makes haste to take back to Gwynedd.

Naturally, when the spell vanishes the following morning, Pryderi understands that he has been tricked. Learning that Gwyddyon was responsible, he prepares to lead a war party against Gwynedd. Math gathers his army. There is a terrible battle, ending in Pryderi's death. But during this time Gilvaethwy has been able to sleep with Goewin. When Math returns he finds out everything and decides to punish both nephews. He transforms them into a stag and a doe for one year, a boar and a sow for a second year, and a wolf and a she-wolf the third year. Finally he decides that their punishment is complete, gives them back their human form, and reconciles with them.

But the problem of the young virgin in whose lap Math must place his feet arises again. Gwyddyon suggests his sister Arianrod. Math has her step over his wand and Arianrod flees, abandoning two newborn infants. One throws himself in the sea. Gwyddyon takes the other and raises him. One day, accompanied by the little boy, Gwyddyon goes to visit his sister Arianrod. She asks him who the boy is. He answers: "This child is your son." Furious, Arianrod refuses to recognize him and accuses her brother of insulting her.[30] Nevertheless she asks him: "What is the name of your son?" As Gwyddyon replies that as yet he has no name, Arianrod says: "I swear it shall be his fate to have no name until he receives one from me."[31] In other words, she curses the child, clearly having no intention of ever naming him. But one day Gwyddyon, disguised as a cobbler, arrives at Arianrod's fortress with the child. Arianrod watches him work. Suddenly the child throws a stone at a bird and hits it. Arianrod laughs and says: "The little one struck him with a sure hand." Then Gwyddyon puts away his things and tells Arianrod that she has just given a name to her own son: henceforth he will be called what she has said, "Lleu Llaw Gyffes."[32]

But Arianrod, angry as ever, declares that he will never have any weapons unless they are given to him by her. Gwyddyon comes back again, in disguise, with Lleu. Using magic, he rouses enemies who prepare to attack the fortress. As there is a shortage of warriors, Arianrod arms the young boy. Then Gwyddyon breaks the spell. So Arianrod is tricked once more; but now she declares that the child will have no woman of the race of men. That is why Gwyddyon, together with Math, creates a woman from flowers: "Then they gathered flowers of oak, broom, and meadowsweet, and by their magic charms made of them the most beautiful and perfect maiden in the world."[33] They name her Blodeuwedd, meaning "Born of Flowers," and then marry her to Lleu.

Blodeuwedd, however, is bored with Lleu. She takes a lover and makes him kill Lleu, who takes flight in the shape of a bird. Gwyddyon searches for his son a long time, finds the bird, and restores him to his human form. Then he takes revenge on the lover and *pursues Blodeuwedd. Though he finds her, he cannot destroy his own creation, so contents himself with turning her into an owl, thereby obliging her to lead a nocturnal life.*[34]

It is possible that the stories of Gwyddyon influenced the composition of the definitive character of the enchanter Merlin. In any case, the unusually clear incest between Gwyddyon and his sister Arianrod can be compared to Merlin's ambiguous attitude toward his sister Ganieda or, if one prefers, to Myrddin and Gwendydd. Like Merlin, Gwyddyon is able to provoke apparitions. He is also a master of illusion, an instigator and protector. Moreover, he plays the same role of dubious go-between for his brother Gilvaethwy that Merlin played for Uther Pendragon. These are elements that, while not conclusive, do suggest a certain relationship between the two legends. Finally, there is the role played by Gwyddyon in a mythological battle related in the *Book of Taliesin*, the famous "Battle of the Trees," or "Cad Goddeu," in which it is clearly stated that the Britons were losing until Gwyddyon brought about their veritable resurrection by transforming them into trees, so that they were the victors.[35] This power of plant magic granted to Gwyddyon is very important, not only because the theme of the marching forest is typically Celtic,[36] but because Gwyddyon's name refers to trees. In fact it contains the word *gwydd* or *wydd*, meaning "woods" (Breton *gwezen* or *koad* from the Gallic *vidu*).[37] Even so, it is rather remarkable that the name of a mythological figure related to Merlin derives from the word "wood," when we know that Merlin is the "madman of the wood."

There are many other examples in European folktales of the hero who learns astonishing things in the heart of the woods, usually perched in a tree. In oral tradition, passed down through the centuries from generation to generation, it certainly seems that science and knowledge are linked to the tree. It is from the Tree of the Knowledge of Good and Evil that Adam and Eve picked the apple that was to prove fatal to humankind. For knowledge is reserved to the few and is not for "the common people." It is secret; those who possess it guard it jealously by a system of exemplary prohibitions and punishments, clear signs of power that must always insist on excluding the masses from knowledge since knowledge itself confers power. If someone acquires this power, it is because he is mad, like Merlin, or because, by chance, he was in the right place at the right time.

A typical example is a Percheron tale, L'Aveugle-né, found at the end of the nineteenth century in the region of Rémalard (Orne). Abandoned by his guide in the midst of a forest, the hero takes refuge in the fork of a tree. From there he hears three animals gathered at the foot of the tree who are speaking among themselves. In this way he learns how to cure his blindness (with the leaves of the oak tree in which he sits); how to cure the king's daughter; and how to make an arid countryside fertile by digging a well.[38] The fact that this character is blind makes him a seer of the otherworld: he can in this way comprehend the language of animals by returning to primitive times, the Golden Age, when this was possible. Above all, thanks to this knowledge, he acquires the power represented by the princess and the fertility represented by the well.

And it is again in the oral popular tradition that we discover the last traces of the "wise" Merlin, the young child who speaks. The legends of Merlin and Taliesin intersect here in a purely hagiographic Christian context that is quite edifying. It is an account found in Armorican Brittany at the end of the nineteenth century that, in its simplicity, even naïveté, carries us very far back, to the foundation of Celtic mythology.

> ——— THE TWO BIRTHS OF KONÉRIN ———— <

Konérin is an adolescent. On his way to school one day, he meets wicked people who tell him that they have been searching for him for a long time in order to kill him. He protests that he has done nothing to them, but in vain; he must choose between being stabbed or being burned alive. He chooses the fire. The wicked people seize him and burn him upon a pile of sticks. A little later, two beggars pass by the ashes and see among them an uncooked apple. One of them suggests eating it, but the other retorts that if this apple did not burn it is because God wanted it so and it must remain intact. They carry away the apple and pass by a hut where a woman is spinning. One of the beggars speaks to her; learning that she has an unmarried daughter, he asks if she is still virgin. Raising her voice, the woman swears that her daughter is virgin. Then the beggar presents her with the apple, saying that she must give it to her daughter to eat when she complains of a stomachache, for the young girl is at risk of a serious illness. The beggars leave. That evening, in fact, the girl complains of pains in her stomach. Her mother gives her the apple to eat. Soon the girl is pregnant, which causes a great scandal. However, the parish priest seems to understand the situation. When the young girl gives birth to a boy without having suffered any of the pains of childbirth, he himself comes to take the infant to the church baptismal font. And when he asks for volunteers to be godfather and godmother, the infant begins to talk: "I have no need of a godfather or godmother. Saint Konérin I was once, Saint Konérin I am now."[39]

The theme of oral impregnation is developed very clearly here. The second irregular birth of Konérin, like that of Taliesin, gives him strength and wisdom that he did not formerly possess. In the Christian context, he is a "saint." In a pagan context he would be the "druid" or the "bard"— in any case, wisdom personified. This is what allows him to defy the established order, the ethics of the milieu in which he appears. He is, indeed, a disturbing child, not only because he exists but also because he speaks. And, as we know, what is most disturbing in Christian civilization is the devil, that is, he who "sets himself against." So there is not much distance between devil and saint. That is why Merlin is the son of a devil and a holy woman.

A situation analogous to the story of Konérin is found in another Armorican folktale. This time it is not a question of a second birth, but of the first. Yet here, too, since the father, or rather the "sire," is a fantastic being, the child will inherit superhuman powers, like Merlin himself.

THE RED APPLE

A widower with a daughter marries a woman who also has a daughter. The first one is beautiful, the second very ugly. The beautiful daughter, walking on a heath, finishes a song of the korrigans.[40]
They bestow all kinds of blessings on her and make her even more beautiful than before. Seeing this, the stepmother decides to send out

her own daughter, who returns uglier than ever because she was not
able to finish the song of the korrigans. The stepmother decides to take
revenge; she gives her stepdaughter some apples to eat, among them a
red apple obtained by magic. The girl eats the red apple and becomes
pregnant; furious, her father sends her away. In the woods she gives
birth to a son of "thirty-seven colors." As the unhappy girl laments,
the newborn child begins to speak to her. He consoles her, goes to the
castle to ask for food and, by his cleverness, succeeds in marrying her
off to a handsome prince. On the day of the wedding he transforms
himself into a red apple on the table and says: "Now I will go to the
top of the tree from which I came." [41]

In this tale from Port-Louis (Morbihan) we find, without doubt, the
story of Merlin's birth. Of course, his name never figures in this original folktale. Still, his image is present in this tradition handed down
from generation to generation. It is a proof of it. The korrigans or the
witches replace the devil. And in this case, the mother's goodness and
beauty, symbol of her virginity and purity, protect the child from the
harmful and demoniac powers that animate him and make him the de-
liverer of judgments, profoundly good, returning balance to the world.
It is the demiurge Merlin in his pacifying and positive modes. Once
again the devil has been tricked.

Another version of this tale comes also from Port-Louis but this time
is about a young woman who mocks the small stature of the korrigans.
They avenge themselves by making her eat nuts, one of which impregnates her while her husband is away for many months. Fortunately all
ends well; the young child makes the truth known and returns to the
tree from which he came, in the form of a nut. [42] Everything occurs as if
the popular tradition were haunted by the story of the fatherless child
intended for a great destiny and able to know the secrets of the world—
as if, in popular wisdom, there were a need for Merlin, under any name
he might have, under any circumstances that might befall him.

It is to Ireland that we turn once more to conclude this brief foray
into the texts that parallel the story of Merlin. The following tale is
also based on a historical personage—Mongan, son of Fiachna, who,
like Suibhné, was king of Dal n'Araide, and who died in 615. Surely it
is not by chance that the territory of Dal n'Araide, adjoining that of the

Britons of Strathclyde, was the setting for the double theme of Merlin, that of the mad king and that of the infant sage, or prophet-child.

> ——————— STORY OF MONGAN ———————<

One day when King Fiachna has gone to Scotland to help his ally Aedan mac Garbrain, who allowed Saint Columcill to settle in Iona, his wife, whom he had left in the fortress of Moylinny, sees a very handsome man of royal aspect coming toward her. This man tells her that Fiachna will be killed in battle the next day unless she consents to join with him to produce a son destined for greatness. The woman accepts "to save her husband's life." It is then discovered that this strange man is none other than Mananann mac Lir, one of the chieftains of Tuatha Dé Danann,[43] those gods of ancient times who live on the knolls of Ireland and on islands in the ocean. When Fiachna returns victorious and unharmed from his expedition, his wife tells him the whole story and he seems to take it well. And so Mongan is born. When Mongan is three days old Mananann comes for him and takes him to the "Promised Land."[44] Raised and educated in a magical country, Mongan thus acquires some of the wisdom of the Tuatha Dé Danann, that is, druidic wisdom, notably, he can change his appearance as he wishes. Once he has returned to Ireland and succeeded Fiachna, he marries the beautiful Dub-Lacha. But having promised him an obligatory gift,[45] he is bound to give his wife to the king of Leinster. Dub-Lacha tries to gain time and obtains a delay of one year before sharing the bed of the king of Leinster, although he keeps her a prisoner. One day Mongan assumes the appearance of the monk Tibraide and disguises his steward Mac an Daimh (whose wife had been obliged to follow Dub-Lacha) as a cleric, and the two of them enter the king of Leinster's castle under the pretext of confessing Dub-Lacha. Of course Mongan avails himself of the situation to satisfy his desire for his wife under the very nose of the king of Leinster, while the lookouts are rather perplexed: they see Tibraide and his cleric inside the castle, and a second Tibraide, who is the real one, outside. But finally Mongan can delay no longer.[46] He finds a hideous old woman, transforms her into a lovely young girl, and leads

her to the king of Leinster's castle, introducing her as his latest con-
quest. The king of Leinster seems strongly attracted to the girl he
believes so lovely. Mongan suggests exchanging her for Dub-Lacha.
The king accepts and Mongan hastens to depart with his wife. One
can imagine the king of Leinster's disappointment when, on the disso-
lution of the spell, he finds a hideous old woman in his bed the next
morning. [47]

One cannot help but be astonished at the parallels offered by all these diverse legends, Welsh, Irish, British, or simply continental. But the one about Mongan has the merit of uniting the figure of the magician endowed with the gift of prophecy and that of the child whose irregular birth is due to the intervention of a diabolical power, in the correct, etymological sense of the term. The incubus who is Merlin's sire is not much different from the Celtic god Mananann, and if the circumstances of the primary scene are not strictly identical, the woman is always of good faith and the result is the same: the child is an exceptional being gifted with supernatural powers. Thus Lailoken, Suibhné, Konérin, and Mongan are only names valid in a certain context for a certain public. They are multiple faces of the same mythological being who is simultaneously prophet, magician, and extraordinarily gifted child; abnormal to the point of madness; wise like Taliesin; fierce like Gwyddyon; righter of wrongs like the little boy of "The Red Apple"; or even a saint like Salaün ar Foll, that poor devil who, in the fifteenth century, lived near Lesneven deep in the woods, in his ecstasy endlessly repeating "Itron Varia" (Madame Marie, or Saint Mary), and in whose honor the magnificent chapel of Folgoët, in Finistère, was built: and that being is our Merlin the enchanter.

Part 3

The Divine Couple

It must be acknowledged, therefore, that the figure of Merlin the enchanter is the synthesis of a series of more or less complex symbioses, drawing upon the characteristics of certain heroes or gods of the Celtic pantheon as well as more historical elements, from which emerges the figure of a king who went mad, abandoned society, and took refuge in the woods. At the center is the dominant personage of Merlin-Lailoken in the geographic context of the Britons of the north, located between the Solway and the Clyde, and in the chronological framework of the second half of the sixth century.

But these observations pose problems, for we are in the presence of a mythological figure. And how can we tell if this is a historical person who became mythological, or a highly divine being, historicized before being reclaimed by fable? The process by which historical persons are deified, euhemerization, is well known and has been prevalent for centuries for sometimes diverse reasons—for religious or political objectives, or quite simply because of a more or less unconscious tendency to put a halo around extraordinary people. In this case Merlin the enchanter would be merely the sublimation, the apotheosis, in the strict sense of the word, of a poor madman made famous by his predictions.

In fact, it is more complex than that, and one must be wary of giving a single answer to matters that bring into play both the memory and the sensibility of various peoples. For example, we know that the legend of Tristan and Iseult is based on an ancient myth whose archetypal formulation is found very early on in Ireland.[1] Now, King Mark of Cornwall is a historical king, sovereign of the double kingdom of Domnonée, that is, Cornwall-Devon in Great Britain and the north of the Armorican peninsula, better known on the continent by its cognomen of Konomor (Cunoworos). On the other hand, it has been proven that the name of Tristan (Drostan, then Drystan, in Welsh) is Pict in origin, and that his country, Loonois, is none other than Lothian, a region lying in the ancient domain of the Britons of the north, south of Edinburgh in the country of the Votadini (Gododdin). The funerary column of Tristan, called "son" of Cunoworos, has been found not far from Tintagel, scene of part of the legend. So, what is this all about? Is it another matter of rivalry between a father and son which then becomes a veritable epic, drawing upon mythological sources for its details? We have seen other examples of this kind; after all, the famous Trojan War was nothing but a merciless battle between Asian and European Greeks for the economic supremacy of the Aegean Sea, camouflaged as the abduction of the beautiful Helen by the handsome Paris. We also know that in Roman history characters often appear who never really existed; they are simply great Indo-European divinities turned into historical figures, such as the famous Horatius Cocles (none other than Wotan) or Mucius Scaevola (who is none other than Tyr) in the writings of Livy.

It seems that the exact point of departure for a legend cannot be determined. It can also be a matter of myth itself, immutable and immanent, actualized by a real event, transmitted through real events from generation to generation, charged each time by mythological residues from the unconscious. By analyzing these legends in depth, we can perceive that although a legend is never created in the absence of an actual historical fact, this fact either becomes part of a preexisting mythic structure or of a setting propitious to the analogic evocation of certain mythological themes. This is what happened in the case of the Armorican legend of the city of Ys. The actual point of departure appears to be the catastrophes that occurred at the end of the Bronze Age as a result of a sudden climatic change (going from dry cold to temperate humidity), catastrophes that manifested themselves especially in the inundation of ancient human habitations near lakes and along the sea by the suddenly advancing waters. The same theme is found all around the Baltic, the length of the north Sea, and in the British Isles. And it is specifically localized at the extremity of Armorican Brittany. But on its way there it acquired various elements—mythological, psychological, sociological, philosophical, and religious—and these expressions influenced the meaning and made it truly the "Celtic myth of origins."[2] This is also true in the case of Vercingetorix: it is not by chance that he appeared to the Romans as the supreme chief of the Gauls, for he had been raised in the very distinctive perspective of the myth of the King of the World, and he simply embodied, made real, a preexisting myth in a framework determined by external circumstances.[3]

This is why it is important to be very cautious in assessing the origins of a well-defined mythological figure. In the case of Merlin the enchanter we have the image of a colorful character endowed with certain powers that he uses as he thinks best, possessing the gift of prophecy; a man of the woods but also a completely refined scholar whose somewhat mysterious birth, ambiguous conception, paradoxical life, and incomprehensible disappearance open wide before us the doors of a magical, not to say divine, domain. Perhaps he is a real man ranked among the gods. Perhaps he is a god who became a historical hero. Perhaps he is an exemplary being, the incarnation of an immanent myth that was only waiting to be personified once again.

First of all, the name should give us pause. It seems that at the beginning of this whole story, Lailoken-Llallogan was the person's actual name; yet it is the name Merlin that has prevailed, and in addition to accepting it we must attempt to explain it.

The name Merlin appears for the first time in the *Vita Merlini* in its Latin form Merlinus. All of the Welsh versions (all subsequent to Geoffrey of Monmouth) give as an equivalent Merddin or Myrddin (the Welsh *y* is pronounced *eu* and the *dd* is pronounced like a *z*, whence the Breton *Merzinn*). If Merlin really is a Briton of the north, logic demands that the original name be *Myrddin*, and *Merlinus* only a latinized transcription, a normal occurrence in a text edited in Latin. This is the current and commonly accepted opinion, as an internal *z* in a word is not easy to pronounce for a speaker of Latin or French or even of English. As Geoffrey of Monmouth, though Welsh, was a scholar educated in Norman schools this softening of *z* into *l* in his writing does not seem incongruous. We must then ask ourselves about the meaning of the word *Myrddin*. Phonetically, it can hardly derive from anything but *mort-dunum* (maritime fortress), second and third terms of the name of the city of Caerfyrddin (Kaermarthen), where Vortigern's envoys discovered the fatherless child. As Geoffrey's text adds—and perhaps it is an interpolation—after the name Merlinus "qui et Ambrosius dicebatur" (who also was called Ambrosius), it might even be a cognomen. Thus Merlin would be a certain Emrys Myrddin, that is, "Ambrosius of Kaermarthen" or, more precisely, "Ambrosius of the Maritime Fortress." This seems to be corroborated by the *Historia Britonnum*, which does not give the name Merlin to the young hero of the episode, but the names Aurelius Ambrosius. It could explain the absence of the name Merlinus in a ninth-century text, when the hero's surname had not yet been given to him or was still too little known. Nothing contradicts this interpretation, especially if Merlin was really a native of Caerfyrddin and had entered the service of Gwenddoleu, lord of the north. But we do not know that.[4]

This hypothesis has the added merit of suggesting an equally logical explanation should the name Myrddin substituted for that of Lailoken-Llallogan. In the British tradition, the complete name of our protagonist would then be Llallogan Myrddin, in the Latin tradition, Lailoken Merlin. Why not?

The problem is that the name Merlinus does not appear in any manuscript prior to that of Geoffrey's *Vita Merlini* in 1132, nor does the name of Myrddin. We have, therefore, no proof that the name Myrddin predates that of Merlin. And who could disprove that the opposite occurred? The name Merlinus, given Geoffrey's dazzling success, would then have passed into Welsh in a celticized form and been substituted for that of Llallogan. This hypothesis is no more absurd than the other.

But what then is the significance of the name of Merlin? It is possible to link it to the twelfth-century English word *merilun*, which has clearly given us "merlin" in modern English, the name of a type of falcon very well known in that era, when all the nobles survived by hunting. After all, Gawain, Arthur's nephew, bears the Welsh name of Gwalchmai, or "Falcon of May," and Arthur's name itself refers to the bear.[5] Why could Merlin not be the "merlin," a surname that could have been given to him by storytellers describing him in the heart of the woods while hunting in order to eat?[6]

But the remaining major obstacle to this hypothesis is that the legend of Merlin, like Arthur's, concerns only Celtic- and French-speaking peoples, at least in the twelfth century. We must remember that in Great Britain the language of the intellectual elite was French, imposed by the Anglo-Norman dynasty and then revived by the Plantagenets, who were Angevins. How would an Anglo-Saxon term turn up in a French-British story? The only possible solution that remains, then, is to make of Merlin an adjective derived from the French word *merle* (blackbird). Not only is this not absurd, it is in all likelihood the best answer to the problem of Merlin's name: the poet-enchanter is a mocker, insolent and impertinent, who spends his time singing and playing tricks. What better name could one find for him than one that comes from the blackbird?

This is not to deny Merlin's Celtic origin; it is merely a matter of his name. We know that it is not his original name, and that we are probably speaking of Lailoken-Llallogan. But it shows that in the twelfth century, probably through Geoffrey of Monmouth this prophet-bard and magician who was, above all, a man of the woods, was given a French name expressive of his intimacy with the forest and the animal world. Because of the role of animals in general, and birds in particular, in druidic practices and beliefs, we may accept as decisive the hypothesis that the name Merlin derives from the French *merle*.

In any case, mythological and religious traditions give great importance to surnames and epithets of all kinds: is not Venus "the Beautiful," Pluto "the Rich," Belenus "the Brilliant," Bran the Blessed "the Raven"? Why shouldn't Merlin be "the Blackbird"? For, as he is presented to us in the Arthurian romances, Merlin far surpasses his historic human condition. One would almost think him a demigod, or a god incarnated to influence the destiny of men. In this sense he is the demiurge, arranging a world he did not create but to whose equilibrium he contributes, by his counsel and magic powers, to everyone's satisfaction. Is it not he who sets into motion the famous Round Table "that turns like the world"? Is it not he who decides everyone's destiny, playing with the established rules, routine, and morals, sending knights on adventures they do not understand but that have a purpose, hidden as it may be within the perspective of a universe where time no longer exists? One could say, as in Vigny's definition in *Chatterton* of a poet, that he reads in the stars the road pointed out by God. That is why he is divine. He is Hermes Trismegistus of the esoteric tradition. He is the god who sees and speaks, the Aius Locutus of the Romans. But it is not in a temple built in the center of a city that he exercises his ministry. It is in the heart of Celtic forests.

This is a fundamental difference. Celtic civilization was never urban; it was always rural or sylvan. Pastoral at the outset, Celtic society evolved slowly toward an agricultural system, first in Gaul, where proximity to the Mediterranean favored the evolution, and later in Ireland, the westernmost point known at the time. It was from this system, barely evolved from pastoral customs, that Merlin emerged: a druid from antiquity thrust miraculously into the heart of a Christianity that no one dreamt of discussing but which everyone interpreted in his own way. And, in himself, Merlin crystallized all that official Christianity had not been able to salvage, all that was considered as diabolical because it clashed with imported theoretical norms mostly ignored by a people attached to its ancestral customs and mental structures, its deep beliefs rooted in the virgin earth. This explains in part why Merlin takes refuge in the forest; why he lives in a tree, invisible to the common man; why he succumbs to Vivian's ambiguous charms, willingly allowing himself to be enclosed in that prison of air where he can continue to observe a world in disorder.

For Merlin, in fact, is not alone. The image of the hermit is impressed upon us because it corresponds to the attitude of withdrawal attributed to Merlin, withdrawal from a society no longer capable of understanding his counsels or his warnings. That society would spin aimlessly until the final catastrophe foreseen by the prophet-enchanter—the battle of Camlann, a symbolic battle if ever there was one, in which father and son would kill each other to the ultimate grief of a barely stable kingdom. After Camlann there is no longer any question of Merlin. Only the hand of Vivian will be seen recapturing Arthur's sword and submerging it in a lake. For Vivian is the Lady of the Lake, also divine, with the face of a mother goddess—a perverse little girl, taught by the old enchanter, who suddenly finds herself mistress of a situation she had not foreseen but is obliged to resolve.

Vivian is close to Merlin. Vivian or someone else, perhaps Gwendydd. We are speaking of a complex character, one whom it is essential to define if we want to understand anything about Merlin.

4

$\mathbf{V}$IVIAN OR GWENDYDD?

 Which is the true name of Merlin's companion? This is our first difficulty. In the Welsh poems attributed to Myrddin she is called Gwendydd and is the poet's sister. In the *Vita Merlini* she is still his sister but is called Ganieda. In the other texts she is no longer sister but lover, and even so her name varies from one work to another, from one manuscript to another, and sometimes even within the same manuscript.

In the later text of Thomas Malory, *Le Morte d'Arthur*, her name is Nimue. In the Huth *Merlin* she is designated as Niviene, and in the *Vulgate Lancelot* as published by Sommer, we find the names Uiuiane (in *The History of Merlin*), Nymenche (actually *Lancelot*), and Niniane (*The Book of Arthur*). In a single manuscript in the Bibliothèque Nationale de Paris we find Uiuiane and Uiniane several pages away from each other, and in another manuscript Uinaine, Uiane, and Uiuiane. This means that, taking into account the ambiguity between *v* and *u*, and the confusion always possible between *u* and *n* on the part of successive copyists, the name of Merlin's companion does not seem to have been determined right away. It is not until the sixteenth and especially the nineteenth century that the form *Viviane* wins out over all the others—in the French domain, of course.

So it is very arbitrarily that we speak always of the fairy Vivian. This usage is now well established, however, and Vivian has been much in vogue as a given name. But it does not appear to be Celtic, at least at first sight, and above all it is very difficult to connect it with Gwendydd-Ganieda, or with Merlin's wife in the *Vita Merlini* (the only text in which a wife is mentioned, and even here her role is negligible), Guendoloena, a latinized form of the well-known Welsh name, Gwendolyn. We have, therefore, five principal versions of the name of Merlin's companion. In the Welsh tradition: Ganieda and Gwendydd. In the continental tradition: Vivian, Nymenche (to which we may add Nimue), and Niniane.

In Merlin's case, the name Ganieda appears first. The manuscripts containing Gwendydd, supposed to be the Welsh form of Ganieda, are all subsequent to Geoffrey of Monmouth. But the passage from Ganieda to Gwendydd remains quite obscure. Gwendydd is easy, even too easy, to understand: the word means "white day." The adjective *gwynn* (feminine *gwenn*) can certainly be found in Ganieda in the contraction *gan*, but the ending of the name, *-ieda*, seems to have little connection with the Welsh *dydd*. We must suppose then that both Gwendydd and Ganieda were borrowed from an older common form meaning, more or less, "Blanchette," or "Blondinette," or simply "Belle" (*gwynn* means "blanc" [white], but also "beau" [handsome] and "blond" like its Gaelic equivalent *finn*, both from the Gallic *vindu*).

Nymenche (and Nimue) is much simpler. The name points to a distinctly Welsh model, or at least an insular Brittonic one: it contains the word *nem*, meaning "heaven" (in the religious sense of the term), found also in the Welsh *nef* (pronounced *nève*, which explains the variant Niviene), the Breton-Armorican *nenv* (pronounced *nan*), and the Gaelic Niamh. In fact, in 1907 the scholar Lucy-Allen Paton linked Nymenche to an epic Irish heroine named Niamh, who played a role somewhat analogous to that of Vivian. In the narrative "The Death of Cuchulainn" she is instructed by King Conchobar to imprison the hero Cuchulainn to prevent him from throwing himself into a fatal battle. And Niamh is a fairy, a figure from the otherworld. It is an interesting hypothesis: Nymenche would then be the "Celestial One," the "Fairy" par excellence, resembling in broad outlines the very ethereal personage of Vivian, even though more closely identified with springs, lakes, and rivers.

The name Niniane figures in numerous commentaries and hypotheses. First we may ask whether Niniane came into use after Vivian, the result of a confusion with Vivienne (the feminine of Vivien) because of its nasality. Though possible, it cannot be proven without patient research into the origin of the form Niniane.

This form could come from the same word, *nem*, but would imply a Breton-Armorican model *nen* or *nan*, therefore strongly nasalized. It is an interesting idea, since Niniane is always placed in "Little Britain," and it is in the Armorican forest, Brocéliande, that Merlin meets her. And later, when she appears as the Lady of the Lake, Vivian will abduct Lancelot to the Armorican peninsula to educate him in her enchanted domain. Now, at a short distance from the Forest of Paimpont, which is considered to be the Forest of Brocéliande,[1] there is a river called the Ninian: it originates in the Côtes-d'Armor, passes through Morbihan, skirts the forest of Lanouée, crosses the territory of Helléan (where we find one of the components of Bréchéliant, the ancient name of Brocéliande), and empties into the Oust southwest of Ploërmel. And the name of Ninian, rather widespread in Armorican Brittany, is that of a saint who evangelized the Britons of the north and the Picts of the south at the end of the fifth century. The name is assuredly Celtic, even Brittonic. It may even come from the same root, *nem*, and could be an adjective meaning "celestial." If so, there is no question that Niniane is the feminine of Ninian. Niniane would therefore be "the Celestial One."

But some scholars have seen in Niniane a distortion of the Welsh Rhiannon, the name of a heroine in the first and second branches of the *Mabinogi*, whose meaning is generally accepted as "Grande Reine" [Great Queen] (Rigantona).[2] This is the opinion of the Welsh Celtic scholar John Rhys; it has also been taken up by the scholar Roger Sherman Loomis, but is disputed by Eric Hamp for phonetic reasons. To be sure, phonetic rules do not always apply to proper names (there are many examples of this) but the figure of Rhiannon hardly corresponds to that of Vivian apart from the role of the mother goddess that can be assigned to them both. If the name change from Rhiannon to Niniane actually occurred, it could only have happened by way of the Armorican form Rivanone, the name of the mother of the holy bard Hervé,[3] and also by way of the form Niviène. All of this seems somewhat hazardous and indecisive.

Another hypothesis is rather comical even though it was upheld by serious professors whose names are best not mentioned. It traces the origin of the name Niniane to the phrase from the text of *Merlin* according to which the young lady "was baptized Vivian, a name that in Chaldean [sic] sounds the same as *noiant* (or *nient*) *ne ferai* (nothing will I do) in French."[4] In other words, the confusion appears to come from an epithet, *nient ne*, misunderstood, shortened, and added superfluously to the name of Vivian. It is quite clever but, in the end, rather ridiculous.

Still, it is true that Niniane appears to be the feminine form of Ninian; that the existence of the name Ninian has been established; and even that there was a Saint Ninian who lived, fifty years earlier, in the land of the historical Merlin, giving his name to a river in Armorican Brittany. In fact Ninian is closely linked to freshwater, whether lakes (the Lady of the Lake), springs, or rivers. She always meets Merlin by a fountain, chiefly by the Fountain of Barenton, of which we will speak again. The first "trick" she teaches Merlin is the power to make a river appear where there is none (and in this case she must be compared to numerous British saints who cause springs to gush forth). Her name is associated with that of the Ninian River. When she has put Merlin to sleep—or confined him, if you like—she becomes the Lady of the Lake, and it is in her castle under the lake that she raises Lancelot. It is also in a lake that she arranges for Arthur to obtain his sword Kaledfoulch, and she takes it back from him in the same lake after the battle of Camlann. Finally, we are told in the continental accounts that Vivian's father, a certain Dyonas, was the godson of Diana, and it is by the Lake of Diana that Vivian takes Merlin for a walk. Because of all of these aquatic references, we have come to see Vivian-Niniane as a kind of water divinity, or nymph. And the patronage of Diana should not surprise us.

There was in fact an attempt to explain Niniane's name as a distortion of the name Diana. It is not an absurd hypothesis. From a logical point of view it is even seductive, since Diana is a divinity of forests as well as of springs. And then Diana, the ancient Indo-European Artemis, was actually a solar divinity before the reversal of trends that led to the masculinization of the sun and the feminization of the moon.[5] Such a hypothesis would restore Niniane to her true dimension of protective and fruitful divinity, dispenser of light, heat, and life. In any case, her character, in all the texts, is distinctly solar, especially when in opposition to Morgan, who is distinctly obscure and somber, and who represents a force of darkness.

Behind the Roman visage of Diana is the great Indo-European goddess of primitive times, known in Rome as Anna Parenna (Anna the Purveyor), in India as Anna Pourna (the same meaning), in Ireland as Ana or Dana, and in Wales as Don, mother of Gwyddyon and Arianrod. We know that she is the same personage as Cybele and we shall see what conclusions we can draw concerning the ties between Vivian and

Merlin, with Vivian playing the part of Cybele and Merlin that of Adonis.

We are left with the name Vivian. If it had derived from a Welsh or Breton-Armorican word, it would begin with *gu* (like Gwendydd or Ganieda). If it came from a Celtic word, it can only be an Old Celtic word in which the initial *v* had not been transformed, as is the case in all the developed Brittonic languages. If not, it is not Celtic—or at least not Brittonic.

Vivian was understood by medieval copyists to be the feminine form of Vivien, a very well known name shared by the heroes of several *chansons de geste*. Vivien was, in fact, the favorite nephew of William of Orange and played an important role in the struggles against the Saracens in the south of France, where he was even looked on as a saint. In Occitan, the language of the land in which his legend is strongly localized and implanted, the form of his name is Vézian. It is not difficult to recognize in this a Celtic name whose Welsh equivalent is Gwyddyon, that is, "the Savant," "the Clairvoyant." Vivian would then be the "Savante" or the "Clairvoyante," which is not incompatible with her image. Even so, it is difficult to accept this hypothesis of the transformation of an Occitan word of Celtic origin to its corresponding French word. The character of Vivian as described in the *chansons de geste* really has nothing in common with Merlin's legend, still less with some feminine legend or other. And the hypothesis, though linguistically plausible, is hardly credible from the mythological point of view.

On the other hand, since Merlin is surrounded by people whose names often include the adjective *gwynn-gwenn*, "white" (Gwenddoleu, Gwendydd-Ganieda, Gwendolyn-Guendoloena), it is possible that the name Vivian comes from a word containing the Celtic *vindu*, which means "blanc" [white], "beau" [handsome], or "blond" [blond]—something like Vindiana, leading, after the loss of the interconsonantal *d*, to the form Viviane, later confused with the feminine form of Vivien. This solution has the merit of establishing an almost perfect correspondence between the name of Ganieda and that of Vivian, who would then be "Blanchette," "Blondinette," or the "Belle."

It was in this spirit that in 1945 the scholar Arthur Brown suggested that the name of Vivian was the end product in French of the Gaelic Be-Finn (pronounced Bé-Fionn), a fairylike figure of Irish legend.[6] Be-Finn means "White Woman" or "Beautiful Woman." It is the surname of the heroine Etaine in a famous narrative[7] and is also the name of the mother of the hero Fraech, who is described to us extensively in another narrative.[8] And the hypothesis according to which Be-Finn became Befionn, then Bevionn, then Vevionn before arriving at Vivian is not phonetically impossible. The only problem is the passage from Gaelic to French: there is no example of direct transmission between the two languages and we must assume a Welsh or British intermediary. But even here we find the meaning "white woman"—all the more interesting since in folk traditions fairies often are called "white ladies."

In Irish mythology, moreover, Be-Finn, the mother of Fraech, appears as the doublet of her own sister Boann, or Boinn, who is described as a true Queen of the Fairies. Boinn has given her name to the most famous megalithic monument in Ireland, the *sidh* of Brug-na-Boyne, otherwise known as the Newgrange burial tumulus, as well as to the Boyne river and numerous springs. The name Boinn is not only very widely known in Irish toponymy but is found in the Massif Central in France, at the exact limit of the territories formerly occupied by the Arvernes and the Vellaves, specifically in the commune of Saint-Jean d'Aubrigoux (Haute-Loire). There is, in fact, a Gallic site there—destroyed by the Romans and never rebuilt—probably a druidic sanctuary, located by a spring called the Fonboine. It is certain that this does not mean "good spring." It is really Boinn's name that we find there,[9] though we do not know how it got there, or how it has endured until the present day.

Thus Be-Finn or Boinn is closely bound up with the cult of springs and rivers. She is Queen of the Fairies, but also an aquatic goddess. The name Boinn is easily explained: there is an ancient Bo-Vinda, also called "the White Cow," as Be-Finn corresponds to an ancient Be-Vinda. The transition from *be* to *bo*, or vice versa, is extremely easy; the confusion is almost to be expected. In fact, this is the most satisfactory hypothesis for explaining the name of Vivian. In the final analysis what stands out is the idea of a white, blonde, and beautiful woman regarded as Queen of the Fairies (the White Lady), as a solar divinity (the blondness), and especially as a divinity of woods and springs. In this way the problem of the concordance between the name of Ganieda-Gwendydd and that of Vivian is resolved. In any event, this seems the most plausible and, pending further information, the most acceptable hypothesis.

There is more. We know that there is no lack of doublets in Celtic mythology, nor in other mythologies. Often divinities have different names, which does not prevent them from designating the same material or spiritual forces, or from having the same basic characteristics. Boinn also appears under the name of Brigit, daughter of the god Dagda, who was so honored in pagan Ireland that, after its conversion to Christianity, she was made the famous "Saint" Brigid of Kildare, probably confused with a holy woman who founded a monastery on the site of a druidic sanctuary. (Kildare is actually "the Church of the Oaks"; for a long time the Christians maintained a sacred fire there.) The legend of Boinn-Brigit takes place not only in an aquatic context, but also in the context of the druidic forest. This statement goes far to explain the true personality of Vivian.

Finally, and it is here that we return to Merlin's own legend, Boinn has incestuous relations with her father, the god Dagda. As the entire history of Merlin is overlayed with an incestuous atmosphere, we can only regard Vivian as one of the medieval faces of that great Celtic goddess of waters and forests whom some called Brigit, other Be-Finn, others Boinn, but who is eternally the same, engaging with her father or brother or son in the sacred incest that is the highest mark of the divine privilege.

5

SACRED INCEST

 At the very least, Merlin's attitude toward women, or, if one prefers, toward woman, is rather strange. In the *Historia Regum Britanniae*, he has neither wife nor mistress. At the beginning he is seen only in the company of his mother, who is the daughter of the king of Dyved. This is also how we learn that Merlin is of royal blood, the heir of the king of the Demetae. When Geoffrey states in the *Vita Merlini* that Merlin was king in Britain, perhaps he is thinking of that. In any case, the story of the fatherless child born to the daughter of the king of Dyved seems to be a case of matrilineal descent as was often true among the Celts. In Ireland the famous king of Ulster, Conchobar, is always called the son of Ness, which is his mother's name; and his sovereignty was acquired through his mother. The hero Cuchulainn himself is above all the son of his mother, Dechtire, for his unresolved paternity is variously assigned to Sualtam, his putative father; Lug, the great god of the ancient Irish; or, as is most likely, his uncle Conchobar, who had committed incest with his own sister. In Wales the historicized gods Gwyddyon, Amaethon, Gilvaethy, and Arianrod are the children of Don, as are also the Irish Tuatha Dé Danann, and the name of their father is utterly unknown. In all of these legendary accounts it is clearly the nephew who inherits more or less from his maternal uncle, as does Tristan from Mark, Gwyddyon from Math, the original Gawain from Arthur,[1] and Constantin, who actually succeeds Arthur, according to Geoffrey, and who is his sister's son.

This was a practice very prevalent among the Celts and, according to Caesar, an absolute custom among the Picts of Caledonia. It is not an Indo-European practice; the Celts of the British isles inherited it from the indigenous people whom they no doubt celticized, but from whom they borrowed a good many beliefs and customs inexplicable when compared with other Indo-Europeans.[2] For we are talking about an ancient society of a gynecocratic type hardly compatible with the patriarchal regimes characteristic of the people referred to as Indo-Europeans for want of a better term.

In the *Historia* as well as in the continental versions of the legend, Merlin has no amorous adventures. It must have been Robert de Boron who, rather late in the day—when Merlin already was the "decaying enchanter," in the words of Guillaume Apollinaire—recorded the episode of Merlin and Vivian. Certainly he did not invent it. He took it from the *Vita Merlini* or from one of the Welsh versions of the Merlin legend that he could have known. But the problem is that in the *Vita Merlini* the object of Merlin's great love does not seem to have been his wife Guendoloena, but his sister Ganieda. It is quite possible that before the horror of such a situation, intolerable for Robert de Boron, who was a Cistercian and one of the most reliable guarantors of Christian morality, the poet wished to substitute a new person with no connection to Merlin's family. To her he assigned the role of perverse but cunning young girl, profiting to the utmost from the old enchanter's knowledge to become in turn the great enchantress, heiress to the powers of the great pagan goddess of the Celts. It is true that unconscious expressions have a difficult time of it. Is not Christianity's Holy Virgin the latest and most beautiful image of this Alma Mater whose virginity is debated according to the meaning one attributes to the term, but who for millennia nourished the hopes of believers of all the religions prior to Christianity?

Then Merlin meets Vivian. This happens by a fountain to remind us that Vivian is an aquatic goddess, and in a forest to remind us that she is a sylvan goddess, as well. This Vivian is absolutely *virgin*, that is, obstinate as to her availability. She knows nothing. She is not even self-sufficient: one might call her a "daddy's girl," and she says so clearly. It is not by chance that the name given her by her father means, supposedly in Chaldean, "Naught will I do." But, as it says in the text, "woman is more cunning than the devil." And the devil is Merlin. Vivian will learn from Merlin everything that she wants to know.

Here we are in the presence of Merlin's professorial vocation. In this respect he can be compared to a great druid deep in the forest, teaching the ancestral philosophy to those willing to follow his digressions. In the continental texts there are only two pupils, both young women: Morgan and Vivian. In the *Vita Merlini* his sister Gwendydd is his pupil and we learn almost by chance that he had a man as a pupil, as well— Thelgesinus, otherwise known as the bard Taliesin. This vocation of successfully teaching young women seems to echo an event contemporaneous with the earliest writings on Merlin: the completely authentic story of Abelard. And when all is said and done, is not Merlin's confinement in the forest of Brocéliande equivalent to the castration of Master Abelard?

So if one believes in the Arthurian romances, Merlin teaches his art to two women: Vivian and Morgan. His relationship with Morgan is not delineated, but in describing her it is said that she was extremely playful, "the most ardent and most lecherous woman in all Britain," and it is carefully noted that she studied with Merlin and acquired all of his knowledge.

It is necessary to explain how a mortal—Arthur's sister—is elevated to the rank of a superlative magician and is the incarnation of the mother goddess of the ancient Celts. Note that contrary to what occurs in pure Celtic texts, it is not women who teach men, but the reverse: it is the sign of a patriarchal society that is reacting forcefully against the gynecocratic tendencies of an earlier civilization. For in all the Irish or Welsh texts of that era, women teach magic to men. The young Peredur, equivalent to the Perceval of Chrétien de Troyes, acquires knowledge from the witches of Kerloyw.[3] The hero Finn mac Cumail is educated by women who are warriors and sorceresses. Cuchulainn learns the art of war and magic from the mysterious and formidable women Scatach, Uatach, and Aifé, with whom he enters into temporary marriages.[4]

In the French texts, after having become the Lady of the Lake, Vivian will resume the role of her ancient Celtic sisters by undertaking the education of young Lancelot, as well as that of Bohort, future hero of the quest for the Grail. But in the beginning she would be nothing without Merlin. The same is true of Morgan le Fay, mistress of Avalon, found in the texts of classical antiquity with the features of one of the mysterious women of the Isle of Sein, seers and magicians with the power to unleash or calm tempests. Morgan, who does not appear anywhere in the Welsh texts except in one passage of the *Vita Merlini*, seems to have been created by the authors of the French romances, but this is not true. She is one of the faces of the mother goddess, and if we search through Welsh mythology we discover her under the name of Modron (maternal), that is, the Gallic Matrona, eponym of the Marne. And even though the Irish name Morrigan is in no way linked to Morgan,[5] they perform identical functions.

In the Celtic tradition, as elsewhere in numerous "archaic" civilizations, the initiation into knowledge does not take place without specific sexual relations between master and disciple. One could say that knowledge is transmitted as much by the psychosensory activity awakened by sex as by reasoned intelligence. We in the West no longer understand this truth, so much has classical morality, inherited from a Christianity that was also poorly understood or poorly integrated,[6] cut us off from the realities of both body and spirit; so much have all sorts of prohibitions distanced us from the very principle of passing along traditional data, always valid through their various transformations, always challenged, always comprehensible on several levels. Without any doubt, Christian civilization caused this abandonment of psychosensory transmittal. But as Celtic civilization was essentially an oral one, it is not surprising to discover in it the marks of such transmission, which defies the laws of post-Aristotelian Mediterranean logic. These reflections lead us straight to the incest, real or latent, that is an integral part of the relations between figures in the Merlin epic, as well as in the entire Celtic cycle.

If at first we limit our reading to the *Vita Merlini*, we can have no doubt about the privileged relationship that Merlin enjoys with his sister Ganieda. He tolerates only her presence. He cares nothing about his wife Guendoloena, who can remarry as she wishes. It is different with Ganieda: Merlin even appears jealous of his brother-in-law, Rydderch. And the episode of the leaf in Queen Ganieda's hair can be interpreted in two different ways. Either Merlin is jealous of Ganieda having a lover and wants to take revenge by denouncing her to her husband, or he knows very well what has happened because he himself is her lover and wants to cause a rupture between Ganieda and Rydderch. In the corresponding episode of the *Life of Saint Kentigern* we know nothing of family ties between the queen and Lailoken, but the situation seems to be the same: a kind of vengeance on the part of the hero toward the unfaithful woman, or the desire to provoke the breakup of the official couple.

But upon Rydderch's death the situation becomes even clearer. Ganieda and Merlin are together when Rydderch dies. Merlin learns of this death by divination and orders his sister to go and deliver the funeral eulogy, which is rather surprising, since usually this function is performed by the official, or "household" bard. It should have been up to Merlin to go, especially since he does not seem to be suffering from madness at that moment. In fact, in the *Vita Merlini* he never appears to be a true madman. He merely refuses to return to society, although in that era the madman had his place there; he was regarded as worthy of interest and was listened to as someone having the power to "communicate the incommunicable."[7] And Ganieda, having accomplished this duty, returns to Merlin and decides to live with him. Here we have a brother-sister couple in which the woman becomes clearly privileged. Indeed, Ganieda begins to prophesy in her turn, and even better than Merlin. She has been initiated into prophesying by her brother and has learned so well that she is able to surpass the master. Henceforth Merlin will be silent: he will occupy only a secondary place. Ganieda is on the point of becoming the Lady of the Lake, absolute mistress of the sylvan domain that she herself had caused to be built, and in which one can imagine her keeping her brother, outside of time and space. Upon reflection, it is Merlin's confinement by Vivian. Of course, in the *Vita Merlini* Geoffrey makes no allusion to incestuous relations between Merlin and Ganieda, but the situation is perfectly equivocal, and if we admit that Ganieda corresponds to the character Vivian, there is no possible doubt. There are courtly and refined French versions, rewritten by the Cistercians or by clerics who collaborated with them, that are much watered down. The Welsh poems attributed to Myrddin are much more specific. They appear to refer to a tradition that Geoffrey did not even use, perhaps because of the risk of profoundly shocking his public.

Indeed Myrddin, alone in his forest, even in his apple tree, often complains of being abandoned. He does not seem to be a voluntary recluse, like a hermit choosing to live removed from the world, but a prisoner. And he grieves because Gwendydd does not come to see him. This is similar to what Merlin says to Vivian upon awakening in his magic castle after his confinement: "What would I do if you didn't come to see me?" And then, in the Welsh poems, there is the matter of a battle that Myrddin supposedly waged for a white maiden. It can only be Gwendydd. There are some fragments here that suggest a complete "saga" of Myrddin in the northern British or Welsh tradition. This might explain the mysterious battle of Arderyd; it would doubtless be the key to the problem of the relationship between Myrddin and Gwendydd. In any case, his dialogue with Gwendydd as he lies dying is significant: Gwendydd speaks to him in accents so touching and ardent that once again no doubt is possible—there was an incestuous relationship between Merlin and his sister.

There is nothing in the theme of fraternal incest that can surprise us. It is a theme that has been developed in every mythology and offers itself as the image of perfect union, of the *dyad* par excellence, with all its esoteric, mystical, and theological extensions. It is obviously the myth of Castor and Pollux before moral censorship masculinized one of the Dioscures without taking into account that this led to the development of another theme, homosexuality. It is the myth of the two children of Leto, Apollo and Artemis, who divided between themselves the light of the world, and spent their time seeking each other in order to couple in the rare moments of eclipse, privileged but dreaded moments of the conjunction of all the forces that give life to the world. It is the myth of Zeus and Hera, of Jupiter and Juno: the fact that they are brother and sister, children of Chronos and Gaia, does not prevent their sacred marriage, symbol of the equilibrium between Heaven and Earth. It is also true that in ancient Egypt the marriage of the Pharaohs with their sisters was obligatory, and that this practice existed also in ancient Persia, in Armenia, and in the Inca society. In Japan and among the Eskimos, who originally appear to have shared an identical culture, the myth of the Woman-Sun and the Man-Moon exemplify the primordial couple, brother and sister who are at the same time lovers and spouses.

If we truly understand the myth of Psyche, we find in it the same meaning. A narrative of the Cherokee Indians based on the same structure helps us to understand it: the Sun is Psyche and her brother, the Moon, is Love. The prohibition placed on Psyche against looking at her love in the light of day refers to the perpetual pursuit between sun and moon, but Psyche, who is determined to know the identity of her lover, darkens his face with soot, and thus realizes that he is her brother the Moon.

It is in the so-called primitive civilizations that fraternal incest seemed to be held most sacred, though subject to major interdictions. A legend of the Trobriand Islands recounts that the magic of love was born as a result of the transgression of fraternal incest. A woman has two children, a boy and a girl. One day the sister goes to look for wood; when she returns and enters the house, she asks for the water her brother is supposed to have brought back.[8] But the mother claims that she has no time to bother with that[9] and tells her daughter to go for the water. But on the way the girl knocks over a vessel in which her brother had boiled oil with mint.[10] A few drops of the oil fall on her and she is impregnated by the power of magic.[11] Rushing to her brother, who is bathing, she undresses, exciting his desire; they couple in the water.[12] And as both of them take pleasure in this, they often repeat the carnal act in a state of exaltation so intense that it borders on mystical ecstasy. Later on, a sorcerer who has seen them in a dream discovers them upon the rocks, entwined and dead,[13] a flowering mint growing across their bodies.[14] From that time on, mint boiled in coconut oil, a beverage over which an incantation is recited, is the basis of the ritual of love.[15]

In the Celtic domain the incidents of incestuous love between brother and sister are quite numerous. The most famous concerns King Arthur himself, who has sexual relations with one of his sisters (it is not specified which one; perhaps it is Morgan). But he does not realize that she is his sister, according to texts always concerned with dealing tactfully with the morals and customs of the society for which they are intended. The result of that incest is Mordret (Medrawt), who will dig the grave of the Arthurian kingdom, proving, according to the logic of Christianized accounts, that the transgression of incest leads inevitably to catastrophe. In Irish epic, which preserves many metaphysical elements of the druidic religion despite historical revision, the most famous case of this kind is the conception of the hero Cuchulainn, resulting from the relations of King Conchobar of Ulster with his sister Dechtire. We have two versions of this narrative;[16] both are somewhat modified and rather strange, as if someone had wanted to disguise the reality through allegedly logical explanations.

Indeed, in one version Dechtire takes to her bosom the child who has just been born to the wife of the host who receives Conchobar and his company. But the child dies. Afterwards the god Lug appears to Dechtire, telling her that she is pregnant with him. She is in fact pregnant, which occasions gossip among the Ulates, who believe that Conchobar is the father. The king hastily marries his sister to a certain Sualtam. But Dechtire secretly aborts and with Sualtam conceives another child, who will be Cuchulainn. We can see how muddled the story is and how the hero has had three births. In the second version Dechtire has fled with fifty maidens without Conchobar's permission, and they reappear as birds. The Ulates go after them, and Conchobar spends the night in a house where there is a woman with whom he wishes to make love. She refuses on the pretext that she is pregnant, but a young boy is found on the king's breast. We learn that he is Dechtire's son, so here, too, incest is more than conclusive. In any case, Cuchulainn has a mythical father, Lug; a social father, Sualtam; and a physical father, Conchobar.

Another example even closer to Merlin is the relationship between Gwyddyon and Arianrod. In this case as well, the texts provide few details; it is Gwyddyon's determination to raise young Lleu and have him recognized by his sister that leads us to our conclusion. Besides, Gwyddyon is never shown with a woman; Arianrod never appears with a man. The union of brother and sister also engenders an unusual person for, on close examination, Lleu is another aspect of the famous god Lug (the names Lleu and Lug, moreover, are akin to each other), whereas Cuchulainn is really a sort of incarnation of Lug. One could go even further, for in the Arthurian romances Vivian has an adopted son, Lancelot of the Lake, who represents the god Lug Lamfada (Lug of the Long Hand), and whose exploits and heroic character he shares.

In the archaic version of Lancelot's adventures, before he is linked to the Arthurian legend—that is, in the *Lanzelet* of Ulrich von Zatzikhoven[17]—the Lady of the Lake, who is not named but in whom we recognize Vivian, already has a son before she abducts young Lancelot. But this son remains concealed in a fortress because of a curse laid upon him: he has become a coward, and all those who enter his fortress, even if they are the most courageous in the world, become cowards in their turn. It is certainly a strange story, all the more so because the Lady of the Lake's son is named Mabuz (a name of Celtic origin based on *mab*, "son"), and is also found in Welsh legend in the form of Mabon, son of Modron (Matrona), another representation of the mother goddess.

Now, this Mabon, known in Gaul according to inscriptions as Maponus, an epithet for Apollo, was abducted from his mother and held captive in a subterranean prison at Kaer Lloyw (Gloucester), and it is Arthur and his companions who, in the story of "Culhwch and Olwen," will come to free him. In *Lanzelet* it is Lancelot who, after multiple adventures, will lift the curse and deliver Mabuz, by which he will learn his name. We perceive that the Lady of the Lake abducted young Lancelot only so that he would free her son Mabuz.

There are, therefore, clear connections linking Vivian, Modron, and Dechtire. This is also the case with Conchobar and Merlin, if only because of the incest that places them in the ranks of the divine. For incest is forbidden to common mortals, being reserved for elite beings only, those strong enough to support the magic shock of such a union. It is primarily a matter of hierogamy, a symbolic union between two beings who share an identical birth. The myth of the primitive androgyne is always present: from the moment when the species was sexed, or divided, into male and female, each of the components dreams only of rejoining its complementary half. And what reunion could be more ideal, more significant, than the one between brother and sister?

It will be said that this all lies in the realm of fantasy, and without doubt, the mythology gives form to the most varied fantasies of human beings. But we must remember what Caesar said about the Britons, especially about the Picts, whose tradition was matrilineal and whose sexual promiscuity was shocking. We must also consider the words of the Carolingian chronicler Ermold the Black, who described in the ninth century the state of the Armorican peninsula at the time of the military expedition of Louis the Pious. He portrays the Armorican Britons as true savages and adds: *"coeunt frater et ipsa soror"* (book 3, verse 1301), that is, "the brother lies with his own sister." One wonders if in the ancient Celtic civilization fraternal incest was, if not an institution, at least a custom. And we know that customs do not originate by chance. Often they have a religious or metaphysical foundation that is no longer understood but that is constantly renewed on a subconscious level.

As it has matured in the imagination of writers, it has even become a literary theme. Even so, this theme is never gratuitous. We have only to think of the behavior of Lord Byron toward his half sister, with whom he consciously engaged in sexual relations. It was a solemn affirmation of something, the power of a sacred union damned by the conformist morality of the society of his time, a society more and more detached from its mythical roots.

Let us look at the case of Chateaubriand. The author of *Atala* was in love with his sister Lucile, that much is obvious. And Lucile was in love with her brother. Chateaubriand described it in *René*, giving the adventure an indisputable moral conclusion; the meeting of Amélie and René in the convent where she takes the veil is heartrending, but it is the only possible solution for escaping the transgression of the forbidden. But in the *Mémoires d'Outre-Tombe* the great writer, probably the most perceptive of all Celtic authors, analyzes the basis of the problem with a candor that allows us to understand the situation. Chateaubriand and Lucile passed the same dreamy childhood in the groves of Upper Brittany and within the austere walls of the chateau of Combourg. Lucile introduced him to poetry. She made her brother dream, transmitted some of her powers to him; as he wrote, "on the Caledonian heath Lucile would have been the celestial wife of Walter Scott, endowed with second sight; on the Armorican heath she was but a lone woman gifted with beauty, genius, and unhappiness." All this is clear. Lucile is the fairy, the prophetess. Chateaubriand himself is the enchanter. The legend of Vivian and Merlin crosses the threshold of the unconscious mind and is embodied in real people. Through the mists bequeathed by Ossianic poetry reexamined and corrected by MacPherson, Chateaubriand could not help thinking of the Fountain of Barenton, which he had occasion to visit, and where he claims to have evoked the shades of heroes of bygone days. Incest, yes, without a doubt, even if only psychoaffective. And Chateaubriand would bear its mark all his life, projecting on both his heroines and his mistresses the face of his beloved sister. It is the proof of the spell that can be created by the myth of Vivian and Merlin.

It is also the appearance in man's affective life of that idealized image of woman—of that brother-being, or of that sister-soul, whatever one wishes to call it—which is simply the dreamer's double. In the final analysis Vivian is Merlin's double, a double who is ethereal, airy, angelic, or demonic as the case may be. She is Chateaubriand's famous "Sylphide" who haunts the forests and is sometimes seen on the curve of a path or near a fountain. She is the one whom the author of *Atala* also called his "demon." She can only be a divine personage, a fairy, a prophetess, a Beatrice leading the poet to the "sacred fields," to use Nerval's expression.

For Nerval, too, relived this theme of Merlin and Vivian. The image of Sylvie, superimposing itself on his feverish imagination, the image of Adrienne, glimpsed on a holiday evening in a meadow by moonlight, facing an old chateau in the style of Louis XIII, would inspire in him a passionate search for woman—for the eternal sister who is also lover, wife, and mother. There are many other cases where incest appears in the troubled waters of dream. Isis, Venus, Mary, mother, daughter, sister: she embodies them all plus something else that the author of the *Chimères* would never discover. Unless it was the final image borne away by the poet when he hanged himself from a street lamp in a sordid alley of a Paris sunk in mud and misfortune. *The thirteenth returns, it is still the first. . . .* The multiple faces of the goddess disconcert those who do not know how to recognize her.

In the archaic Welsh version of the account of the Grail, the hero Peredur often meets a woman who guides him in his adventures. She has different names, different faces, different roles. She is, nevertheless, the one called the "empress," the uncontested sovereign of those regions where dawn and dusk mingle in an eternal outpouring of lights and shadows. Vivian or Gwendydd, Niniane or Ganieda? No matter the name, she is always the same; it is she whom Merlin calls on with all of his force, since she is indispensable to him if he is to be wholly himself. The same is true in ancient Hindu mythology, wherein each God is inoperative, nonexistent, and impotent without his female double, his *shakti*, his source of power at his side. And the *shakti* is always of the same essence and the same origin as he who puts into action the force she incarnates. This explains the importance of incest as the purest and most perfect union of two beings who are called on to change the face of the world. It is from this perspective that the divine couple, for Merlin and Vivian are such a couple, derive all of their symbolic value.

All the same, there is usually an identification between mother and daughter, and so the sister can be either the mother or the daughter. Queen Iseult of Ireland is originally the sorceress who heals Tristan. Soon she becomes Iseult the Blonde, the daughter, endowed with the same powers, the rejuvenated figure of the ancient queen of the fairies. In "The Education of Cuchulainn," at first the young hero is initiated by the sorceress Scatach and afterwards by Uatach, the former's daughter. This means that in most mythological themes incest can not be reduced only to relations between brother and sister but can also involve relations between mother and son and between father and daughter. Such is the case in the *Story of Taliesin*. When Gwyon Bach is ingested by Keridwen in the form of a grain of corn he is Keridwen's lover, and when he is born as Taliesin he is her son; yet both are the same person. Here we encounter the myth of Cybele and Attis. And it implies a very clear interpretation of the famous "operation of the Holy Spirit," by which Christ is begotten.[18] Incest exists, then, as a necessity: it is the means of the rejuvenation of the divinity, of his metamorphosis. The old sun Osiris, after coupling with his sister Isis, becomes his own son, the young sun Horus. And if we read the Bible literally we must consider Japheth's descendants the results of incest practiced by Eve and Japheth.

And it is in the Bible that another type of incest is found: that of the daughters of Lot who mate with their father to assure the continuation of the race. This utilitarian and primordial purpose is put forward as if to excuse the act itself, scandalous in the eyes of the law. Lot, moreover, was not a conscious participant in this operation and it is made very clear that the entire fault, if there is any fault, lies with his daughters. It is the sign of a gynecocratic era in which the male was nothing outside of his procreative role. But it is also the proof that relations between father and daughter can be favored in certain circumstances. This type of incest is found in a context similar to the legend of Merlin.

We have said that Vivian can be considered the equivalent Be-Finn or Boinn, the queen of the fairies of Ireland. Boinn, divinity of springs, lakes, and rivers, is the other name of Brigit. And Brigit is the only daughter of Dagda, the great Irish god who is one of the famous Tuatha Dé Danann, whose name means "Good God," and who is sometimes known by the circumlocutory cognomen Eochaid Ollathir, that is "Eochaid (knight?) Powerful Father" or "Father of Everything." Now Dagda, as we will see, is the druid-god par excellence and has many things in common with Merlin; and in the Irish tradition we are told that Dagda had "adulterous," meaning incestuous, relations with Boinn,[19] the wife of his brother Elcmar, and so his own sister-in-law as well as his daughter. It is with Boinn that he has a son, Oengus, also called Mac Oc,[20] who is destined for great things. Later on, according to one version of the legend, Oengus disposses him of his residence of Brug na Boyne by way of a very specious contract.[21] Another version asserts that it is his putative father Elcmar whom Oengus dispossesses in this manner.[22] Be that as it may, it is a clear-cut case of incest that, because of the identification of Boinn with Vivian, returns us to the matter of Merlin.

6

G THE OD CONFINED

 It comes as a surprise to all who follow Merlin's adventures that the old enchanter succumbs so easily to Vivian's perverse charms, allowing himself to be confined in the prison of air when, on the one hand, he knew the future and, on the other hand, possessed superior magical powers. Despite attempts to explain Merlin's attitude in terms of his mad passion for Vivian and so to arrive at a pretty conclusion concerning the power of love, the real problem is ignored. Why does Merlin, of his own free will, decide to have himself incarcerated?

The first answer comes to mind from a comparison with the *Vita Merlini*: Ganieda, seized by prophetic frenzy, begins to make predictions, and at that moment Merlin says that he himself will never again prophesy because Ganieda is superior to him. It is a confession. His powers are now weaker than those of Vivian. It is indeed a true transference of power. Divinities, whoever they are and whatever form they take, are subject to destiny: they must be born, accomplish their mission, and then die or disappear to make room for younger divinities. Symbolically, since mythology portrays a divine personage according to the concept of that god during a particular period, it is necessary to adapt or transform whatever aspect can no longer be felt or understood by an evolving society. It is true that each age has its gods; that is why there are so many battles between gods in mythological accounts, so many divine metamorphoses, so many dismemberments, so many disappearances or concealments. In the story of Dagda, he does not die; he is simply removed from his principal home by his son, Oengus, but is obviously diminished by the adventure. It is almost the same with Merlin: he does not die but is simply put out of the way. This allows for the possibility of encountering him again later under another name, another aspect. He is simply in a state of suspended animation, like Arthur on the Isle of Avalon, or like Cronus, whom Zeus put in chains on an island somewhere in the west. When a regeneration, meaning a revolution, occurs, the old god will be freed and will take his place in the world, renewing it and restoring all of its vitality. The same may be said for the myth of the Golden Age, the messianic myth, and the myth of the Grail, in which the old, impotent king laments while waiting for the "Young Son" who will restore prosperity to the Waste Land.

In any case, Merlin has voluntarily chosen what might be called his retreat. In the *Vita Merlini*, it is he who ardently desires to live in the woods. His madness is just a logical pretext advanced to justify this obvious abandonment of his territory. And in the poems attributed to Myrddin we see that his "madness" is far from certain. In the French version of the legend there exists an episode which has received too little attention: the stroll that Merlin and Vivian take along the shore of the lake of Diana.

It is Merlin who calls the tune. He asks Vivian if she wants to see the lake of Diana. She answers, "To be sure. There can be nothing of Diana that does not please me, for all her life she loved the woods as much and more than I." That answer already suggests a possible identification between Vivian and Diana-Artemis, and it is Vivian herself who announces it. She defines herself as a sylvan divinity. Merlin then shows her the tomb of Faunus where these words can be read: "Here lies Faunus, friend of Diana. She bore him a great love and wickedly caused his death. She was his reward for having served her loyally." When Vivian asks for an explanation, Merlin tells her the story of a strongly heroic Diana bearing little resemblance to her image in the Greek legends. This Diana, who lived in the time of Virgil, had made her home in the forest of Brocéliande because it was the most beautiful of all the forests in which she had hunted. She ordered a beautiful manor built near the lake, and became the lover of Faunus, the son of the king of that country. Their liaison lasted for two years, but Diana became infatuated with another handsome young man, Felix. He refused to see her again unless she rid herself of her first lover, thus claiming exclusive possession of Diana. But Diana knew that Faunus would never leave her, and so she had recourse to great treachery.

On the lake shore was a fountain that healed all wounds. (This re-

calls the famous Fountain of Health of the Tuatha Dé Danann in Ireland, in which the god Diancecht had placed all the herbs of the island, and which healed the gravest illnesses and wounds.[1] It also recalls
the cauldron of the Welsh hero Bran and the one found by Peredur in
his peregrinations, a cauldron that healed and revived.[2]) Now, one day
when Faunus had been wounded while hunting, Diana had the fountain emptied. As Faunus complained of not being able to take care of
himself, Diana told him to lie down in the fountain, saying that she
would cover him with the healing herbs. But she let the stone slab fall
down again on Faunus and, as the most refined touch of all, had molten
lead poured into a hole so that her lover's body was burned very quickly.
Having rid herself of Faunus, Diana went off in triumph to look for
Felix who, outraged by her wickedness, cut off her head. As for the
castle, it was destroyed by Faunus's father.

It certainly seems that Merlin intentionally tells this story that so
prefigures his own demise. Curiously, however, there is a detail in this
account that is found only in Malory's English version: the large rock
under which Nimue immures Merlin, that is, puts him to death. In any
case it is a confinement; assuming that Vivian identifies with Diana,
she must understand the profound meaning of the narrative, all the
more so since, after hearing it, she asks Merlin to build her a magnificent castle. This Merlin does. The magical castle now rises on the site
of the lake, yet if someone were to reveal its secret the castle would
vanish before him and be engulfed by the waters. We have here the
theme of the invisible castle in which Merlin will be held, and of the
magical castle in which the Lady of the Lake will raise Lancelot.

Vivian does not appear to be troubled, however. She avails herself of
the opportunity to ask Merlin how to confine a man forever. There is a
kind of dialogue of the deaf between them. In any event Merlin cannot
be the dupe of a game played by one he loves so madly. He is the
master of magic, master of illusions created at will (like his other pupil,
Morgan, mistress of the Valley of No Return where she imprisons knights
unfaithful to their ladies) but he is no longer master of his destiny. And
matters must unfold, since it has been determined by a superior power
that they do so.

Besides, Merlin's role is finished. He began his career very early,
prophesying to King Vortigern that he would be defeated; leading Uther
Pendragon to victory; arranging the conception of the future King

Arthur, having him crowned, and giving him useful counsel to stabilize the ideal society of the Arthurian knighthood; establishing the Round Table; and revealing some of the mysteries of the Grail. But that is the limit of the magician-prophet's intervention, at least in this appearance. He has played the role of a messenger of God. He has shown the way. Perhaps it is time now for the wise man to retire and ponder the dark times to come. His magic is not lost, for he leaves two pupils, Morgan and Vivian. Morgan will be charged with Arthur's long, deathlike sleep and future reappearance. Vivian will have the duty of turning a young fugitive child into the shining knight, Lancelot of the Lake. If we can believe the *Vita Merlini*, he leaves a third pupil as well, the bard Taliesin whose task is to relate the great secrets of the world, at least those that can be transmitted to ears that know how to listen.

According to the standards of Indo-European tradition, so much involved with triads and tripartitions, Merlin is a kind of organizer god. If in Hindu mythology, at least in its simplified form, Brahma is the Creator, a superior being without direct action, and Shiva the destroyer of creation, Vishnu is the organizer of the world—and Merlin is his equivalent. But Vishnu is not always there: he sends his various avatars, such as Indra, to realize the patient work that takes place through the ages. As Merlin sends out Arthur, whom he wanted and, though he did not sire him, "fabricated" by his machinations. And Vishnu, like Merlin, retreats from the world.

Other than in the passage in Malory where Nimue appears to kill Merlin by crushing him under the great rock raised by his magic, we find not the slightest allusion to Merlin's death, except in a conversation he has with his sister Gwendydd, but even this is only a sequence of regrets: we do not see the poet die. So Merlin is not dead; he is simply hidden. And the fact that he is confined in a prison of air or a glass castle can give rise to numerous commentaries.

First, it is important to compile a list of the different descriptions of the place in which Merlin is confined, according to the multiple versions of the legend.

1. In *The Story of Merlin* it is an invisible castle surrounded by walls that are translucent but insurmountable.
2. In the Didot *Perceval*, in which there is no mention of Vivian, after the quest for the Grail Merlin retires to a house he has built near the

castle. He is with his master Blaise in this *éplumoir*, but when he is in residence there no human eye can see him.

3. In the romance *Méraugis de Portlesguez* this "*éplumoir* Merlin" is a large rock that overhangs a river, on which live nine sorceresses.

4. In *The Life of Saint Kentigern* Merlin, or rather Lailoken, prophesies upon a large rock that overhangs a river.

5. In Malory's *Le Morte d'Arthur* Merlin is literally "entombed" under a great rock by Nimue.

6. In Geoffrey's *Vita Merlini* Merlin retires with his sister Ganieda to a residence in the middle of the woods. The principal dwelling, reserved for Merlin, has seventy doors and seventy windows from which astronomical observations can be made.

7. In Triad 113 mention is made of the disappearance of Myrddin, who had gone by sea to look for the House of Glass.

8. In one of the poems attributed to Myrddin, he describes being in an apple tree, which is understood to be invisible to those passing by.

9. An eighteenth-century text (*Iolo Manuscripts*) states that the thirteen magical objects of the Isle of Britain were taken by Myrddin to the House of Glass.

10. The Irish text of *The Madness of Suibhné* describes the life of the mad king in a yew tree in the middle of the forest.

It can be seen that a simple rock figures in two of these ten descriptions: on top of this rock Lailoken prophesies, and under it Merlin is treacherously "entombed" by Nimue. The remaining eight descriptions, although different, are analogous or corroborate each other.

Indeed, the detail of invisibility is latent everywhere in the account of Suibhné, and quite specific elsewhere. One does not see Merlin in the *éplumoir* that bears his name and on which are nine sorceresses. In the dwelling where Merlin lives with Blaise he is invisible from outside. In the house with seventy windows, reserved for Merlin alone, one can very well imagine the prophet observing the outside world without being seen. As for the detail of the seventy windows, obviously it refers to the invisible prison of air whose walls are insurmountable, and to the house of glass. Here we are in the presence of a very old myth, particularly conveyed by the Celts whether in Ireland, in Wales, or on the continent. As we know, Nennius, or at least one of the authors of the *Historia Britonnum*, retold an adventure in which the ancestors of the

Irish, navigating the ocean, encountered a tower of glass in which there were people. But when they spoke to them, these people did not reply. Though they tried to take the tower by storm, the attempt turned into a catastrophe and most of them were drowned. This theme must have been known in classical antiquity, for in Latin poets such as Ovid we find references to these "silent ones" who live in the middle of the ocean and do not answer those who address them.

But what is interesting is the tower of glass in which these "silent ones" are confined. If they are silent they must belong to the otherworld. Therefore, the tower or house of glass *is* the otherworld. When, in the twelfth century, the Abbey of Glastonbury was designated by order of the Plantagenets as the famous Isle of Avalon where Arthur sleeps, watched over by Morgan, the name "Glastonbury" was explained as meaning the "City of Glass"—the Kaer Wydr found in the poem "Remains of the Abyss" attributed to Taliesin.[3] Perhaps we should see in this tradition the memory of old Celtic camps that were vitrified (at least their walls—the result of fire vitrifying the siliceous components, as in the Camp of Péran, not far from Saint-Brieuc), but its origin certainly seems to be older, and rests on analogical connections comparing transparency and insurmountability.

The first analogy concerns water, which is also insuperable and yet translucent. It is known that the dwelling place of the spirits is always on the other side of a river or on an island in the sea, for according to an old belief, the spirits cannot cross a liquid element. This brings to mind the intrauterine situation, in which the fetus floats in amniotic liquid. This is the reason that heaven, especially the Celtic one, is often represented as an island.

The second analogy is also aquatic but relates directly to ice. It is very likely that the legends of the isle of glass came into being largely as a result of icebergs, those impressive and most inexplicable floating mountains encountered by navigators. If we believe the Irish texts concerning the Tuatha Dé Danann, moreover, they had arrived at "the islands of the north of the world," which would imply a hyperborean influence; the ramparts of ice are thus completely integrated into beliefs about a mysterious country, separated from the rest of the world by insurmountable walls that have the appearance of glass.

The third analogy follows from the second. Icebergs and walls of ice can reflect sunlight with great intensity, from which emerged a new mythological concept incorporating the sun into that mysterious and impenetrable domain. The otherworld will become the domain of the sun, the palace of the sun, and as the sun is a female element, imagination will people this island or fortress with strange women ruled by a sun-woman even more beautiful than the others, mistress of life and death, a mother divinity like Morgan, or like Vivian in the prison of air where she holds Merlin. Therefore it is not surprising to see so many islands and castles inhabited solely by women in Celtic legendry, whether Irish, Breton, or continental. And thus the elements that make this feminine representation a divinity of the heavens and a divinity of water at the same time are combined: in fact, she is the virgin mother, heaven and water. She gives life. She is the mother of gods and of men.

In addition, this island or fortress of glass, translucent and sparkling, sometimes opaque, evokes the idea of whiteness, from which comes the symbolism and richness of white since, not being a color, it contains them all. Fairies, therefore, will be white ladies, and many mythological heroines have names that refer to whiteness.

And what about human fantasies? Those shining walls that are almost transparent, yet conceal what goes on behind them, excite the imagination to the highest degree. They develop what could be called the "voyeur complex." We want to see, we want to know. Mystery provokes curiosity. And we can imagine that on the other side of those walls the strange beings who live in the house of glass are also voyeurs, observing human behavior. For the gods have the reputation of knowing everything that happens on earth. In his house of seventy windows Merlin will be able to observe not only the stars, but men as well. Yet he will not be seen. The fantasy of a two-way mirror is not far from these mythological considerations, and there is never anything gratuitous in human behavior. Everything relates to more or less unconscious myths that are relived according to each person's experience.

There is another fantasy grafted onto this "voyeurism": the recreation of the orginal scene, meaning parental coitus. Indeed, it is in this cosmic "egg" that life is born. The desire to see into it implies the desire to return whence one came in order to be born again under better conditions. One one hand there is a terrestrial paradise inside the insurmountable walls, and on the other hand all the riches that one could want. It is therefore necessary to undertake an expedition either to carry off the riches of the otherworld or to live there for a while in order to undergo a regenerative cure. This is the sense in which the isle of glass or the house of glass is described to us as an orchard where the fruit is ripe in every season, where time no longer exists, where everything is beautiful and bathed in the beneficent and regenerative rays of the sun. The house of glass is nothing but a *serre* [greenhouse] in which grow the most beautiful flowers and fruits of the world, and it will be seen that the term *enserrement* [confinement] referring to Merlin is not fortuitous in this context of the Golden Age, lost and then found again. It is, then, the enclosed space protected from all inclement weather, the miraculous orchard in the heart of an ice-pack, in which all the rays of the sun converge—a place that is sometimes the sun itself—where the gradual transformation and rejuvenation of people and things takes place.[4] In the final analysis, it is the maternal womb.

Numerous Irish legends describe this isle of glass. The enclosed world where Merlin is confined in Vivian's agreeable company is easily recognized. *The Voyage of Maelduin*, a very beautiful and extremely poetic narrative, is tale of a hero and his companions as they roam among magical islands. One of them is an "island on a pedestal." Another one is at the bottom of the sea: the water is limpid and, leaning over the edge of the ship, they can see the roofs of houses (the myth of the city engulfed, which is simply a variant of the city of glass). Elsewhere an island is surrounded by a wall of insuperable waves. Finally they approach an island on which stands a magical fortress protected by four walls, one of them crystal. They reach the fortress by a glass bridge and are welcomed by a woman of great beauty who serves them marvelous food and exquisite beverages, recalling the Feast of Immortality, or the Feast of the Grail.

In another account the principal character is Art, son of King Conn of the Hundred Battles. As the result of a fairy's magic incantation he must seek a young lady whom he has to marry but whose place of residence he does not know. He comes to a magical island and is lavishly received by its queen, Creidé, who installs him in a "chamber of crystal. Beautiful was the appearance of this chamber with its crystal doors and inexhaustible cisterns, for though they were never filled they were always full." The hero remains for a month in this crystal chamber where all the rays of the sun converge, and there he acquires a new strength, an energy enabling him to face the worst perils. One cannot help but compare this crystal chamber with the alchemical athanor—

the retort, sometimes clay and sometimes glass, used in the conversion of the raw material for the preparation of the Philosopher's Stone, source of all wealth and knowledge, but also a universal cure.

Exactly the same description is found in an important fragment of *The Story of Etaine*, one of the oldest Irish mythological accounts. The heroine has been entrusted by her father to Oengus so that he may take her to his foster father Mider, who is in love with her and marries her. But in a fit of jealousy Mider's first wife, the magician Fuamnach, transforms Etaine into an insect that Oengus, the Mac Oc, plucks from his coat. "Oengus places her on his chest in a fold of his coat. He takes her to his dwelling (Brug na Boyne) and to his sun chamber of sparkling windows. . . . He placed crimson ornaments there . . . the Mac Oc fell into the habit of sleeping next to her in the sun chamber every night, and he comforted her until her joy and her color returned, then he filled the sun chamber with beautiful green plants, and the insect thrived on the flowers of these good and precious plants."

This "sun chamber," a reduced image of the house or the isle of glass, is a very widely known theme. The text of the *Folie Tristan* gives us a rather precise description of it. Tristan has disguised himself as a madman in order to penetrate the fortress of Tintagel so that he can approach Iseult without being recognized. He amuses King Mark and his knights. He proposes to the king to exchange Iseult for his own lady love. And when the king asks him where he will take the queen, he answers that he has a crystal chamber in the air, suspended between heaven and earth, a magical chamber where the sun enters and the most marvelous flowers bloom. Thus Iseult will truly be in paradise. Obviously there are several levels on which this description can be read. On the level of the imaginary, it is ideal happiness, the seventh heaven. But it is also the glorious isolation of two people who love each other and no longer need anyone else. This is the theme of the legend of Tristan and Iseult: that the two lovers, united by a perfect love and having no need of other members of society, are not only no longer useful to that society, but are even harmful to it and must therefore be eliminated, pursued, and destroyed. For love is incompatible with the norms of a society built upon marriage. This isolation can only occur under certain circumstances, outside of time and space, from which comes the notion of the crystal chamber—the equivalent of the chamber of the sun in the Irish texts—placing the lovers halfway between heaven and earth, no longer completely human but not yet gods. And that is where the gradual maturation of people occurs, in the framework of an enclosed paradise, shielded from a hostile world and in constant communication with the living forces of nature symbolized by the sun.

Besides, this fantastic and paradisiacal situation had happened before to Tristan and Iseult, in the forest of Morrois according to the common version of Béroul, in a grotto according to the advanced version of Gottfried de Strasbourg, which in this is very much like the prototype of the legend, the Irish story of Diarmaid and Grainne. For the forest and the grotto clearly represent that enclosed and feminine world in which sensitivity rather than logic reigns, a world in which truly "the heart has its reasons that reason cannot know." But in both episodes, in the forest and in the grotto, the heroes, no doubt unprepared for this trial, fail in their attempt to restore the Golden Age. That is why the so-called madman Tristan imagines, in his daydream, a life with Iseult in that crystal chamber—the chamber in which the insect Etaine is being refreshed; in which Art, son of Conn, is being regenerated; in which Merlin wakes from his magic sleep under the attentive and passionate eyes of Vivian.

Such a concept presupposes a sublimation of love, which is considered the prime mover of every step toward the divine. The *Lancelot* of Chrétien de Troyes shows us this, thanks to an apparently "courtly" theme that is in reality dependent on primitive myth. Queen Guinevere has been abducted by Meleagant, a kind of underworld god, and taken by him to the kingdom of Gorre (or Voirre), that is, "the city of glass" of ancient traditions. Lancelot and Gawain launch a search for the one they love, each in his fashion. In order to reach the kingdom of glass, which is clearly presented as the otherworld, for it is the "country from which none returns," it is necessary to cross strange bridges. One is the Bridge of the Sword: a sharp sword is placed over a rushing torrent and can be crossed only by wounding oneself horribly. The other is the Bridge Under Water: it must be discovered at the risk of being swept away by whirlpools. These are shamanistic concepts; Mircea Eliade has noted parallels between the text of Chrétien de Troyes and the beliefs of Asiatic shamanism. The water is the wall, equivalent to the walls of glass surrounding the island, or the house in the middle of the sea or lake. Crossing it is a transgression of a prohibition and few are capable of undertaking it. Lancelot will take the Bridge of the Sword. Gawain will take the Bridge Under Water. In the end it is Gawain who will bring back the queen, renewed by her stay in the City of Glass. Lancelot, who is not yet at his level, will have to remain in a tower for long months before facing Meleagant in a decisive combat that will give him the right to lay claim to Guinevere. It is perhaps because he entered the forbidden city by the Bridge of the Sword. Perhaps the initiatory road passes over the Bridge Under Water, because water is the true frontier that separates the world of the living from that of gods and heroes. But the text of Chrétien de Troyes is too overloaded with the sociological elements of his era; we can no longer accurately distinguish the threads of the original myth.

In *The Story of Merlin*, on the other hand, the threads are old, even though they can be transcribed to a psychological plane. Certainly Merlin agrees to vanish to the other side for love—a mad love—as he says himself, for he loves his love more than his freedom. But this interpretation, however attractive from a uniquely literary and poetic perspective, does not obscure its metaphysical and religious realities; it is in the closed vessel of the crystal chamber that the perfect fusion of two alchemical elements, represented by Merlin and Vivian, can take place. Merlin in his wisdom has understood this completely, and so allows himself, in full consciousness, to be swept into the adventure. There, it is no longer the world of illusion over which the old enchanter reigns, but the world of supreme realities, to which he aspires and which only the female figure of Vivian is capable of procuring for him by her love.

And besides, Merlin's confinement in the aerial fortress is completely in character. We must not forget that in all versions of the legend Merlin is the man of the forest. This aerial fortress or house of glass in which he finds himself is an enclosed world in the middle of the forest inside whose invisible walls is an otherworld, an orchard. The dyad, the sacred union of the god-brother and the goddess-sister, is achieved in this orchard. Withdrawn from the world because they are living an absolute love that by its nature cuts them off from society, Merlin and Vivian are sufficient unto themselves. They return to the primordial condition of Adam and Eve before sin, before they became aware of the outside world. Being cut off confers on them a fresh virginity, that is, a new potential for living. More than ever, Merlin is the man of the forest and the druid-shaman. In the perpetual transformations of divinities, the stages are not necessarily identical. A god who is active, a generating force, an organizer of the world, can become the *deus otiosus* who withdraws to his ivory tower, as Vigny said, in magnificent isolation. Merlin is in a state of dormition, as is Arthur himself. They will return, more powerful than ever.

In this sense the god's confinement, far from being a catastrophe, is a regeneration of the functions he embodies, especially as a mediator between man and nature. For he is a man of the woods, master of plants and wild animals; he is a druid, magician, and priest, and, like the shamans, a medicine man. It is from this perspective that he is so valuable to an era in which civilization, crushed by industrial centralization, is cut off from the deep roots that once nourished it with the juices of earth.

PART 4

The Man of the Forest

In all accounts of him, whatever their circumstances, one motif dominates the description of Merlin: his special alliance with trees. Above all, Merlin appears as a man of the forest. Whether he has retreated to the prison of air, the house of glass, the *éplumoir*, a tree (an apple tree), or a house of wood, one constant is obvious. There is even an evident play on words between the *maison de verre* ["house of glass"], the *pays de verre* ["country of glass"], and the *vert* [green] of the trees in all the French texts.[1] It is noteworthy enough to connect the myth represented by Merlin to a "tree cult," or at least to metaphysical elements of an indispensable complementary character between man and nature. The myth of Merlin and the legends that bring him to life clearly refer, therefore, to a naturistic type of religion like the religion of the Celts, or druidism.

Unquestionably, Merlin is the man of the forest. If he has occasion to move in established society, whether in an ancient kingdom (since Geoffrey tells us that he was a king) or in King Arthur's entourage, he does not make his home there. He is seen arriving at Arthur's court unexpectedly, coming from somewhere else. He is, in short, a marginal figure who deigns to enter the social world only to give counsel, make prophecies, or perform a magic feat. As soon as he has accomplished his design he returns to his own domain. And this domain is the forest. This is what he will do, with his sister or with Vivian, when he definitively renounces the world. And it will be but the continuation of a situation that he has experienced already.

It is difficult to really explain someone without looking attentively at his environment, by which he is conditioned and which it might be said justifies his behavior. Merlin occupies a space that is very firm and well defined, and corresponds to the place of the cult of the ancient Celts. It is a sacred space, a sanctuary in the heart of the woods.

7

S THE
ACRED CLEARING

 We now know that the Celts had never built temples before the Roman conquest and, on the periphery of their domain, in some cases not before they came under the Mediterranean influence.[1] Greek and Latin writers never used the words *naos* [temple or shrine] and *aedes* [temple] to designate the Gallic sanctuaries, and we know of only one example, and that questionable, of a pre-Roman temple in Great Britain, at Heathrow in Middlesex. Julius Caesar, who knew Gaul comparatively well, does not speak of a single constructed temple. Though Suetonius accuses him of having pillaged the *fana* and the *templa* of the Gauls, he means Cisalpine Gaul, that is, the plain of the Po, long under Roman, or at least Etruscan, influence.

On the other hand, the testimony of Latin authors regarding religious centers located in the midst of forests is perfectly clear. The most famous is that of Lucan, in the *Pharsalia*. In fact it evokes the Gallic druids "who live in the deep woods (*nemora alta*) and retreat to uninhabited forests. There they practice barbaric rites and a kind of sinister cult." It is noted in the manuscript that in this place "they worship the gods in the woods without recourse to temples."[2]

The Latin term used by Lucan, *nemus*, which really means the "sacred wood," the "sylvan sanctuary," is not in doubt. But another passage of the *Pharsalia* tells us even more about this subject. The poet tells us how, near Marseilles, Caesar destroyed a sacred wood in which tree trunks, roughly sculpted, were "sad representations of gods." He adds that barbarous rites in honor of the gods were practiced in this place, and that sumptuous offerings were brought there. And, of course, every tree trunk was splashed with human blood. There is also a rather detailed and poetic description of springs that gush forth in the darkness and shadowy thickets which no wild beast could approach. All this recalls the wooden statues found in the sanctuary of the sources of the Seine, as well as the legend of the Fountain of Barenton; near it was the "Lord's Copse," a privileged place where there was "neither fly nor venomous beast." Lucan insists on the wild nature of this sacred wood: although a priest officiated there for the *dominus* of the site, people never came near, but abandoned the place to the god, and "the priest himself feared his approach, being afraid of the master of the woods."[3]

Lucan also speaks of the superstitious terror of the natives when they were asked to cut down the trees "that the hand of man had never touched since the most remote times." It is certain that the sanctuary itself had always been subject to a strict interdict among the Celts; thus, in the temples built in the Roman era, whose plan in no way corresponds to a Roman sanctuary, there was necessarily a *cella* to which the public was not admitted. This *cella* was a sort of "holy of holies" to which only the priest had right of entry. This observation is corroborated by a text of Pomponius Mela who informs us that "the druids teach many things to the highest nobility of the nation, secretly, for twenty years, either in caves or in distant forests."

The Celtic temple was, therefore, in the midst of nature and absolutely removed from the social life of the group, as opposed to the custom of all Indo-European peoples—especially the Romans—and of Christians, as well. We must believe that the druidic religion was markedly different from other religions and that, in any case, the sense of ritual was very different from that practiced elsewhere. There was no question of a collective cult, in which the whole group was united; this was a kind of worship that could be engaged in only by initiated priests, in the name of the community, but apart from it. That is why a sanctuary isolated in the heart of the forest was the best place for the celebration of druidic religion. The testimony of Dio Cassius concerning the revolt of the British queen Boadicea demonstrates this again: the historian observes that the British have sanctuaries (*hiérra*) dedicated to the goddess Andraste in a sacred wood (*halosos*). And Tacitus, who relates the events of A.D. 60 in Great Britain reports that on the Island of Mona (Anglesey) there were sacred woods "devoted to barbarous superstitions," subsequently destroyed by order of the consul Suetonius Paulinus. Caesar himself alludes to the role of the forests in the practice of druidism when he describes the great annual assembly of the druids in the land of the Carnutes.

This tradition was not forgotten by the peoples who were first romanized and then Christianized. Indeed, there are still many reminders of the cult of trees and rocks in isolated places in the midst of forests. How many allegedly modern superstitions are merely the continuation of these naturist cults celebrated in the most deserted places? And it is certainly not by chance that the first evangelists of the Celtic world, the Irish and Britons in particular, were in the habit of living in hermitages completely removed from social groups. We see here the stability of a custom which originated very far back in time, probably in an age before the advent of the Celts. This shows that the druidic religion, despite a certain Celtic Indo-European framework, was nevertheless the survival of ancient religions practiced by natives colonized by the Celts.

In any case, trees seem to have played a great part in the mythology and religion of the ancient Celts. We should not exaggerate the importance of what Pliny the Elder tells us about gathering mistletoe from oaks,[4] but there really is a druidic ceremony in which the symbolism of the oak is emphasized. According to Pliny, moreover, "druids" comes from the Greek name for oak (drus). While etymologically incorrect, this provides an analogous relationship, as knowledge is linked, in Celtic languages, to the name of the tree.[5] And though what Maxime de Tyr says may be debatable, he definitely attributes to the Celts a belief according to which "the oak is the representation of divinity."[6] Because of its distinction and strength the oak has always been a ready image by which to convey the concept of divine omnipotence, and one comes across it frequently in Celtic legends and in that strange tradition expressed in the Welsh "Cad Goddeu" of which we have spoken,[7] where the Britons are transformed by means of magic into trees and are victorious over their enemies.

Other trees seem to have been honored by the Celts, notably the yew, whose wood was used to make magic wands for the druids and whose name, eburo-, is recognizable in the name of certain Gallic peoples like the Eburovices; the birch, which appears to have been the tree dedicated to the dead; and the rowan, utilized in magic incantations. Then there is the hawthorn, traditionally associated with belief in fairies, and the hazel, the tree of divination always used by dowsers. The apple tree plays a significant role: it is the tree of Paradise, the fruit-bearing tree par excellence. The apple is the tree found on the magical isles where heroes and gods live, the Insula Pomorum of Geoffrey of Monmouth, the Isle of Abalum in ancient texts, where Baltic amber is found, the Emain Ablach of the Irish, the Ynys Affallach of the Welsh, and the Isle of Avalon in the romances of the Round Table.

And it is in an apple tree that we find Merlin in the poems attributed to him, an apple tree invisible to ordinary mortals. Elsewhere, Merlin's abode is in unspecified trees. In the parallel legend of Suibhné he takes refuge in a yew tree. It is a fact that the act of climbing a tree or staying in one is a ritual gesture that has numerous counterparts in shamanistic traditions.

During an initiation ceremony of future shamans among the Bouriates, the "father-shaman" climbs a birch tree and makes nine incisions at its crest. After he has descended to the foot of the tree, each candidate ascends in turn. They are all overcome by ecstasy while climbing and, upon reaching the top, they begin to shamanize, that is, to recount strange visions. It is obvious, says Mircea Eliade,[8] "that the birch tree is the symbol of the cosmic tree or the axis of the world and that consequently" a shaman who climbs to the top of it "is considered to occupy the center of the world; in climbing up it, the shaman embarks upon an ecstatic voyage."

There is a striking analogy between this ceremony and the behavior of Merlin—or of Suibhné—in his tree. At that moment Merlin is an authentic shaman embarking upon an ecstatic voyage and ready to prophesy, or to express what he sees and feels. Perhaps this shamanistic ceremony and Merlin's behavior belong to the same ritual as that of the druids in their oak tree as they cut off the mistletoe. In any event, the similarity can only stimulate profound reflection on this theme. "In a number of archaic traditions, the Cosmic Tree, expressing the sacredness of the world, its fruitfulness and its durability, corresponds to the ideas of creation, fertility, and initiation, in the last instance with the idea of absolute reality and immortality. The Tree of the World becomes, therefore, a tree of life and of immortality."[9]

The ascent of this tree, possible only for certain individuals, is a defiance of natural laws. It is a transgression of a prohibition, permissible only to a privileged person, since the completed ritual leads into the otherworld. The person who finds himself in the tree—or who is hanged from it in certain cases—acquires a special knowledge of what transpires in the celestial world because of his position as an intermediary. He is truly the medium, interpreting humans to gods, and gods to humans. He is shaman. But he is also prophet and seer. It is from this that Merlin, perched in a tree or confined in a forest, derives all of his significance. We are reminded of Odin-Wotan, hung by his feet for three days and three nights from the ash tree Yggdrasil, or the Tree of the World, above the fountain of knowledge, who acquired in this way the sacred art of reading runes. And as Claude Gaignebet says, we must not forget that "the knowledge of Trees is, in the *Book of Adam* (a biblical text considered apocryphal), one of the diabolical learnings that the sons of the Gods taught to men when they became enamored of their daughters."[10] The fall of the angels consisted of their union with women. Is Merlin not the son of a devil and a young woman? Has he not acquired his gift of prophecy, his knowledge, and his magic powers as a result of this ambiguous birth?

In any case, Merlin possesses the knowledge of trees in the same way as do the sons of men and the fallen angels, as does the Germanic god Odin-Wotan (in whose name we find the name of the tree). There is no doubt, therefore, that Merlin is a shaman or druid, at once a master of ecstasy and a priest responsible for the ritual of communication with divinity. There is no doubt that he must exercise his function in a clearing in the midst of the woods, a privileged place where communication between heaven and earth is established thanks to the mediation of the trees that stand in a ring around it.

This sacred clearing is the Gallic *nemeton*. The name is found again in the eleventh century in the form of Nemet in the Breton list of titles in Quimperlé, where it designates a forest in Cornwall not far from Locranan (*quam vocant Nemet*); the modern Breton form is Nevet, and an ancient form modified and frozen in *Néant* [Nothingness] can be recognized in the name of a village of the Morbihan in the forest of Brocéliande, not far from the Fountain of Barenton. The basic component of the word is *nem* (which became *nef* in Welsh and *nenv* in modern Breton) meaning "heaven" in its religious sense; it has the same Indo-European origin as the Latin *nemus*, "sacred wood." In Irish, Nemed is the name of the mythical invaders of the island, according to the *Book of Conquests*, a name meaning "sacred." One finds the same term in the name of the heroine Niam, who plays a role in the tale of "The Death of Cuchulainn" and in that of "The Violent Death of Celtchar," and some have not hesitated to establish a link between the names of Niam and Vivian-Nimue.[11]

It seems, then, that before becoming a sacred sanctuary, the *nemeton* was an ideal projection of a piece of heaven on earth, a kind of terrestrial paradise, or rather a magical orchard of the sort encountered in Celtic legends or those of Celtic origin. This idea is closely tied to shamanistic techniques as well, especially to the rite of the shaman's ascent of the tree. Indeed, as Mircea Eliade says, the entire body of religious practices and ideas that make up shamanism "appear to be related to the myths of an ancient era when communications between Heaven and Earth were much easier. Seen from this angle, the shamanistic experience is equivalent to a restoration of that primordial mythic time, and the shaman appears as a privileged being who rediscovers for himself personally the blessed condition of humanity at the dawn of time.[12] In fact, this is Merlin's situation, whether he takes refuge in the forest or is confined by a Vivian whose celestial aspect leaves no room for doubt.

But it is not far from the idea of "sacred" to the idea of "terror." This explains the hesitation of the ignorant or uninitiated to enter this forbidden domain, reserved to the priest who alone had the right to speak to the gods. But perhaps this terrifying aspect of the *nemeton* arises simply from its inaccessibility to whomever has not undergone the ecstatic experience: this would explain the invisibility attributed to the place, an invisibility that in certain texts is translated as "inviolability." Merlin is found in an invisible prison of air because no one else can recreate that privileged situation which restores the dawn of mythic times. And it is not by chance that the authors of classical antiquity insisted so much upon the isolated and formidable aspect of this *nemeton*. Lucan's text, still referring to that sacred wood near Marseilles, is most interesting in this respect:

> *There was a sacred wood that since earliest times had never been profaned. Its interlaced branches enclosed an air of gloom and icy shadows where the sun never entered. It was not inhabited by Pans, country people, or Sylvans, people of the forests, nor by Nymphs. There were only sanctuaries dedicated to gods of barbaric rites. Altars were set up on sinister mounds. All the trees were splashed with human blood. . . . Birds*

*were afraid to perch on its branches, wild animals avoided going to
ground in these haunts. The wind did not sweep through these trees, nor
did the lightning springing from dark clouds. . . . Water flowed copiously from black fountains. Sad formless statues of gods stood upon the
trunks of trees that had been cut down. . . . It was said that tremors of the
earth resounded in the depths of caves, that bent yew trees straightened
again, that the woods shone with the light of fires when none were even
burning, that dragons roamed through the trees. Men did not come near.
They did not want to perform rites to divinities there, preferring to abandon the place to those divinities. Whether Phoebus was at the height of
his course or gloomy night covered the sky, the priest himself dreaded
going there, fearing to come upon the master of that forest.* [13]

This kind of description is obviously designed to strike the imagination of Roman readers and make them understand that in banning the
druidic cult the aim is simply to suppress barbaric and bloody rituals. It
could be an account written by Catholic missionaries in nineteenth-
century Africa. Still, the sacred forest of the Gauls seems to stand outside of time and space, removed from all social life, sheltered from wild
animals and the most destructive natural phenomena. In addition, it is
the site of mysterious and incomprehensible things relating to magic,
or to the irrational ascribed to the otherworld; not just anyone can
enter it, even in the capacity of a priest. It is a terrible and dangerous
place for the uninitiated, those, in other words, who have not attained
the degree of ecstasy sufficient to see beyond the illusory, material aspect of things.

Now, this *nemeton* is not unique. They were everywhere in the territories occupied by the Celts, especially in the western part of Europe,
which was covered in great part by impenetrable forests. We know
some of them, celebrated in tradition and still visible today. One example is the Fountain of Barenton, in the heart of the legendary forest
of Brocéliande, remainder of the immense forest that covered the entire center of Brittany until the High Middle Ages. Then it was gradu-
ally cleared by monks and by the peasants whom they had encouraged
to live in those isolated regions. And it is there that Merlin's shade so
persistently prowls.

8

S THE
ANCTUARY AND THE SPRING

 From all the evidence, the clearing in which the Fountain of Barenton is located dates back to prehistoric
times, as is attested by its dolmen stone, the famous
"stairway of Merlin" that juts out over the basin where
the waters collect. The fountain's old name is Belenton,
in which Bel-Nemeton is easily discerned. This place was, therefore, a
sacred clearing. In the Gallic era it was dedicated to Bélénos (meaning
"brilliant"), the solar god of the Gauls, as is shown by numerous Gallo-
Roman inscriptions. It is surprising that this fountain was never Christianized, since most springs in Britain and elsewhere were taken over
by Christianity and placed under the patronage of one saint or another. The Fountain of Barenton remained pagan throughout the centuries, but this did not prevent the inhabitants of the region from visiting it, in processions led by clergy, during years of drought.

For this fountain has a magical-religious role: it produces rain. Local
tradition relates that its water cures madness (hence the name of the
neighboring village of Folle-Pensée [Mad Thought], or *Fol-Pansit*, "that
cures madness"), returning to the theme of Merlin as the madman of
the woods. Also, when water is poured on the stairway, a dreadful storm
is likely to arise. This belief goes back to earliest times; there is an
account by the twelfth-century Norman writer Robert Wace, who speaks
of "Bréchéliant, where Britons who make up tales often go" and who
describes visiting the fountain and taking part in its rite. But "one went
there mad, mad one returned," and Robert Wace was unable to make it
rain.

Nevertheless, this fountain is the setting for several episodes of the
legend of Yvain, or the Knight of the Lion, as recounted by Chrétien

de Troyes and an anonymous Welsh author in the twelfth century, in which it is the "fountain that causes rain to fall." This is how Chrétien de Troyes describes the fountain and its site:

> *I noticed the tree and the fountain. I can say of the tree that it was the most beautiful pine tree that ever grew upon the earth. I believe that not a single drop of the heaviest rain could have passed through it: water could not penetrate its foliage. I saw the basin [goblet] hung from the tree: it was of the finest gold that could be found, even in these times, at fairs. As for the fountain, believe me when I say that it boiled like hot water. The stairway was made of a single emerald pierced like a goatskin bottle, with four rubies more dazzling and more crimson than the morning sun when it appears on the horizon.* [1]

The description by the author of the corresponding Welsh text, "Owein," or "the Lady of the Fountain," is more sober and realistic: "You will notice a plain, a kind of large irrigated valley. In its center you will see a great tree: the tips of its branches are greener than the green of pinetrees. Beneath the tree is a fountain and on the rim of the fountain a marble slab, and a silver basin is attached to the marble slab by a silver chain so that they cannot be separated." [2]

In fact, the stairway is a large stone that came from an ancient megalith, but the site is presently comparable to the one described by the old authors. The pine tree is particularly remarkable. It was mentioned by medieval writers because it was a relatively rare species in Britain at the time, and it makes a great deal of sense that it appears as the central pivot of a clearing in the forest. It is, indeed, that famous cosmic tree that the shaman ascends. It is the Tree of the World from which Merlin prophesies. We really are in a *nemeton* that constitutes, as Eliade says, "the central opening of the world," where the heavenly and earthly worlds meet. And to make the sacred character of the place even more complete, there is the spring, inverse symbol of the tree, representing the link with the subterranean world, another aspect of the dwelling place of the gods. And the spring adds the idea of fertility, its waters welling up from the earth as milk issues from the mother's breasts, or as blood nourishes the fetus, floating in water, by means of the umbilical cord.

This explains the importance of the spring in the *nemeton*. It is a point at which all the forces of the world and of the otherworld converge. There the priest or magus, he who is able to avail himself of these forces, can learn all the secrets of life and death and act upon the unfolding of events. The three permanent elements, Earth, Air, and Water, will in this way be provisionally transformed, in a transitory fashion, into what is habitually called the fourth element—Fire, symbol of the Spirit manifesting itself and creating. One involves the other, since all creation implies an incarnation, each of which requires the appearance of an opposite by which the individual realizes his own existence.

The legend of Yvain certainly takes into account the sacred and extraordinary nature of the sanctuary of Barenton. Indeed, when a knight goes there he must attempt an adventure, that is, submit himself to a trial. There is an interdiction upon the place; no one is to enter it. When an intruder arrives unexpectedly, therefore, he must perform a task that will determine whether or not his trespass is valid. If it is not, he will be eliminated. If it is, he will become master of the place, the *dominus loci* of which Lucan speaks. This is why he must conform to the ritual: taking water from the fountain and pouring it on the steps, an eminently symbolic gesture suggestive of the son spilling his sperm on his mother's belly—a perfect Oedipal situation if ever there was one. And, as a profound taboo has just been violated, nature attacks: the country in which so abominable an act has occurred must be destroyed. And so we have the storm and the tempest that lay waste the region and leave not a single leaf upon the trees—except for the pine tree, which is the Cosmic Tree, untouchable, the pivot without which the world would not exist. The region is now devastated, sterile, like the Waste Land of the legend of the Grail. Consequently, the power and even the virility of the *dominus loci* are affected, since he was not able to prevent the sacrilege, incest. The intruder did not know what it was that he did. He had simply been told to accomplish an exploit; he did not seek to know why. In the account of Chrétien de Troyes it is a rustic, a "wild man," who sends the knight to the Fountain of Barenton, and this wild man is obviously one of Merlin's aspects. In the folktales of all of western Europe, and particularly in the oral tales of Armorican Brittany, this theme is frequently encountered in an identical form, embellished with local variants and different inventions: there is always a foolish, even imbecilic young man who is given a test, not knowing what it is about. Sometimes it is to kill a serpent, or to give a cake to an old woman who reveals herself as a fairy, or still again to carry this woman's firewood. If he does not succeed at the test he is eliminated and not spoken of again. If he succeeds—without knowing what it means—he is allowed to cross onto a path that will lead him to royalty. It is quite clear in the legend of Yvain: he sets in motion a tempest, but after the tempest he hears the marvelous song of a multitude of birds in the pine tree. The image is a simple one of that state of beatitude, that paradisiacal state of the child after his first orgasm, phantasmically experienced with the mother. So great is his torpor due to the song of the birds that he is ready to fall asleep, until a black knight comes along and incites him to combat. This black knight is the guardian of the fountain, or the *dominus loci*, but also the godfather; the child knight must fight the image of the father and kill it. Yvain does this; after fierce combat, he mortally wounds his adversary and pursues him to his castle. And there, after various adventures, he weds the widow of the black knight, the beautiful Laudine, and becomes the *dominus loci* in his turn.

The narrative's plot is remarkably clear. The *nemeton* is the site of the experience by which an individual can climb to the top of the Tree of the World and return, in ecstasy, to those earliest times when incest was not forbidden. The proof here is that Yvain marries his adversary's widow—the image of the mother, the incarnation of primordial woman already glimpsed in the form of the stone on which he poured water.[3] We have seen that in the case of Merlin and Vivian fraternal incest, if not explicit in all the accounts, is at least latent; and just as incest is forbidden to ordinary mortals, it becomes an element of initiation for the superior being capable of confronting its terrible dangers. Yvain, the hero of Chrétien de Troyes' account (the Welsh Owein, a semi-historic person) is therefore an exceptional being because he passes the test, attaining royalty by committing incest with the mother with impunity, and accepting all ensuing consequences. Diderot was right when he declared, in his strange *Rameau's Nephew*: "if the little savage was left all alone, if he preserved all of his imbecility and if he joined to the minimal intelligence of the child in his cradle the violence of the passions of a man of thirty, he would wring his father's neck and lie with his mother." This is what Yvain does. It is what the young heroes of folktales do. And it takes place in the sacred space of the *nemeton*.

At Barenton the magical-religious ceremony of the legend has survived in the form of epic accounts. History has failed to retain even more of it because the area around the Fountain of Barenton was the scene of strange happenings during the twelfth century.

In the twelfth century the abbey of Paimpont, established in the heart of the forest of Brocéliande, had become very important and the monks were obliged to establish a second location. The priory of Moinet was created not far from Barenton. We are certain only that there was a cluster of cabins constructed half in stone, half in wood, but from what the texts say there was also a "small but very beautiful chapel."[4] About twenty monks gathered there under the direction of a prior named Éon.

This Éon seems to have convinced himself that he had a divine mission to accomplish. Since the Latin word *eum* was pronounced like Éon at that time, he must have taken literally the words of the liturgy, especially *per Eum qui venturus est judicare vivos et mortuos* (by Him who will come to judge the living and the dead). Apparently he declared himself the judge of the living and the dead and preached a rather peculiar doctrine, of which only fragments remain, seen from the point of view of his accusers. He preached a kind of "peasant communism" as well, participating in acts of banditry against surrounding castles, priories, and churches. Amassing great riches in this way, he redistributed a portion of them to poor peasants, which provided him with a large following. It seems if we believe the evidence, that he was also a magician, or at the very least a noteworthy hypnotist. Certain people who came to visit him were invited to grand banquets where they were served the rarest and most refined dishes. Each guest ate and drank his fill, but moments after leaving the table realized that his stomach was as empty as it had been before.

Other accounts note the magnificence with which he presented himself, always robed in rich habits covered with strange signs, and often surrounded by an unreal light. What, exactly, was he? We do not know. But it is probable that he had formidable parapsychological powers and that he employed them with great talent. It was even claimed that he could move from one place to another without walking. As the reports of the time say, however, "it was diabolical illusion." In any case, the figure of Merlin is not far removed from this story, at once authentic and shrouded in mist.

Éon's activities took place in about 1148. In that same year a comet appeared that terrified his contemporaries, and Éon was given the name "de l'Étoile" ["of the Star"], adding a fantastic aura to his image. And this heresy, for ultimately that is what it was, gained ground around the priory of Moinet, around Brocéliande, and in Brittany. He had disciples even as far away as Gascony. Naturally, the doctrines he propagated started to threaten the Church as well as the established social order. Although it seems that he was not taken at all seriously at the outset, repression struck in 1148.

It was at the personal request of the pope, then in France at the council of Épernay, that he was arrested by order of the duke of Brittany, who was then Conan III. Éon de l'Étoile was immediately brought before the council of Épernay and called upon to explain himself. The record of this trial is perplexing. In all likelihood an effort was made to present Éon as a madman, a visionary; his words were judged to be incoherent. Then, strangely, instead of being condemned to the stake like most heretics, he was simply thrown in prison, where he very quickly died. As for his disciples, they were pursued with the greatest severity. But not one of them renounced his master, and all of them preferred to be hanged or burned at the stake rather than abandon the doctrine of Éon de l'Étoile. The priory of Moinet was razed, and the environs of the Fountain of Barenton were once more deserted. But we will never know the truth about Éon de l'Étoile. Was he simply an impostor? Was he a visionary? Was he a "sorcerer"? Did he have in his possession secrets that sprang from the mists of time? Was he a distant descendant of the druids? It is impossible to resolve these questions. We can be certain only that the story of Éon de l'Étoile, clearly located near Barenton, decisively nourished the legend of Merlin, also located there.[5]

But in the light of history, as well as of legend, the clearing of Barenton presents us with a most authentic aspect of the Gallic *nemeton*. We find once again the strange phenomena that were supposed to have taken place there, the Cosmic Tree, the clearing itself in an uninhabited place apart from societal life, and the spring.

We have said that Vivian can be considered a water divinity because Merlin always encounters her by a fountain, and because the first "trick" that he teaches her is how to make a stream gush forth. We have also said that Vivian, whatever her true name may be, could be the equivalent of the Irish goddess Boinn (the White Cow), and that the name Boinn was found in the Massif Central on the border of the Arvernes and the Vellaves, in a place that had many points in common with the sites of Barenton and Fontboine, near Saint-Jean d'Aubrigoux (Haute-Loire). There too we are in the presence of a *nemeton* that continued to exist even under Roman occupation, until Romans destroyed the dwellings that had been erected there.

The central point is the spring. It exists in an extremely isolated place in the heart of the forest. The constructions appear to have had no military purpose, but to have been used for religious reasons only. In short, it was probably a kind of pagan monastery.[6] There is no documentation concerning this establishment, but archaeology clearly reveals it to have been a sanctuary. It would have been, therefore, a *nemeton*, but more evolved, exposed to Roman technical influences, and including the construction of a temple. This is not an isolated case, for from the time of the Roman occupation the Gauls began to build sanctuaries, some dedicated to Roman gods, others to indigenous divinities. Since the establishment of Fontboine was destroyed by the Romans, it can be deduced that it was an indigenous sanctuary of druidic obedience; indeed, the druids were pursued and tracked down throughout the empire, their doctrine presenting real dangers to Roman society and ideology. And so little by little the druids, even those who had gone to ground in the depths of their forests, were annihilated, at first by Roman temporal power, then by Christian spiritual power.

There are many other examples of sanctuaries that had, as an essential element, a spring in the center. The most famous site of this genre is the sanctuary of the sources of the Seine, where not long ago statues and statuettes made of wood were discovered, either representations of divinities or votive offerings. For springs are associated with the idea of healing with water. It seems that men have always understood the therapeutic advantages of spring water. At the Fontaines Salées, near Vézelay, traces of a Gallic water catchment have been found beneath installations of the Roman type. In the Vichy basin numerous legends mention primitive springs that were removed by the fairies as punishment for transgressions committed by women.[7] The water of the Fountain of Barenton was believed to cure madness; in Brittany the fountain is associated with the cult of Saint Mathurin, under whose patronage are numerous springs with that reputation. And in the forest of Bellême (whose name comes from Belisama, "the very brilliant," a sort of secondary divinity associated with Belenos) in the Orne, ferrous springs are dedicated to "infernal deities" (*diis infernis*). We will only mention the wells found in the many Gallic *oppida* [fortifications built on elevated sites] on the Mediterranean periphery, for they are very numerous and all associate the idea of healing with the concept of the "hole through which one communicates with the otherworld," that mysterious world below that, by virtue of the identity of opposites, is also the world above.[8]

Well known and excavated archaeological sites confirm this opinion that the sanctuary without the spring has no significance. In Great Britain, near the fort of Brocolita (Carrawburgh) on the south side of Hadrian's Wall is such a sanctuary, with a spring dedicated to the goddess Coventina. This spring, which still bubbles, was covered originally by a temple that was Celtic in type but of Roman construction, containing a basin into which monetary offerings were tossed. Also found nearby are altars and carved plaques from the temple itself. Among them is a plaque depicting the goddess Conventina leaning over a leaf floating in the water, holding a water plant in her right hand and in her left, a goblet from which flows a stream of water. It is an advanced form of sanctuary but the characteristics of the Gallic *nemeton* are recognizable.

The practice of throwing coins into the spring or into consecrated water appears to have been quite common in the Celtic world, and in our time we can see that many fountains that were Christianized are the scene of identical operations.[9] It is the same at the Fountain of Barenton: the basin contains small coins, and it is the custom for young women to toss pins into it to ask if they will be married within the year.[10] The lake of Llyn Cerrig Bach on the isle of Anglesey (Ynys Mon) contained a fabulous treasure, discovered in 1943: a great quantity of weapons, chariot fittings, tools, chains, cauldrons, and bronze plaques decorated with motifs in the style of La Tène, all representing sacrificial offerings made between the middle of the second century B.C. and the second century A.D. And the Greek author Srabo discloses that near Toulouse there was a temple that contained an inviolable treasure, the famous "Gold of Toulouse." He adds that throughout Celtic Gaul great quantities of gold and silver were immersed in lakes because the treasures became in this way completely inviolable. This is a reference to the belief that wells, fountains, and lakes are privileged places through which there is communication with the otherworld.[11]

The medicinal role of the spring is obviously linked with its magical or religious aspect. In the end, only the gods can cure disease. The same concept has endured to the present time and explains both the success of thermal cures and the pilgrimages to Notre Dame de Lourdes. At the archaeological site of Glanum in Saint-Rémy-de-Provence (Bouches-du-Rhône), a site occupied successively by Celts, Greeks, and Romans, this famous healing spring can be seen. It probably gave rise to the entire complex of sanctuary and city, especially as the name Glanum refers to an Irish term, *glan,* meaning "pure." There is no doubt that the waters of Glanum spring "purified," or "cured" the sick who came there—even then—in pilgrimage.

And that recalls the famous "fountain of health" of Irish epics. It is described for us in the narrative of "The Battle of Mag Tured:" "Diancecht (druid and god of medicine), his two sons and his daughter . . . sang a spell over the fountain called Health. They tossed into it mortally wounded men whom they tended, and live beings came forth. The wounded were cured by virtue of the song of four doctors who were around the fountain. . . . The fountain has another name, Lake of the Plants, for Diacecht had planted there a blade of every grass that existed in Ireland."[12] It is not far from this fountain of health to the miraculous cauldron, found in Welsh tradition, that resuscitates the dead and heals the wounded, obvious archetype of the Holy Grail of Christianized legends.

The explanation of this belief is simple. The spring exists in the ideal place—where exchanges occur between worlds, where divine force manifests itself without restraint, where conditions exist by which the paradisiacal, original condition of humanity in the time of the Age of Gold, or of Eden, is restored. Drinking that water, or performing a rite over it, is to participate in this restoration, to return to the state of innocence and purity that characterize the world *before the fall,* regardless of what was responsible for human degeneration. What is essential is to drink from the source of life. But that is possible only if the spring in question is sacred, if it is in a privileged place that is the ideal projection of a part of heaven on earth.

So the *nemeton* is the druidic temple, in the heart of the forest, removed from the social group of which it is nevertheless the indispensable spiritual complement. It implies a durable connection between humans and nature, being considered not as another living being, as in the romantic perspective, but as the receptacle of the whole potentiality of being. It is this meaning that can be attributed to certain Irish or Welsh poems, particularly the famous "Cad Goddeu," that evoke the passages of the being through its different forms, animal or vegetable, not to say mineral. It is in no way about an ordinary doctrine of metempsychosis. No text mentions this, and if it has been much spoken of with regard to the Celts, it is because the theme of metamorphoses has been elaborated on without true understanding.[13] The only tangible druidic doctrine on this subject concerns the community of existence of beings and things, their membership in the same world, the feeling that nature is a totality to which the human being fully belongs.

It is in this context that Merlin appears, in an age when druidism, in its form of structured and hierarchical religion with a regularly taught doctrine, had long since disappeared from all of western Europe. If we can assert that there is druidism behind the character of Merlin, it is because druidism left traces in the oral traditions and legendary narratives collected or organized throughout the Middle Ages. On this basis, Merlin is indeed the personification of the druid, even of the druid-shaman as he might have been imagined around the year 1200. But he is a multiform figure and it is not unusual to find him elsewhere than by a fountain in the *nemeton*. And it is not unusual to recognize him in forms that are unconventional yet expressive of the essential characteristics of the wild man, the madman of the woods, the man of the forest.

9

R THE USTIC AND THE MADMAN

 In *Yvain*, by Chrétien de Troyes, when Calogrenant or Yvain makes his way to the Fountain of Barenton, he has a surprising encounter that is nevertheless the essential element of this quest for the *nemeton*. This is how the poet from Champagne describes the character Yvain meets:[1]

A rogue resembling a Moor, impossibly repulsive and hideous, a creature uglier than one can say, was seated on a stump holding a large cudgel in his hand. I approached the rogue and saw that he had a head larger than that of a horse or other animal, bushy hair, a skinned forehead wider than two handspans, ears as hairy and large as those of an elephant, heavy eyebrows and a flat countenance, eyes like an owl, the nose of a cat, a mouth that opened as wide as a wolf's, the sharp red teeth of a wild boar, a red beard and a twisted mustache; his chin met his chest and his back was long, crooked, and humped. He leaned on his cudgel and was dressed peculiarly, not in linen or wool, but hung from the rogue's neck were two recently flayed animal skins, from two bulls or two oxen.

The description is picturesque and rather gripping. This account by the Welsh author of "Owein" is less detailed but perhaps more precise:

. . . you will see a large black man, at least as big as two men of this world: he has but one foot and a single eye in the middle of his forehead; in his hand is an iron cudgel, and I can tell you that there are not two men in the world who would not find it a burden. He is not a wicked

man, but he is ugly. He is the keeper of the forest, and you will see a
thousand wild animals grazing all around him. [2]

Here then is the *rustic*, the Wild Man. There is a description comparable to Chrétien's in *Aucassin and Nicolette*, that thirteenth-century
"chantefable" [prose recitation interspersed with sung verses] that so
often borrows elements from the Arthurian romances. One might also
compare this rustic to the "Hideous Maiden on the Mule," messenger
of the Grail, Wolfram of Eschenbach's *Kundry la Sorcière*, abundantly
described by Chrétien in his *Perceval*. She appears to be the feminine
equivalent of the rustic. In any case, an element common to both
Chrétien and the Welsh author should be noted: the cudgel. As to the
rest, despite the common features of ugliness and size there are notable
differences. Among these, it should be pointed out that the man in
"Owein" is one-eyed, has only one foot, and is the guardian of the
forest. If he is one-eyed and lame, he is the image of two ancient Indo-
European divinities, gods of the first and second functions: the German Odin and Tyr, and the Roman Horatius Cocles and Mucius
Scaevola. This is a curious finding. As for the fact that he is the guardian of the forest, the Welsh author, like Chrétien, describes the wild
animals who are grazing near him and who obey him; for he is also the
"master of animals."

We come across this rustic, who is not exactly a giant, who in any
case is not a malevolent infernal monster—for he is not wicked—many
times in Irish epics. In "The Feast of Bricriu," he is the one who arbi-
trates the disagreement between the hero Cuchulainn and his two companions, Conall and Loégairé, concerning "the Hero's Morsel." [3] And in
the strange account of "The Destruction of the House of Da Derga" he
appears again under the name of Fer Caille, literally "Man of the Woods,"
and is described in this way: "He had coarse, frizzy hair; if a sack full of
wild apples had been emptied onto his skull, all of the apples would
have stuck in his hair and not one would have fallen to the ground. [4] If
his head had been thrown against a branch it would have been impossible to disentangle his head from the branch. Each of his shins was as
long and thick as an oxen yoke. Each of his buttocks was shaped like a
cheese on a willow twig. He carried in his hand a pole whose iron tip
was black and forked, and on his back a black-spotted red pig that

cried continually." Here again is the ugliness, the coarseness, the wildness, as well as the iron point, equivalent to the cudgel, and the pig suggests he is also "master of animals." And as the tale continues, we find Fer Caille in the company of his wife, as ugly and monstrous as he is.

These various descriptions of the rustic correspond to the portrait of the Wild Man in the French text of *Merlin*, the Wild Man who clearly states that he is "Merlin, King Arthur's councillor":

> He had a head as large as a calf's, round and prominent eyes, a mouth that went from ear to ear, thick lips always half-open through which his teeth protruded, feet turned inside out, black hair so long and coarse that it covered his belt. He was tall, bent, amazingly old and hairy, clothed in a wolfskin. And his ears, large as winnowing-baskets, hung down to his knees so that they could be wrapped around him when it rained. Finally, he was so repulsive to look at that no man lived who would not be afraid of him. As he walked, he struck the oaks with great blows of his cudgel, and brought with him, like a shepherd with his flock, a horde of stags, does, deer, and all manner of russet animals. [5]

The similarity is striking, and here again we find the gigantic stature, the ugliness, the cudgel, and the activity that characterizes the Wild Man: looking after wild animals. Details like the presence of stags and the wolfskin need to be taken into consideration. But most important of all is that this description of the rustic refers to Merlin himself.

The Wild Man who shows the knight Yvain the way to the Fountain of Barenton, then, is Merlin. It is he, in fact, who is in charge of that fountain, with which his name is still associated. He is the true master of the *nemeton* of Barenton, and if he allows someone to go there, it is in order to put him to the test. The priest of the place is Merlin, the druid-shaman in a state of ecstasy at the top of the Cosmic Tree, that is, the pine tree of Barenton. As for Vivian, she is present in the fountain in her capacity of aquatic divinity. The dyad exists: Vivian rules over water, Merlin over the forest. And Merlin corresponds to a mythological figure that Celtic tradition has not forgotten, as it is found in numerous texts of different origins, including the Irish texts which are apt to be oldest. Who, then, is this mythological character disguised as the "man of the woods"?

We find him in the Irish account of *"The Drunkenness of the Ulstermen."*

During a turbulent night, after a banquet washed down too copiously with wine, Cuchulainn and the warriors of Ulster find themselves at the house of their enemies, Ailill and Mebdh of Connaught. Inevitably there will be conflict. But among the ranks of the Ulstermen appear various Tuatha Dé Danann, in particular Oengus and another person who is described as follows: "a man with a great eye, enormous thighs, wide shoulders, of a prodigious size, completely covered by a vast gray cloak" and who holds "a thick iron cudgel in his hand." This person strikes the nine men of his company with the maleficent end of his cudgel and kills them with a single blow. But he places the beneficent end of the cudgel on their heads and revives them. Curoi mac Dairé, Cuchulainn's enemy, recognizes him at once and remarks to Queen Mebdh: "It is not difficult, it is Dagda." We must consider, then, an identification between Merlin the enchanter of the Arthurian romances and the famous Irish god, one of the chieftains of the Tuatha Dé Danann, Dagda, sometimes called Eochaid Ollathir ("Powerful Father," or "Father of All") or Ruadh Rofhessa ("the Red of Great Learning"). And it is known that Dagda enjoys incestuous relations with his sister Boinn, in whom we have recognized one of Vivian's aspects. At this point, these are no longer simple coincidences.

What is equally remarkable is the marginal and anachronistic aspect of the Wild Man, or Dagda who seems to rise from earliest prehistory. First of all, we seem to be speaking of a very ancient divinity, predating the Celts; then, it is confirmed that this person stands outside time and space and has succeeded in restoring, for himself, a primary time incomprehensible to ordinary mortals. In the account of "The Battle of Mag-Tured," Dagda goes to spy, for the Tuatha Dé Danann, on their enemies, the Fomoré. He presents himself to them in a grotesque fashion and distinguishes himself by his gluttony, devouring in the wink of an eye the contents of a vat filled with food. Naturally, the Fomoré ridicule and laugh at him, which does not prevent Dagda from returning to his people with a detailed description of what is happening in the enemy camp. Concerning this episode, some commentators have concluded that the Christian transcribers of the epic, no longer taking Dagda seriously in his original character of great god of wisdom, wished to mock pagan superstitions. This seems to be an erroneous interpretation. We are, indeed, in the presence of a grotesque character here, but the grotesque has never been a defect; on the contrary, it is often one of the characteristics of the gods. Dagda is without peer, beyond time, beyond space, as is Gargantua, the one before Rabelais as well as the one whom Rabelais described with such precision. He is the monstrous and anachronistic god, the young child gifted with extraordinary power, able to take his father's place and sleep with his mother, the fantastic glutton, the bottomless gulf of knowledge. But his appearance is disconcerting. In the same way that the Jews awaited a certain Messiah and did not recognize him in Jesus, men await a divinity incarnate who is consistent with their fantasies. Now, Dagda-Gargantua runs contrary to these fantasies: instead of the reassuring image of the father, protector of the tribe, they are confronted with the terrifying image of a greedy, gigantic, disheveled, hirsute monster armed with an anachronistic weapon. It is almost derision. He is Ubu the King whose scepter is a small broom. He is Jesus wearing a crown of thorns. But he is also His Carnival Majesty in all his pomp and glory, with his grotesque cortege and ridiculous royal insignia. And if he is His Carnival Majesty, then he is the king of the madmen.

For Dagda, like Gargantua and like Merlin, is a madman. We have, in our times, lost the profound sense of madness. Schizophrenics are excluded from daily life, shut up in asylums, or what pass for such, and paranoiacs are left at liberty, usually given places of the first rank in society.[6] It was not this way in so-called primitive civilizations.[7] The schizophrenic was integrated into the social body and was respected by it as the possessor of a certain wisdom, a certain knowledge. And then it was the madman, he whose head was empty, who had attained the state of ecstasy, and so was in contact with all the spiritual powers. The madman was the visionary of the gods, the sacred medium who was listened to, and who pointed out the road to be followed. But this madman was a schizophrenic. The paranoiac was excluded, banished from society, because he was dangerous, bloodthirsty, and the instigator of catastrophes.

The theme of the madman is closely linked to the theme of the rustic. We can see this in the Arthurian romances when Lancelot, deserted by Queen Guinevere, runs away to the forest, mad with grief, and begins to live like a wild animal. The same thing occurs in *Yvain* by Chrétien de Troyes: when the hero, driven away by his wife for having broken his word, finds himself in the forest, he becomes a rustic, a wild man, eating like a wild animal. And when Tristan wants to rejoin Yseult, who is a prisoner at the court of King Mark, he disguises himself as a madman the better to approach her—but this madman is a rustic with all the attributes of one, the marginality, the roughness. In the *Vita Merlini* Merlin lives in the forest. But when he attends the wedding of his former wife he is astride a stag and becomes the master of wild animals, like the rustic who guides Yvain to the fountain of Barenton. At that moment Merlin is declared "mad," and his behavior confirms it.

The madman acts in a manner that is not only anachronistic, but also *diabolical* in the etymological sense of the word. This is to say that "he sets himself against" whatever is considered normal, and turns into derision the famous "that which goes without saying" of Roland Barthes. The madman disturbs the order of the world. And that, paradoxically, constitues his positive effect, for he obliges men to reexamine the world, to challenge it, and to find new solutions to their problems. Diogenes is mad when he walks in full sunlight with a lighted lantern while saying "I am looking for a man." But that is without any doubt the most honest and reasonable attitude that a human being can have. For the madman knows what others do not.

That also explains the numerous representations of the madman hanging from a tree, head down, as in the Tarot. The madman is inversion incarnate. His head is upside down. But, since what is up is identical to what is down, everything depends on the way in which one looks at things. Where is reality and where is illusion? When one looks at the image of trees reflected in the still water of a lake, one has the right to wonder where reality lies: above the water's surface or below it. The madman has chosen that which is below. When he reaches the top of the Cosmic Tree, Merlin, the druid-shaman, sees the world in a completely inverted manner. And when he makes prophecies he describes that inverted world that others do not recognize because they have not completed the same ritual of regeneration. This explains the importance of considering Merlin in his various aspects, which always correspond to a situation that is inverted in relation to the norms in effect. He is the son of a devil and a maiden, which points rather clearly to his double nature and to his ability to turn upside down to see something other than what is seen by the people around him. He will be ridiculed. But he will be feared, for whoever has strange visions is feared. He not only risks being misunderstood; he risks the stake for nonconformity to dogma. For he is the Devil—from which sometimes comes the image

of a horned god—from which comes Merlin mounted on a stag, hurling one of the stag's horns at his rival. And it is not far from horns
(*cornes*) to a crown (*couronne*), even if etymology is not a factor, for folk
tradition laughs at linguistic rules, much preferring a kind of phonetic
cabal where the analogy of form and function play the principal part.

The madman is also the one who speaks an incomprehensible language. All the pythias or sibyls had need of an interpreter. The sound
of the voice was not enough: if the Pythia of Delphos, intoxicated by
the inhalations and fumes rising from cracks in the earth, prophesied in
a hoarse voice in the midst of an ecstatic trance, she needed the aid of
a priest to be understood by those who consulted the oracle. But Merlin has no need of an interpreter because he also belongs to the ordinary world; existing halfway between man and the devil, he knows the
words that must be said in each of the worlds he frequents. He does
not need to be possessed by the god because he himself is that god,
and is also a man. It should not be forgotten that the legend of Merlin's
birth is presented, in the French *Vulgate,* as a sort of grotesque parody
of the birth of Christ. Instead of the Holy Spirit who impregnates the
Virgin, it is the devil's spirit that through trickery penetrates the body
of Merlin's mother. Satan, or the Destroyer, the Hebraic Shatam, had
wanted to have on earth a being who belonged to him, an Antichrist.
Merlin will always carry this grievous heredity that is not without ambiguity. He says to no avail that he will use his supernatural powers
only for the triumph of good; he escapes from Manichaeism, for he
shares in both natures, and the good that he saves or defends is not
necessarily the good recognized by theologians or by the common
people. And it is always because he surprises and disquiets that Merlin
occupies a privileged place in the social group to which he belongs
through his mother. King Vortigern respects him even as a child because his words frighten him. Uther Pendragon venerates him because
he is a "seer." Arthur obeys him because without him he would not even
be king. And here we come across the peculiar relationship between
the king and the druid in Celtic society, a relationship found again in
the Middle Ages, in history as in legend, in the pair often formed by
the king and his jester. Alexander the Great had Aristotle as his tutor.
Nero had Seneca. What does that mean? Are not philosophers there-

fore like jesters, madmen, devils, and "those who prevent things from running smoothly"?

Yes, because the madman is, paradoxically, a wise man, and the art of wisdom is nothing other than philosophy. Merlin is a philosopher, as were the druids, according to the authors of classical antiquity. Having reached ecstasy up in his tree, he can teach whoever wants to listen a special Wisdom.

That is why Merlin is presented to us as the madman of the woods. Men live in palaces. He will live in a tree. In their discourse men describe what they see. In his prophecies Merlin will describe what he does not see but what he knows. Men obey the laws of society. Merlin puts himself outside of that society and recognizes no laws other than those of nature, in which he participates. Men scrupulously observe prohibitions. Merlin makes fun of prohibitions and sleeps with his sister. His head really is upside down, like the Hanged Man of the Tarot. Morals, customs, social life, and various prohibitions no longer exist in the world attained by Merlin, that of the dawn of time. And if Merlin reaches it so easily it is because he is the incarnation of divine power, because he himself is the god who rules the world, the demiurge. He is not the Creator. But he is the organizer.

This is why Merlin must be studied in his essential aspect of *druid* or *shaman*. His retreat to the heart of the forest, his gift of prophecy, his magic powers, his mocking attitude toward society, his "confinement" in nature, his Wild Man appearances, his flagrant anachronism, all induce us to see in him something other than a simple "enchanter." He is much more. He symbolizes, in fact, all that remains of druidic learning, scattered throughout popular oral tradition and recovered during the Middle Ages, by fragments, in accounts whose meaning we no longer comprehend very well but that are the final teachings of the ancient Celts.

PART 5

The Great Withdrawal

What is most interesting to us as members of an industrial, technologically advanced civilization dedicated to a concrete universe and to the imperatives of a centralism with universalist tendencies, is the contemplation of Merlin's separation from the society of his time. He has accomplished the great withdrawal. As the character, whether actual or imaginary, is the incarnation of a myth, it remains to discover the profound meaning of that myth as well as what impulses or drives belonging to men and women at the end of the twentieth century it may conceal. Any person descended from the past and more or less brought back to life from the darkness that surrounds him is of interest only to the extent that he corresponds to what we think. Merlin's passage turned out well. It is important to explain why and how his ritual ascension to the summit of the Cosmic Tree was crowned with success.

All that is needed to do this is to recapture the elements brought to light in the course of analyzing Merlin's legend. Each of these elements, placed in its original context, supplies the answer, for each one of them exists only in relation to another. In this way a chain is formed whose apparent diversity only confirms its single identity. Merlin can belong to all ages and to all systems of reference even if our image of him is marked too heavily by the imprint of a moribund feudal civilization resulting in the triumph of the clerical class. Merlin is the wise man par excellence, and wise men have no era and no age. If Merlin is able to rejuvenate his appearance, to present himself as an old man or a young boy, there is a reason for it: he is the model of those who want to abolish time and space. It can be said that this is the purpose of all religions, understood properly, and certainly of all teachings the least bit esoteric. Prince Gautama became Buddha, or the Enlightened One, when he understood the vanity of the world, or at least what the world had become after the great division established between man and nature. But not only the Orient became aware of this disequilibrium. The West understood it as well but, for quite complex reasons, efforts were made to ignore this discovery. The example of the Gallic and British druids, tracked down by the Romans because they taught a doctrine that did not conform to Roman imperialism, confirms that voluntary concealment in the West. As for the Irish druids, never subdued by the Roman armies, they blended with and were taken over by the zealots of triumphant Christianity, zealots who probably used the same techniques as they had, and presented themselves as miracle-workers for the same reasons. We know the result: lost in a false synthesis of eastern Jewish mysticism and the aggressive rationalism of the Romans, western spirituality was crushed by a politically strong Christianity, in which the Church was at first temporal because it could take the place of the civil order inherited from the Roman Empire. Only the great mystics of Christianity such as Francis of Assisi, and most of the great heretics, would keep alive the flame that sought only to illuminate the world. But it burned in the darkness of crypts, within the walls of certain monasteries, and also in forest hermitages where human beings relearned contact with God in total harmony with nature. It is in this perspective that the figure of Merlin appears. He is not a Christian priest; he is not a monk; he is not a hermit in the medieval sense of the word. But he is the druid, the shaman, to whom everyone looks. He astonishes; that suffices to make him an exceptional being. He is regarded with suspicion because whoever has a certain vision of things that does not conform to the accepted one must be "diabolical." And yet, seen from this point of view—of marginality and a return to nature—Merlin's case cannot help but be interesting.

10

Ⱨ EIR OF THE DRUIDS

 When the figure of Merlin emerged from the shadows, during the twelfth century, it had been a long time since the druids had vanished completely and druidism had become a mystery as spellbinding as it is today. In assembling the various elements of the legend, however, Merlin is incontestably the heir of the druids, even if only through his identification with Dagda, that Irish god who is also the druid-god, the all-powerful medicine man, the great shaman.

The Irish narrative of "The Battle of Mag-Tured" begins: "the Tuatha Dé Danann were in the islands in the north of the world, learning science, magic, druidism, witchcraft and wisdom. . . ."[1] In other words, the Tuatha Dé Danann, or "People of the Goddess Dana" had brought to Ireland the knowledge and techniques of druidism, but this druidism had originated in the north of the world. Was it the geographical north, the land of the "Hyperboreans," or, on the contrary, a mythical north, symbol of the pivot around which the earth is deployed? It is difficult to say. Note that druidism is put on the same level as wisdom and science, but also magic and witchcraft. We know that the word *magus* often designated a druid in ancient and medieval texts. Witchcraft, though considered diabolical, was also seen as a reflection of ancient ritual practices from the time of druidism—practices much disparaged, even dishonored, and driven out by the established order. But Merlin seems to be as expert in wisdom, science, or even druidism, as in magic and witchcraft.

But those famous "islands in the north of the world," whether real or mythical, are the image of the Celtic paradise, that Land of the Fairies so often sung of by the poets. They are mysterious lands ruled always by women, dispensers of knowledge, initiators of the men who venture among them. There one finds the apple trees that bear fruit all year round. How is it that Merlin, *dominus loci* of the *nemeton*, has supplanted the fairy or goddess who was originally enthroned there? For the legend of Merlin gives the noble role to man: it is Merlin who initiates Morgan and Vivian, who will then reign in their turn, either on the Isle of Avalon or in the Lake of Brocéliande, in domains quite comparable to the Land of the Fairies. At first glance Merlin might be considered a victim of women, since he is confined by Vivian. But the truth lies elsewhere. Being the demiurge, the organizer, Merlin is the one who disseminates knowledge. And by forming a sacred dyad with Vivian, he does much more to restore the completeness of the couple than the exaltation of femininity. At this stage there is no more sexuality, no *sex* in the etymological sense, because the division between brother and sister no longer exists. It is the triumph of the original androgyne who has just been resuscitated by Merlin, thanks to his cohabitation with Vivian.

Everything seems to unfold according to the following scenario: Merlin, endowed with extraordinary powers (due to his birth and diabolical antecedents), goes to seek his double. This double can only be an extraordinary woman, worthy of him, and his peer. Where is she? By a fountain, of course, since she is a water divinity. In this way the legend adapts itself to the original theme, the voyage of the young hero to the Land of the Fairies so often described in Irish epics, particularly in *The Voyage of Bran Son of Fébal*.[2] Perhaps it is there that we should look for the explanation of what is said in one of the *Triads of the Isle of Britain*, in which Merlin disappears at sea during an expedition to the House of Glass. In any case, Merlin reaches the Land of the Fairies or the House of Glass, and with a female divinity forms that divine couple essential to supreme wisdom.

But this voyage is extremely ambiguous, as the Irish text asserts regarding Bran. When he is aboard his ship, proudly steering toward the isle of Emain Ablach, he comes across a knight who is riding the waves. The knight is Mananann, one of the chieftains of the Tuatha Dé Danann. And this king of the otherworld is singing very curious words. He says, notably:

Bran finds it marvelous
to cross the bright sea in a boat,
whereas to me, around my chariot, and from a distance,
it is a flowering plain upon which he rides.
What is the bright sea
to the boat with Bran is at its prow,
is a pleasant plain full of flowers
to me, from my two-wheeled chariot.
. . . . Your ship floats above woods
across treetops;
there are woods laden with beautiful fruits
beneath the prow of your little boat . . .

It could not be more explicit. And Bran's voyage to the Land of the Fairies irresistibly recalls the famous Ship of Fools[3] originating in Carnival and afterwards so often revived in the works of hermetic science and in symbolic paintings. We do not know the precise origin of this Ship of Fools, a vessel mounted on wheels that was led in the Carnival procession and was probably its most noticed and extraordinary element, especially from the fifteenth century on. Is it, as has been said in arguing about a ninth-century text from the abbey of Saint-Trond, a recollection of the weavers' shuttle? (The custom of weavers during that part of the ninth century was to go from town to town along the Rhine, with a boat on wheels used to travel over paths and roads.) The processional boat of Isis in ancient Egypt was considered, as well as the naval chariot of the Germanic goddess Nertha. After all, isn't *carrus navalis*, "naval chariot," one of the etymologies, probably unreliable, of "Carnival"? It is true that the word *navette* [shuttle] means "little ship." Be that as it may, the naval chariot or the boat with wheels that travels over roads and across is a strange element found both in Celtic tradition and in the Carnival procession, feast of the fools. Is not this Ship of Fools the ship of Merlin, himself the bard-fool, the prophet-fool, the king-fool, otherwise called the visionary, the scholar, and the one who disturbs?

In any event, the world through which Merlin moves in his quest for the House of Glass is a place where the most unlikely exchanges occur.

One cannot help but think of this description in *L'Ile Tournoyante* [the Whirling Isle] as we will discover it in *The Story of the Holy Grail*:

> *At the beginning of everything, the four elements were confused. The Creator separated them. Fire and air, which are all brightness and lightness, immediately rose toward heaven, while water and especially earth, which is simply a heavy accumulation of filth, fell down below. But from having been mingled for so long, it was inevitable that the four elements would have reciprocally exchanged some of their opposing properties. As a result, when the Sovereign Father . . . had cleansed the pure air and the bright fire, shining and warm, of all earthly things, and the cold water and the heavy earth of all heavenly things, the residues formed a kind of mass or smoke, too heavy to rise into the air, too light to stay on the earth, too humid to mix with fire, too dry to combine with water. And this mass began to float through the universe until it arrived above the Western Sea, between the isle of Onagrine and the Port of Tigers. There, inside the earth, is an immense quantity of magnetic material whose force attracted and held the ferruginous parts but without sufficient power to prevent the parts of fire and air from carrying the mass away toward the sky; it remained, therefore, on the surface of the water. It then began to pivot on itself according to the movement of the firmament to which it belonged by virtue of its igneous parts. And the result was that the people of the country called it* island *because it was in the middle of the sea, and* whirling *because it swung in this way.*

The description is certainly curious. It goes beyond the imaginative fantasy of the author. One draws from it, in fact, quite intelligent reflections on the reciprocal action of elements among themselves, and on the appearance of a fifth element, the magnet, that is, the element that makes things coalesce. We are in the presence of a true treatise on alchemy: it is really a description of the dissolution of elements contained in the raw material of transmutation and of the coagulation of those elements that are *residues of the normal world*, being thus imbued with a certain occult power in order to arrive at the elaboration of a perfect matter, the one called the Philosopher's Stone. Thus it is a rather bizarre illustration of the famous alchemical council *solve et coagula*. It is also the proof that an entire ecstatic experience that constantly refers to alchemical practices is defined in the character of Merlin. For of necessity the operation on matter has its counterpart in the operation on spirit. One does not exist without the other. Merlin in his tree or the shaman in his birch tree is the Philosopher's Stone, with all that entails concerning the reconstruction of the world. If the Philosopher's Stone represents matter in its state of perfection, Merlin in the *nemeton*, forming the ideal couple with Vivian, represents the discovery of the perfect world before the fall or corruption. And in what container does this creation occur? In an *athanor*, in the vocabulary of alchemists, that is, in a vessel of glass. Merlin's house of glass is no different, like the chamber of crystal in Irish legends and the story of Tristan.

But no matter how charged it is with alchemical elements, this description of the Whirling Isle has its source in a serious author of classical antiquity, the Greek geographer Polybius, who refuted an opinion of the navigator Pytheas, explorer of the islands of the west and north. "Pytheas has deceived the public," states Polybius, "concerning Thule and its neighboring countries by saying that there is neither land nor sea nor air in these areas, *but a mixture of all the elements*, rather like a marine lung, and by placing the earth and the air and the sea above this lung which links all of these parts without offering the possibility of sailing or walking on this matter."[4] And according to Pliny the Elder, this sea is called Marimaruse,[5] or "Dead Sea"; the term is typically Celtic.

The theme of this quest of Merlin's for the fortress of glass, which is the *nemeton* in its purest form, spread almost everywhere, as is shown by certain tales of the oral tradition. One of them, that has multiple and various versions depending on the region, contains a play on words between *verre* [glass] and *vert* [green]. It is "La Montagne Verte" [The Green Mountain] of which the most complete version was found in the Rouergue in the heart of Occitan country.[6] The version closest to the Celtic model, "Les Femmes-Cygnes" [The Swan Women], comes from Armorican Brittany, specifically from the island of Molène.[7]

>———— THE GREEN MOUNTAIN ————<

A young peasant loses everything gambling, even his house. He goes to the cemetery to hang himself when a somber person appears and gives him a pot full of gold. The sole condition he imposes is that the pot be returned to him completely empty, after a year and a day, at his castle, which is somewhere on the Green Mountain. The time elapsed, the hero goes to seek the Green Mountain. He meets some old men who are not able to tell him which road to take because they are not old enough to know. Finally, a very old woman reveals to him the location of the castle and gives him the means to enter it. Following her advice, the hero comes to a lake in which three female ducks are swimming. He plucks a feather from the white duck and she instantly changes into a ravishing maiden. She tells him that she and the other two ducks, her sisters, are the daughters of le Drac, and she warns the hero that her father will try to detain him by subjecting him to all sorts of tests. She also offers to help him if he will marry her. Le Drac does indeed subject the hero to various tests which he passes, thanks to the white maiden. The last test consists of going to look for a bird on a glass tower so smooth that it is impossible to climb it, particularly as there is no ladder in the castle. The only way is for the hero to boil the maiden in a cauldron, dismember her, take all of her bones and place them end to end, and thereby reach the summit of the tower. Afterwards, he puts the maiden together again in the cauldron but forgets one small bone of her foot. Le Drac, defeated, offers him one of his daughters in marriage, but says that he must choose the one who loves him without being able to distinguish among them, all three being dressed alike and having their faces hidden. Naturally, he recognizes her because of the missing little toe. The marriage takes place, but le Drac wants to kill his daughter and son-in-law. They flee. Le Drac pursues them, but thanks to the magic of the maiden in white, they transform themselves, outwitting le Drac several times and finally causing him to drown. Then both of them take possession of the castle on the Green Mountain, with its treasures and secrets.

THE SWAN WOMEN

Every day a young shepherd sees three swans alight by a lake, divest themselves of their covering of feathers, and bathe. His grandmother *explains to him that they are the three daughters of an enchanter. She reveals how he can penetrate the enchanter's castle, which is a "castle of gold and crystal suspended in the air between heaven and earth." The shepherd then goes to the lake. When the swan women have bared themselves, he takes the plumage of one of them and hides it. The maidens want their feathers back, but he agrees only on condition that they take him to the enchanter's castle. Once there, he hides in the chamber of the maiden whose plumage he had stolen. But the other two maidens wish to share the shepherd with their sister and threaten to reveal everything to the enchanter. The maiden and the shepherd flee with the enchanter's treasures; he is unable to catch them.*

The theme developed here is exactly the same as that of Paris meeting Aphrodite, Pallas, and Hera on Mount Ida—at least before the Greeks turned this initiation myth into a moralizing beauty contest, useful for explaining the Trojan War. In its original form, Paris steals Aphrodite's clothing and agrees to return it only if she promises to give him Helen, the swan maiden. Paris's goal is to reach the Castle of Glass, where the harmonious fusion of opposites takes place in a return to the original circumstances of the dawn of time. The castle on the Green Mountain (*montana verde*) is described by a play on words on "verre" [glass]. The castle of gold and crystal in "The Swan Women" is even more unequivocal. And in another Breton tale, "The Voyage of Izanig," the hero goes to seek his sister who has married a mysterious and luminous person (the sun). After traveling through countries where everything is confused, where time and space no longer exist, he arrives at the Château Vert (Kastell Glaz) [Green Castle]. Here the play on words exists in French (between *vert* and *verre*) as well as in Breton, where *glaz* (blue or green) evokes ice and glass.

Note that if the castle of the enchanter, or of Le Drac, or of the devil always conjures up glass, the daughter of the master of the place is always characterized by the color white; she is a white swan, a white duck, or a maiden in white.[8] This invites comparison with the name of Merlin's companion in all versions of the legend (Gwendydd, Ganieda, Vivian, and even Boinn, the "White Cow"). Since the folktales have kept the basic form of the original myth, we deduce that Merlin without his companion is again nothing; he attains wholeness only in Vivian's company, only because of his union with her. In reality, the young hero of the folktale who marries the devil's daughter marries his sister, since Merlin is himself the devil's son, but a son rejected by the father because he does not obey the line of conduct that had been established in bringing him into the world. It is a question of the struggle between the devil, possessor of all power, and the devil's son, who has the complicity not of the mother, but of the sister.[9] Having become invulnerable through union with his sister, he recovers the half of the diabolical powers that had been denied him because of his crossbreeding with the human race. The incest between Myrddin and Gwendydd, or between Merlin and Vivian, is thereby justified.

If the hero of the folktale is the equivalent of Merlin, what powers does he obtain in the castle of glass, that is, at the top of his tree in the center of the *nemeton*? The gifts of clairvoyance, metamorphosis,[10] and invisibility; influence over the elements; comprehension of the language of animals and power to command them are given him, as well as the gifts of medicine and resurrection of the dead; the gifts of causing springs to flow and making visible people and things that do not exist; power over the vegetable kingdom; ubiquity; and the ability to fly through the air. All of these powers are those attributed to the druids by Irish and Welsh literary traditions.

Indeed, druids were the "augurs" of the Celts. In the Irish epics, they make prophecies constantly, foretelling victories and catastrophes, indicating the destiny of a child to be born, specifying at what moment and in what way such or such a person will die. There is nothing new about that—the priests of most ancient religions claimed, by reason of their position, the right to determine the future in the name of the divinities they represented or incarnated. "There is only one God," says widespread proverb; but from the moment the druid takes on the incarnation of god, he is divine, as he participates fully in divine wisdom.

The gift of metamorphosis is much less common in religions, though even today, in the countryside, Catholic priests have the reputation of doing "physical tricks."[11] Nevertheless, the druids, at least in the epics, are accorded the ability to transform their aspect and sometimes to change themselves into animals. In the same way, they can metamorphose the appearance of other human beings. This happens in an account of the Leinster cycle concerning the hero Finn and his son Oisin (Ossian): Oisin's mother is a woman who was turned into a doe through the magic of the Black Druid, and her son Oisin bears that name because it means "fawn." The Irish hero Mongan, son of Fiachna, in reality the son of Mananann, can change his aspect at will, assume that of another, and metamorphose other people. In the very curious tale of the "Two Swineherds," the heroes are rivals who confront one another in different forms: first as two swineherds, then as two champions, two demons, two worms, and finally as two bulls. And the mythical druid-hero Tuan mac Cairill lives for twelve hundred years, first in the form of a man, then in the form of an ox, a goat, a bird, a salmon, and finally again as a man. In the Irish narrative of the *"Siege of Druim Damhgaire,"* three magicians with druidic powers transform themselves into sheep, and a druid raises the level of a hill and changes his adversaries (also druids) into stones. In this narrative, the victorious druid is dressed peculiarly in the hide of a brown bull with no horns, and a strange headdress consisting of a speckled bird. And in one of the battles of the *Tain Bo Cualinge* the goddess Morrigane assumes the form of a crow.

There are many other heroes, heirs to druidic wisdom, who transform themselves or others. The bard Taliesin, who inadvertently drank the three drops that impart knowledge, is a typical example.[12] King Math of Gwynedd metamorphoses his nephews Gwyddyon and Gilvaethwy into animals, and later, with Gwyddyon's help, creates a woman out of flowers. And Gwyddyon transforms his own appearance at will, for he has inherited the "magic" of his uncle Math. We know that *magic* often means *druidism* in medieval texts which, in Wales as on the continent, never use the word *druid,* long since gone from the vocabulary.[13] Owein, son of Uryen, has at his disposal a "flock of crows" that are really fairies.[14] In fact, it is his mother, Modron or Morgan. And according to the *Vita Merlini,* Morgan can change herself into a bird. This recalls the famous text of Pomponius Mela regarding the "priestesses" of the island of Sein, who "knew how to take the form of whatever animals they wish."[15] The theme is mythological; it occurs in Ireland in the *Tale of Étaine* with the transformation of the heroine into a puddle of water, a worm, a butterfly, then a woman once more, at the will of the female magician Fuamnach.[16]

Merlin is inevitably the heir to this tradition. He himself changes his aspect, appearing at various times as a young boy, an adolescent, an old man, a beggar, a woodcutter, a wild man, and sometimes even an animal—especially a stag—as in the text of the *Vulgate*. The episode in the *Vita Merlini* in which he is mounted on a stag is merely a rationalization of the myth. And he particularly knows how to transform humans and things, as is shown in the adventure of Tintagel, in which he permits Uther to assume the form of the duke of Cornwall, and in the transformations he performs in the Vivian's presence. He is also master of the vegetable kingdom; we shall see later on what conclusions can be drawn from this fact. He can cause springs to flow and is master of the mineral kingdom. He is, therefore, as much the heir of the druids as of the holy miracle-workers. In certain episodes of the Arthurian romances, he can restore life to knights who are dead or on the point of dying. So he is also the medicine man, the shaman who, by means of his ecstatic voyage, goes to the otherworld in search of the soul of the person who is ill or dead, and brings it back with him. And if he has the gift of ubiquity and can fly through the air like a bird, it is because he possesses a strange power that the Christians recognized in the druids of Ireland even as they called it "witchcraft" or "devilry." When Saint Ronan cursed him, Suibhné began to fly through the air like a bird. The significance of the anecdote is that in cursing him, Ronan excluded Suibhné from the Christian community; Suibhné immediately returned to his pagan state with all its attendant powers. The saints and bishop-priests of Irish Christianity had, themselves, inherited a goodly number of powers from their predecessors, the druids. Merlin, like Suibhné, is a kind of bird-man. There are comparisons to be made with shamanism, all of whose practices tend to make of the shaman, or of those whom the shaman wishes to initiate, strange beings endowed with supernatural powers. By means of their psychic force shamans manage to persuade a man that he really is an animal, and to make him act like one. The experience has been verified many times, and physical evidence established. Is the shaman, then, an illusionist, a hypnotist? Perhaps. So is Merlin, then, like Éon de l'Étoile, who seems, more than anyone else, to embody Merlin's myth. But that does not explain everything, for it concerns only the techniques employed. We must question the benefit of these psychic transformations of human beings. We must also understand why it is so important to the shaman to travel through the air and transport himself psychically from one place to another. There are two specific answers to these questions. First, the shaman recreates the original human condition. This is why he must transform himself or the other into an animal—to be privy to the secrets of a being able to *feel* the inexplicable, that which human logic cannot recover. Next, as the voyage to the otherworld constitutes the essence of shamanistic thought and cannot be accomplished by normal means, the gravity that holds the body to earth must be abandoned in order to enter forbidden domains, forbidden only because the means of entering them is unknown. That is what sets the shaman apart from the society in which he lives: he is able to move by setting aside gravity, and he can enclose his soul in the body of any animal so that he can experience a different world—the world of instinct, fundamentally opposed to the world of intelligence. Merlin's case is not in any way different.

There is also the famous gift of invisibility. We know that this gift was taken just as seriously by the Christians. A text which serves as the introduction to the *Lorica*, the celebrated hymn of Saint Patrick, tells us that Patrick, whose enemies lay in wait for him, sang this hymn and his enemies no longer saw him. Instead of the saint and his companions, they saw stags with a fawn. The text tells us that this hymn was composed to protect body and soul against "demons," that is, against magi of all kinds. This gift of invisibility, or *feth fiada*, is the privilege of the Tuatha Dé Danann, who obtained it after the division of Ireland with the Gaels, when they were forced to take refuge in the hills and islands. It allows the Tuatha Dé Danann to be invisible to ordinary mortals. But certain druids also have this gift, which they cannot reveal, for at that moment the magic power of the *feth fiada* would be completely destroyed. At least that is what Cuchulainn says to his friend (and adversary) Ferdead in the *Tain Bo Cualinge*. There is a famous legendary episode around this *feth fiada*, in the beautiful story of Diarmaid and Grainné: the two fugitive lovers are going to be overtaken by Finn and the Fiana, and it is then that Oengus, son of the god Dagda, takes them under the folds of his coat, conferring upon them the privilege of invisibility.

In another Irish text, "The House of the Two Goblets," reference is made again to this characteristic of the Tuatha Dé Danann. The narrative's heroine, a certain Curcog, who belongs to the race of fairies, is with her companions on the shore of the Boyne. All at once the *feth fiada* deserts her. She can no longer see her comrades, but they can still see her. We are then told that she goes from paganism to Christianity and abandons demoniacal practices discover the true faith. Of course she is baptized afterwards.[17] In *Yvain*, by Chrétien de Troyes, the fairy Luned gives the hero a ring that renders him invisible in the castle of the knight he has just slain; and in the Welsh narrative "Peredur," the young hero is given a stone of invisibility by the mysterious empress that enables him to triumph over a monster in a cavern.[18] All this is found again in a tale of Lower Brittany, *"The Marvellous Stone."* It is about a midwife who has come to deliver a korrigan-woman who asks her to take a certain stone and rub the infant's eyes with it. She obeys, but also rubs her own right eye. One day in the market she sees the korrigan-woman help herself generously without paying and without anyone seeing her. When she meets her later, she makes a comment to her about this. Then korrigan asks her with which eye she sees her. "With the right eye," she says. And the korrigan pierces her eye. "From that time on the midwife was blind in one eye and never again saw the korrigans when they were invisible." It proves that popular tradition has maintained this belief in the gift of invisibility of fairies and the people who live underground.

It will be said that this gift refers to the fantasy that men have always had of seeing without being seen.[19] But it is possible that only exceptional people are in possession of the secret. There is no doubt that Merlin is one of them; in the poems attributed to him there is clearly an allusion to the apple tree in which he is located and that is not seen by other humans. And in any case, when he is confined by Vivian in the magic castle he is invisible. The episode of the *Vulgate* in which he tells Gawain what has befallen him leaves no doubt—Gawain hears him, but does not see him through the strange haze that separates him from the enchanter.

By definition the druid, as mediator between divinities and mortals, is the master of the invisible. Merlin is also this mediator. We realize it from the place that he occupies as councillor to King Uther, and then to King Arthur. The two kings undertake nothing without asking his counsel, and even when they claim to be acting of their own free will, Merlin unexpectedly appears to guide them or to amend their plans, deciding himself what must be accomplished. The two kings obey Merlin blindly as if they were of an inferior rank.

This illustrates the place of the druids at the king's side. All the texts, from classical antiquity or medieval Ireland, agree on this point: the druid and the king form an indispensable couple, and in this couple the principal role is played by the druid. Dio Chrysostom states that without the druids "kings were not allowed to act or make decisions."[20] It is a fact that in original Celtic society, which lasted a long time in Ireland, if the king made a decision it was only after the druid had given his advice. It was unthinkable for the king to make his decision alone, just as it was unthinkable, during an assembly, for the king to speak before his druid. Spiritual power has primacy over temporal power even if, theoretically, it is the king who occupies the pivotal place in society. The narrative "The Drunkenness of the Ulstermen" affirms it. The text even adds that "if someone desires to converse with the king, it is permitted only if he first speaks to the druid." And the kings are kings only because the druids have decided that it would be so. It is the same for Arthur: he is king only because Merlin arranged for him to be recognized as such. Caesar tells us that among the Eduens it is the priests who elected Convictolitavis to the supreme magistrature.[21] And if the king breaks his word to a druid, he is cursed. It happens to Conchobar in "The Exile of the Sons of Usnech": he has sworn to his own father, the druid Cathbad, to respect the lives of Usnech's sons, who ravished the beautiful Deirdre; after slaughtering them he is rejected and cursed by Cathbad, and his capital, Emain Macha, is burned down. It is somewhat like the malediction cast by Merlin, in the form of a prophecy, upon wicked King Vortigern.

For Merlin also has the power to curse, to issue interdicts or "satires" against those he judges injurious to the harmony of the world. The Irish druids practiced rituals of execration that were quite formidable. We know, for example, how the *glam dicinn*, a malediction pronounced against an individual or a group, was put into effect. After a period of fasting, seven poets (belonging to the druidic class but of a lower rank) climbed a hill, turned toward the land of the king against whom they were to pronounce the incantation, each of them holding a bramble thorn and a catapult stone in his hand, and performed the ritual. But if the malediction was unjustified, the hill opened and the earth swallowed the poets. The text of "The Death of Cuchulainn" cites numerous resources possessed by the druids, the poets, and the "satirists" for magically defeating an adversary.

An Irish text appears to synthesize all the comparisons that can be made between Merlin and the druids on one hand, and between the druids, Merlin, and shamanism on the other. It is the very fine and strange narrative of "The Death of Muirchertach mac Erca,"[22] a historic figure from the early days of Christianity. His tragic destiny soon made an impression on poets, who created around him a grandiose epic in which druidism and Christianity confronted each other. But the heroine is a witch-woman. Now, contrary to certain opinions expressed over the centuries, of which the figure of the Velléda of Chateaubriand has become the symbol, there were never any druidesses among the Celts. There were only prophetesses, women who were magicians, belonging by right to the druidic class but without the status of priestesses. But in this narrative the woman seems to have all the powers devolving upon the druids.

⟩— THE DEATH OF MUIRCHERTACH MAC ERCA —⟨

King Muirchertach meets a maiden with whom he falls in love. As he himself is married, he proposes, according to custom, that she become his concubine for one year, and offers her the customary gifts for that kind of situation. The maiden asks for as much as she can, and above all demands that he send away his wife and children and have nothing more to do with the priests. The king promises everything she wishes. The abandoned wife goes to the holy bishop Cairnech to protest and, like a druid, he pronounces a curse upon the fortress of Cletech, the king's residence, and on the king himself. He even digs a false grave and utters these imprecations:

> *Everyone will know, forever,*
> *that in this mound is*
> *the grave of the hero Mac Erca.*
> *His deeds were not minor.*
> *A curse on this hill,*
> *upon Cletech and its hundreds of warriors. . . .*
> *May its corn and milk spoil,*

> may it fill with hatred and evil,
> may no king or prince live there,
> may no one leave it in victory. . . .
> Here on this mound, on this day,
> lies the tomb of the king of Ireland.

And Cairnech blesses another place. At Cletech, however, the girl forbids the king to pronounce her name, and so that he will not violate this magical taboo she reveals that she is called Sin (Breath), Rustling, Tempest, Harsh Wind, Winter Night, Cry, Lamentation, Moaning. The king becomes uneasy in her presence, as she seems to him to be "a very powerful goddess." He asks her:

> "Tell me, beautiful maid,
> do you believe in the god of the priests?
> How did you come into this world?
> Tell me of your birth. . . . "

The girl answers:

> "I believe in the same true god,
> savior of my body against death's assaults.
> There is no miracle in this world
> that I cannot straightaway perform.
> I am the daughter of a man and a woman
> of the race of Eve and Adam.
> I look kindly upon you
> provided remorse does not seize you.
> I can create a sun, a moon,
> and radiant stars.
> I can create cruel men,
> implacable warriors.
> I can, without lying, make wine
> from the water of the Boyne, as I can make
> sheep out of rocks
> and pigs out of ferns.

I can make silver and gold
in the presence of crowds,
I can create famous men
for you, now, I say it. . . . "

With a few exceptions, this poem is a résumé of the powers generally attributed to Merlin the enchanter, as well as to Vivian and Morgan. In any case, the story shows us how Sin uses the powers she claims
to possess. She creates armies, pigs, intoxicating drinks. And in the
morning, the king feels very weak. This recalls, naturally, the story of
Éon de l'Étoile offering sumptuous feasts to his guests who, when they
leave the table, feel as hungry and thirsty as they did before. But Sin
continues her tricks. She takes stones and makes from them "men with
goat's heads and blue men." These phantoms rush at the king, who
seizes his weapons and fights them. "He slew and wounded many of
them, but each man he killed rose up behind him." The episode recalls
one of the fragments of the Breton Legend of the Ville d'Is, in which
the foolish young Kristof, who has become a magician, thanks to a
divine little fish, creates soldiers who are always revived and cannot be
killed when he is attacked by the troops of his father-in-law, Gradlon.

Meanwhile, Muirchertach is still embattled before the fortress of
Cletech. Some clerics pass by and are astonished to see him fighting
stones.[23] They make the sign of the cross and the enchantment vanishes. The king repents, confesses his sins, and promises to change his
life for the better. But Sin succeeds in confusing his mind and causes a
violent tempest, the famous "druidic wind," which no one can resist.
Then the king says: "It is the breath of a winter night." These are words
he should never have said, for in doing so he disobeys Sin's interdiction
by twice speaking her name: "breath," and "winter night." From that
moment on, as always happens in such cases,[24] Muirchertach will transgress all taboos and so, of necessity, be led to his death.

Sin causes more and more visions, more and more tempests, and
each time the king falls into the trap and utters the words that he must
not say. In the end, inside his fortress, which is on fire, he drowns himself in a vat of wine. We learn afterwards that Sin was the daughter of a
man who died because of Muirchertach, and that she wanted to avenge
her father's death on the king with whom she was nevertheless in love.

This strange, beautiful, and tragic adventure makes absolutely clear the formidable powers granted to the druids and their successors: the *fili,* the holy bishops, and especially the women magicians who would become the witches of the Middle Ages, destined to be burned at the stake for keeping company with the devil. These witches were also heirs of the druids. In the midst of the twelfth century, Merlin, with an aura of the prestige of accursed knowledge, yet saved by the saintliness of his mother, belongs to the same domain. He is magus, the enchanter, the master heretic, who embodies all the rejected and hidden beliefs, all the dishonored yet coveted practices, all the "diabolical" yet "devilishly interesting" secrets. And Merlin's disciples are two women, Morgan and Vivian, living symbols of witches and of the "sleeping women" who still officiate in the countryside, living images of the fairies who pass like lightning through the folktales of oral tradition.

11

THE

ASTER OF WORLDS,
OR NATURE RECONCILED

 A hero, whoever he may be, a god's prophet or the people's teacher, is basically only an image representing the immense possibilities of the human being who, utilizing only a part of his brain and an infinitesimal portion of his knowledge, forgets that he can master the worlds in which his life unfolds. The wise man's mission consists, therefore, of enlightening others concerning human development. Merlin, in a romantic form or in various disguises, is the hero who, in the words of an ancient Irish poet, "fires up the mind."

Already powerful in the social group into which he was born, both for his special gifts and for his marginal position with respect to society, Merlin consecrates his triumph at the moment of his confinement in the prison of air, or *nemeton*, where he is the demiurge, sage, and prophet.

Like druids and shamans come to the pinnacle of their initiatory quest, what defines Merlin is his power over the elements. By virtue of his breath he is master of the tempest, that famous druidic wind that can chill the world or set it ablaze. It is not by chance that his legend is located at the Fountain of Barenton, over which a tempest is loosed when the rite is performed. Merlin is therefore the master of breath, like young Sin of the Irish account, whose name amounts to an explanation. We know that the importance of breath has been recognized throughout history in rituals, myths, legends, and their varied incarnations, even if only in the Carnival procession entirely dedicated to breath and its exaltation.[1] It is also known that breath is a concept linked to madness, and that the word "fou" [mad] (Latin *follis*) is related to the word that means "soufflet" [bellows]. Hence *le fou* [the madman or fool] is the possessor and master of breath. It is no surprise that Merlin is the madman of the woods.

Merlin is also the master of plants. He has successfully ascended the Cosmic Tree. And the pine tree of Barenton described by Chrétien de Troyes and by the Welsh author of "Owein" is an extraordinary tree which does not let rain pass through it, thus sheltering a protected world out of the reach of storms. If the druids were always associated with trees, if only because of an erroneous etymology, there still must be a reason for it. We know what this reason is because, in Celtic languages, knowledge is linked etymologically to the name of the tree (*vidu*). It is amid the trees, in the *nemeton*, that one obtains this knowledge—in the ordinary sense of the term, since the druids taught their disciples in remote forests, but also in the figurative sense. The tree symbolizes the past (the roots), the present (the trunk and the branches), and the future (the leaves), according to a widely known, grandiloquent image by Victor Hugo, in a poem in which the poet's function is given its rightful place: he is the one who says out loud what others murmur or dare not say, because he draws upon the past to illuminate the future.

We should not be surprised, therefore, to encounter so many references to the vegetable kingdom in Celtic mythology. Trees are wholly separate beings. All that is required is to rouse them, to make them move, as in the "Cad Goddeu," "The Death of Cuchulainn," and Shakespeare's *Macbeth*.[2] It is from plants that Math and Gwyddyon created young Blodeuwedd, the flower-daughter destined for Lleu Llaw Gyffes.[3] It is from a stick of wood that a young simpleton who had become the devil's servant makes an ox in a folktale of Upper Brittany.[4] It is with wands from a yew tree that druids make divinatory incantations;[5] it is with a yew wheel that the druid Mog Ruith (whose name contains the word "roue" [wheel]) unleashes the elements on his enemies in the Irish tale of the "Siege of Druim Damhgaire," one of the texts from which we learn most about druidic practices.[6] It is with the wood of a rowan tree that another druid in the same tale causes a "druidic fire" that spreads everywhere. It is with a divining rod from a hazel tree that the satirists launch their incantantions upon Cuchulainn in the account of the death of that hero.[7] It is again with a divining rod from a hazel tree that dowsers discover water. And what is there to say about the magic wands of fairies, sorcerers, and enchanters? As for the apple tree, it is the tree, par excellence, of the marvelous orchard, and it is with one of its branches that mortals are drawn into the land of fairies.[8]

Not only do druids have powers over the vegetable kingdom, then, but they also use plants to influence other elements. We know that Merlin is able, through "his art," to move enormous stones from Ireland to Stonehenge, and that in Thomas Malory's version he can move aside great rocks. Nimue can do as much, moreover, since she locks up Merlin for good. And if Gwyddyon transforms mushrooms into gilded shields, Merlin changes bushes and pebbles into a marvelous castle. Sin makes stones look like formidable warriors. Nothing is impossible. This is why Merlin creates for Vivian that famous Garden of Joy or Garden of Gaiety that is the ideal *nemeton*, the original orchard, the sanctuary where the Philosopher's Stone will be created.

What also characterizes Merlin, as well as the Irish Dagda, is that he is the master of animals. In the *Vita Merlini* he is riding a stag (which is to say that he has taken the form of a stag) and is accompanied by a wolf (which is to say that he is a wolf). To be master of animals is not only to be obeyed by animals but also to be able to assume their forms. And that is pure shamanism. The legend of Odin shows him asleep, but "he becomes a bird or a wild animal, a fish or a dragon, and travels in the wink of an eye to very distant countries" (*Ynglinga Saga*, 7). This power that Odin possesses of transforming himself into an animal is one of the characteristics of the shaman. But, as Mircea Eliade says, "in mythical times each member of the tribe could metamorphose himself into an animal, which is to say that everyone was able to share in the condition of the ancestor. In our day such intimate relations with mythical ancestors are reserved exclusively for shamans."[9] The same is true of druids in the Celtic society, and for Merlin in his legendary context.

In the story of the *Chevalier au Lion* by Chrétien de Troyes, the knight Calogrenant meets the rogue of whom we have spoken, who is Merlin in one of his aspects. He asks him what he is doing there. The Wild Man answers that he is tending the animals. Calogrenant is astonished: "By Saint Peter of Rome, they (the wild animals) do not know man. I do not believe that it is possible, in the plain or in the woods, or anywhere

else, to tend in any way a wild animal who is not tethered or penned."
The Wild Man answers him: "Nonetheless I tend them and control
them in such a way that they will not leave this enclosure . . . There is
not one of them who dares move as soon as he sees me coming. When
I can hold one of them, I grasp him by the two horns with my solid and
powerful hands, with the result that the others tremble with fear and
gather around me as if to ask my pardon, but no one else but me would
be able to venture among them without being killed. I am the lord of
my beasts."[10]

In the Welsh text of "Owein," there is an analogous episode. It concerns Kynon, who asks the Wild Man "what power he had over these
animals." The Wild Man takes his stick and strikes a great blow to a
stag. "The latter bayed loudly and at the sound of his voice there came
running at once as many animals as there are stars in the sky, to the
point where I had great difficulty in remaining on my feet in their midst
in the clearing; furthermore, there were serpents, vipers, all sorts of
animals. He looked at them and ordered them to go and graze. They
lowered their heads and showed him the same respect as men submis-
sive to their lord."[11] In its severity, the Welsh narrative is more explicit:
the Wild Man, by his voice, and by the voice of the stag, has absolute
power over all the animals of the forest.

This recalls the Wild Man of the *Vulgate*, Merlin himself, who leads
many wild animals and makes his first appearance as a stag. Behind the
figure of Merlin there seems to be a complete mythology of the stag.
We know that the epic of Leinster, or Ossianic cycle, is dedicated in its
entirety to that animal. It describes the vestiges of a civilization of hunters living principally by hunting all species of deer, which evidently led
them to a kind of deer cult. Finn and the Fiana, the heroes of this cycle,
are roving hunters. Finn's true name is Demné, meaning "le Daim" [the
deer]. That of his son Oisin (Ossian) means "fawn"; that of his grandson Oscar means "who loves stags." And Oisin's mother is a woman
changed into a doe by a druid. There are too many precise details for it
to be a coincidence. Are we to conclude that the character of Merlin
retrieves the memory of that ancient cult of the deer? It is not impossible. Merlin actually appears as a stag, or mounted on a stag. The stag's
antlers could be a crown, or at least a headdress, and here again we
converge with the use of masks and headdresses among the shamans,

and also among the druids, according to some texts. And we should remember the Gallic god Cernunnos, quite frequently represented in Gallo-Roman statuary, especially on the altar of the Nautes,[12] and the famous cauldron of Gundestrup,[13] where he sits in a Buddhist position, with long stag's antlers, and surrounded by various animals. There is no doubt that Merlin is one of the aspects of this divinity whom the Gauls named Cernunnos and the Irish, perhaps, called Finn (or Demné).

As the devil's son, Merlin would have to be related to the stag, for in medieval imagery the devil often took the form of Cernunnos. It is common knowledge that the clergy, unable to eliminate from popular traditions certain images from past ages, preferred either to Christianize them outright or represent them as diabolical. That is what happened to the stag god; in Carnac (Morbihan) he became "Saint" Kornely, always accompanied by a horned bull, and venerated as the protector of horned animals. But on the other hand, the conventional image of the devil is that of the same horned god. Another Breton saint, Edern, one of Arthur's former companions in the legend, is also linked to the stag in Armorican hagiography.

But the scene described by Geoffrey of Monmouth in the *Vita Merlini*, in the course of which Merlin pulls out one of his stag's horns and hurls it at his wife's fiancé, clearly refers to the tradition of the cuckold. Claude Gaignebet says that "the entire context of this strange scene is carnivalesque. Merlin the Wild Man, coming out of the woods, causes it to be springtime. By this rite of the transmission of horns, moreover, he establishes the alternation of the cuckolds."[14] Actually, cuckoldry regenerates the world. The female principle changes the male principle. The old male is no longer good for anything. He hands over his function to the young male who, the following year, will be cuckolded in his turn and will pass on his function to another. The procession of the brotherhood of the cuckolds during Carnival is not merely a grotesque spectacle; it is above all a matter of participating, in an almost unconscious way, in the rejuvenation that takes place at this time of the year, of getting ready for spring through the regeneration of the sexual function. But Merlin slays the future cuckold, jealously reserving the function for himself; he is able to do this because he himself is regenerated by means of his ecstasy (his removal to the *nemeton*). He now belongs to all time, or rather, time no longer exists for him and he is the immutable husband, or the immutable lover of the goddess. In other words, each spring Merlin sheds his skin (and horns). From the ritual point of view, this metamorphosis has to be understood as the discarding of a garment and headdress that are out of date, and taking possession of another headdress, another garment. Now, it is known that the druids, after the manner of shamans, often wore the hides of animals and headdresses decorated with horns.[15] Yet the stag is not the only animal whose form Merlin takes. In the *Vulgate*, when he emerges from the forest as the Wild Man, he is dressed in a wolf skin. In the *Vita Merlini*, moreover, it is specified that if Merlin passes the winter in the dwelling built for him by his sister during the summer, he will wander through the woods accompanied by a gray wolf. We find here the same rite of passage as in the episode of the stag. The winter Merlin is sedentary, like nature, but during the rest of the year he is nomadic, confirming the designation of demiurge we have conferred on him. But there is more. In several versions of the legend, notably in the Didot *Perceval* and in Thomas Malory, Merlin has as a companion in his retreat a hermit, his master, whose name is Blaise. Now, we know that in Welsh and in Breton *bleidd* or *bleiz* means "wolf." And one can't help thinking of Saint Blaise, whose name day falls on February 3, one day after the carnivalesque holiday of Candlemas, which goes back to the ancient Celtic holiday of Imbolc. These are further coincidences that reveal an astonishing continuity in the traditions.

For Saint Blaise has his legend as well. We are told that he had been elected bishop of Sébaste in Armenia but had retired to Mount Argée, a peak in the middle of what is now Turkey. Wishing to seize him, the governor of the country sent hunters to the mountain. This detail is quite similar to the story of Merlin, to whom King Rydderch sends servants in order to bring him to the king's palace. The hunters found Blaise seated at the entrance to his cave surrounded by a throng of wild animals drawn up in order, listening to him preach. This detail does not come as a surprise, however, since we recognize in it the Wild Man of the *Vulgate* and of the Yvain-Owein legend.

Blaise was then led away in chains to Sébaste, where he was put in prison before undergoing martyrdom. But during the trip he had two important encounters. One was with a woman who, because of Blaise's reputation for saintliness, came to ask him for a miracle because her pig had just been carried off by a wolf. Blaise got the wolf to give back the woman's pig. [16] We can only recall the wolf of Gubbio with whom Saint Francis of Assisi, the last druid-shaman of the West, made a pact of peace. Blaise's other encounter is with a woman whose child had choked on a fish bone it had just swallowed. Blaise restores the child to life; in consequence, he is invoked for disturbances of the throat.

There are many examples of this kind in Celtic hagiography. Edern protects a stag from the wolf who wants to devour him. Ronan, another hermit of Britain whose hermitage was by chance in the forest of Nevet (Nemet, or *nemeton*) and whose activities resemble those of a druid more than those of a cleric, saves a sheep from a wolf that has caught it: he orders the wolf to set down the animal, and the wolf obeys. It is even claimed that this miracle occurred several times. Saint Hervé, the patron saint of bards (heirs to the druids) is known for having procured the services of a wolf that had devoured his donkey. But Ronan's case is odder, for according to the hagiographer Albert Le Grand, "it was claimed that he was a sorcerer and a necromancer, that he was like the ancient lycanthropes (werewolves) which, by means of magic and diabolical art, transformed themselves into wild animals, and roamed the groves, causing a thousand evils in the country." We definitely recognize Merlin in forms that are continuously different and yet always identical.

Is it correct to say that Merlin and Saint Francis of Assisi are one and the same? Yes, although each of them had a proven historical existence, and the assertion seems shocking. Nevertheless, Merlin and Saint Francis of Assisi are incarnations of the same myth, different yet analogous realizations of the concept of the great brotherhood of beings and things. Merlin in the Celtic domain is also, after all, the Irish Dagda. And from the purely Celtic perspective, druids are inevitably the embodiment of gods, for if all gods are druids, all druids must be gods. There are, of course, mythical hierarchies, for the same reason that there are hierarchies in the druidic priestly class. And the god of the druids, who is also the druid god, is Dagda.

Now, Dagda demonstrates the totality of the being reconciled with himself and with things. For Dagda laughs at morality and the laws of society. He is the father of his own mother, his son's uncle, and the lover and son (Mac Oc) of his own daughter (Boinn, who is the wife of his brother, therefore the equivalent of his sister). Although this seems extremely complicated, it is really very simple: Dagda, in his capacity as a "good god," exemplifies the upward progression of the world. He escapes from time and space because he is himself the past, present, and future. And he has attained this by being at the summit of the Tree of the World. He reigns over stones, water, plants, animals, humans, and gods and is the transcendent image of the fraternal fusion that existed before the separation of the elements, before the knowledge of good and evil. This explains why his cudgel is ambivalent, why it can kill or give life. Since there is no longer any separation, beings have the possibility of undertaking anything, in one sense or another. There is no positive aspect and no negative aspect. This makes Dagda the pivot around which the world moves. The transformation into an animal— meaning the recognition by Merlin, or by the druid, of the primacy of instinctive over intellectual life—is, as in the upward-moving ecstasy of the shaman, the most remarkable of experiences: a transcendence of the profane condition, the recovery of a paradisiacal existence lost at the end of mythical times.

"To learn the language of animals, that of the birds first of all, is tantamount everywhere in the world to knowing the secrets of Nature and consequently having the ability to prophesy. . . . To learn their language, imitate their voices, is tantamount to being able to communicate with the Beyond and with the Heavens."[17] Obviously it is a question of rediscovering the Golden Age, that blessed time when man and beast lived in peace and did not kill each other, for in order to live it sufficed to gather fruit. There was no destruction of life; there was only the absorption of the food supplied by nature to supplement the grain she provided us to live on. A paradisiacal situation, to be sure, but one described by all the legends not only as part of the past but as a goal to be attained. And it is accomplished by the great reconciliation of language. If the Wild Man can assemble the animals around him; if Merlin talks with wild boars, stags, or wolves; if Francis of Assisi, Saint Ronan, or Saint Blaise make pacts with the wolf; if animals speak to humans and humans understand animals in folktales it is because language, as Jean-Jacques Rousseau believed, before serving intelligence was content to support sensibility. If we come to understand this fundamental truth, we may learn to comprehend the language of animals and once again make the pact of fraternity with them that will liberate the world.

This is why music is so important in druidic traditions. Dagda owns a harp. "It is the harp upon which Dagda had set tunes so that they were heard in a particular order." This harp is evidently magical, and has two names, "Table of Oak" and "Air of the World." And Dagda plays "the three airs by which a harpist distinguishes himself: the air of sleep, the air of laughter, the air of complaint. He played for them the plaintive air and their tearful wives wept. He played them the air of laughter and their wives and children began to laugh. He played them the air of sleep and the army fell asleep."[18] The druid god, master of animals, certainly knows the language of animals. It is music, which has no need of words, and expresses totality.

One can easily imagine Merlin with a harp, playing it to charm the animals. For Merlin is also Orpheus. Like Orpheus, he has an "infernal fiancée" whom he must either search for in the otherworld or rejoin in the green paradise of childish loves. But Orpheus made a mistake: he wanted to bring back Eurydice. Merlin, however, remained in Vivian's land of glass. The failure is on the Greek, not the Celtic, side. It is because the Celts always favored instinct over reason. Ulysses blocks his ears, or has himself bound to the mast, which is the same thing, to avoid succumbing to the song of the Sirens. Celtic heroes leap into the sea to join the fairy who sings. All the differences of civilization, of mentality, are illustrated by these two images. Ulysses is afraid to go to bed with Circe. He agrees only in return for strong guarantees. Merlin knows that Vivian is going to lock him up, confining him forever. He accepts this, because he has understood that the lost paradise can be recovered only at the cost of a renunciation, a sacrifice, the retreat from the world of deceptive realities: *the great withdrawal.*

A folktale from Upper Brittany in the form of a poetic children's story provides the key to the enigma. It concerns a little girl whose father has remarried. Her wicked stepmother makes the child work very hard, and the girl's only friend is an old blue bull. One day the little girl learns that the blue bull is going to be killed, so she runs away with him. They both must pass through three mysterious woods, and each time the blue bull tells the little girl not to touch the leaves of the trees. In the first wood the leaves are made of bronze, and all goes well. In the second wood, the leaves are silver, and the little girl clumsily brushes against one of them. Crawling beasts rise up, but the blue bull crushes them. In the third wood the leaves are made of gold and the little girl cannot resist; she touches one. At once ferocious animals appear and the blue bull has great difficulty slaying them. Although the little girl is safe, the blue bull is dying. He makes the little girl promise to bury him under blue stones and then go far away, telling her that she will be happy, but that any time she needs something she is to come and ask him for it. The prediction of the blue bull comes true.[19] The story's theme is very clear. The blue bull is Merlin, who sacrifices himself so that Vivian, in other words, the little girl, may know the lost paradise in its totality. This paradise can be reached only after undergoing trials. The blue bull, dead and buried under blue stones, is none other than Merlin in his prison of air, or of glass. And Vivian is always close by so that she can ask what she wants of him. Thus is brought into being, on a symbolic level, the famous dyad without which the paradisiacal world will not be restored.

"In numerous traditions," says Mircea Eliade, "friendship with animals and comprehension of their language constitute paradisiacal syndromes. At the beginning, meaning in mythical times, man lived in peace with animals and understood their tongue. Only after a primordial catastrophe comparable to the "fall" of biblical tradition did man become what he is today: mortal, sexed, obliged to work in order to eat, and in conflict with animals. In preparing for ecstasy, and during that ecstasy, the shaman abolishes the present human condition and finds again, provisionally, the initial situation."[20] This is why the blue bull, in making the little girl pass through the three woods, causes her to go back, symbolically, in time. The encounter with the animals takes place in a contemporary perspective, with violence and aggressiveness. But the fact that the blue bull is victorious, yet dies as a result of this victory, paradoxically demonstrates the great reconciliation. The little girl, who already understood the language of animals, is now, jointly with the bull, the mistress of animals and brings into being the Golden Age. From now on the Lady of the Lake, formerly the little girl named Vivian, will be able to people the world with new creatures, and nurture heroes and fairies in order to send them out to convert the rest of humankind. For Vivian, the Lady of the Lake, is always the image of the Good Goddess, the divinity associated with Dagda.

The bull, of course, represents a civilization of shepherds, in contrast with the stag, symbolizing a civilization of hunters. We know that the bull plays an important role in the Irish epic of the cycle of Ulster, around King Conchobar and the hero Cuchulainn, who were themselves marked by the image and name of the dog. The story of the blue bull is therefore an incarnation of the myth in a milieu of farmers and breeders. The symbol has a somewhat different value, expressing permanence as the stag indicates the alternation of seasons. Indeed, the bull is the image of strength and fertility, and also of war, because he is the most powerful of domestic animals. Yet he is domesticated and never loses his horns. He is related, therefore, to a sedentary population living all year round on the products of their land. The stag, on the contrary, is a wild animal. He is endowed with uncommon swiftness and agility, and has the privilege of shedding his antlers each year and having them grow back in the spring. This is why Merlin, in the form of a stag, better explains rejuvenation than when he takes the form of a bull. The wolf, also an eternal wanderer, an animal who "rejects the pact of cities," in the phrase of Alfred de Vigny, better expresses the freedom and receptivity demanded by nature. The stag and the wolf, who seem to be Merlin's companions and, most of the time, his symbol, embody Nature's immense virginity.

For that is surely what it means. Nature is at the center of the debate provoked by the character of Merlin in the midst of his different adventures. As heir to the druids, he is just as much heir to a kind of contract that binds man to nature. On one of the carved plaques of the cauldron of Gundestrup, the god with the antlers of a stag, who is seated in the position of the Buddha, is surrounded by animals who appear to obey him. The animal closest to him is a stag. There is also a wolf. And the god, undoubtedly Cernunnos, holds a torque in his right hand and a serpent's neck in his left. The same Cernunnos, however, is shown on the altar of the Nautes with the horns of a bull. He is, then, the god of two civilizations, that of the hunters and that of the shepherds. The torque is a sign of power, the serpent a symbol of knowledge. And above all, on the same Gundestrup cauldron another plaque displays the goddess of birds, that is, the Rhiannon of the Welsh stories, whose birds "put the living to sleep and wake the dead." We recognize in this Dagda's cudgel, and that of the Merlin the Wild Man. The goddess evidently knows the "language of birds." And Rhiannon is one of the aspects of Vivian. In that world of plants and animals in which they are confined, Merlin and Vivian are masters of the destiny of all living beings.

All of this has a meaning. It is not a matter of looking backwards and espousing a return to the past—history can never be remade, and original innocence cannot be recovered by going back in time. It is more a matter of moving ahead to rediscover the *equivalent* of that original situation. Alchemy teaches us that the raw material must be purified before it can be used to create the Philosophers' Stone.

The great lesson of Merlin's legend teaches us to move forward and to practice the great withdrawal that will lead us to the *nemeton* where all the optimum conditions have been recreated that lead to ecstasy, otherwise known as perfect communion with the gods—or with nature, which is identical. When Merlin goes mad at the battle of Arderyd he becomes cruelly aware of reality and can no longer stand to live in a world dominated by contradictions, violence, and illusion. The heartbreak he experiences is what has been called his madness. And so he withdraws. But it is not an escape, for in the woods he will begin to act upon himself and upon things to effect the transformation of being, the maturation that will bring him into full bloom. It is the same when he leaves King Arthur's court to find Vivian in the forest of Brocéliande. He knows that Vivian is going to confine him. It cannot in any way be an escape. It is the great withdrawal that will permit his metamorphosis. In society he was but a chrysalis. In the castle of glass he will be the butterfly who will draw sustenance from the sun's rays.

Why did Merlin accept confinement? Because he understood that to live outside of nature is to dedicate oneself to destruction. In the midst of the twelfth century, a time when the outline of capitalism already began to emerge in the new cities that had given themselves over to the exclusive power of money, the figure of Merlin was a warning. The bourgeoisie, on its triumphant path, and sheltered behind its walls, reconstructed a world to its measure. Its principal edifice was no longer the church, but the town hall, its principal place no longer the cemetery—symbol of the communion between the living and the dead—but the marketplace. A people that places its dead outside the walls of its town and abandons the sacred sanctuary for the temple of wealth, brutally severs itself from its roots. And, cut off from its roots, it no longer knows how to use nature. It thinks it knows: by exploiting it unremittingly—by clearing forests, digging mines, massacring animals, destroying the ecological landscape. The aberrations of the twentieth century are already contained in the steps taken by twelfth-century society. They result in an immoderate use of natural resources *believed to be limitless.* Now our scientists perceive that throughout the centuries humanity has lived in a misleading illusion, that it has lived above its means. So a cry of alarm is sounded. We howl about pollution and poverty. We deplore that the world is becoming sterile and desperately seek remedies for this terrifying evil. But the poets of the twelfth century had already understood this, not only in developing the theme of Merlin, but by stressing the description of the kingdom of the Grail— as a consequence of the Fisher King's wound, the kingdom's lands are sterile and the trees no longer bear fruit.

Above all, they explain the reason for this: the king is wounded, stricken in his virile parts. His impotence leads to his incapacity to govern. And if the king cannot govern, his realm cannot survive, the king being the balancer of opposing forces. We know that life throughout the universe rests upon a fragile equilibrium between the elements; if there is the slightest threat of a breach in this equilibrium, life is in danger. The same thing is true of the human body: the life that animates it is maintained only by an equilibrium that is constantly endangered. The only way to survive, both in one's body and in the universe, is to be constantly vigilant that this equilibrium between beings and things is never broken. But for that one must be aware, and not forget that at the beginning of all is the Spirit—no matter what entity is represented by that word—coordinating everything, keeping it all in balance.

This "naturistic" idea of life and the world, of which the poets of the twelfth century and their immediate successors attempted to remind men, had evidently been drawn by them from the cultural heritage of the West, in all probability the Celtic heritage, orally transmitted from generation to generation. Faced with the Roman pride that claimed the world could be dominated by force and nature made to yield to the will of man, faced with a Christianity that made man the king of creation, subordinating animals and things to his will, druidic doctrine pointed out that man was part of the totality of nature, and insisted on the interdependence of beings and things. This is why the druidic religion was classified as a "naturistic" cult, condensing in this word all of the contempt that civilized people, or those who believe themselves to be, can have for a primitive mentality.

It might be objected that we do not know what the druidic doctrine really was. Perhaps, but we know how the ancient Celts lived, and it is a generally accepted rule that religions reflect the collective mentality of the people from whom they emanate. Now, the principal character-istic of Celtic civilization, irrefutable because of the abundance of proof, is that it was rural, even sylvan, absolutely not urban. There were never any cities in the Roman sense of the word in independent Gaul, pre-Roman Britain, or pre-Norman Ireland. That is a fact. The Celts lived in forests or along the coast and the rivers, in very scattered colonies. The settlement of actual Celtic countries expresses this phenomenon exactly. Urban concentration was limited to places of passage and em-barkation, markets, or, in the event of war, to the occupation of strong-holds that were designed for that purpose but were only provisional towns.[21] The economic activity of the Celts concerned the countryside exclusively. And urbanization came latest and was least important in purely Celtic lands.

This rural and sylvan character of Celtic civilization is the indica-tion of a mentality that seeks to be integrated into a natural context in order to maintain a constant harmony. It is completely different from an urban civilization, which requires periodic harvests from the coun-tryside to provide for the needs of city dwellers who are themselves cut off from all alimentary resources, and who obviously do not under-stand the fragile relations that exist between man and nature. Today the urban phenomenon has overwhelmed the whole world. We are beginning to see its manifold consequences. Let us recall the prophe-cies that Geoffrey of Monmouth attributes to Merlin in the famous passage from the *Historia Regum Brittaniae:*

> *Men will get drunk on wine and will forget heaven in favor of earth. The stars will turn away from them and will obscure their course. Crops will wither away and water will disappear from the earth. Roots will turn into branches and branches will turn into roots. The light of the Sun will*

be eclipsed by the silvery light of Mercury. . . . The chariot of the Moon
will disturb the Zodiac, and the Pleiades will shed tears. Soon everything
will cease to accomplish its function, but Ariane will soon lock herself be-
hind her closed door. The ray's shock will lift up the seas, and the dust of
ancient times will rise up again. Winds will clash and their din will be
lost among the stars.[22]

Whoever is the true author of these prophecies, they refer to Celtic eschatology. Strabo says the druids taught "that one day water and fire will reign,"[23] but Celtic eschatology is clearly different from Germanic eschatology. It is not a "Twilight of the Gods." It is not nonexistence or the negation of functions, the degeneration of natural hierarchies, that cause the end of the world, but a dislocation of the field of action of sacred functions including, inevitably, respect for the harmonious relations between man and nature. Then, as the goddess Morrigan says at the end of the account of "The Battle of Mag-Tured":

I shall not see a world that will please me:
summer without flowers,
livestock without milk,
women without modesty,
men without courage,
captives without a king,
trees without fruit,
sea without yield . . .[24]

The druids had to guard and carefully preserve the world's delicate balance, both on the material level, by supervising the distribution of labor and production, and on the spiritual level, by a subtle play of rules and magical interdictions, and by maintaining a complex system of hierarchical values and functions. For Celtic society could have seemed, to observers who were uninformed or unable to comprehend the profound meaning of its institutions, to have had "anarchistic tendencies." It is true that it leaned toward libertarianism, relying on the free will of individuals. But that did not prevent it from being firmly structured in a way that was completely the opposite of Roman methods.[25] Indeed, its rural civilization predisposed Celtic society to be a horizontal one, based on the equal relationship among its different constituent groups, with a strong propensity for autarchy, if not self-government. Roman society, on the other hand, urban and developed around the axis of Rome, could only be of a vertical type, assuming a strong central power to insure the cohesiveness of the whole.

This Celtic society must be taken into account in studying the matter of Merlin. Let us not forget that before withdrawing to be near Vivian, he leaves a sort of testament with King Arthur in the form of various counsels, especially advising the establishment of the famous Round Table "that turns like the world." Arthurian society is a true microcosm organized according to standards that strangely resemble those of the ancient Celts. Having satisfied his political mission in that world, Merlin can cross over to the otherworld embodied by the *nemeton*.

For the universe of the *nemeton* is no different from the universe of the *sidh*, described many times in Irish stories and the vestiges of which often appear in the Arthurian romances. The universe of the *sidh* is that of the heroes and gods of ancient times, the Tuatha Dé Danann in Ireland, the fairies of popular legend, or even the subterranean world of the korrigans in Armorican Brittany. But there too everything is organized, everything obeys rules. On the other hand, the standards are not the same as in the terrestrial world.

Indeed, the *sidh* often appears as a universe contained inside a prehistoric mound or tumulus, or as an island in the middle of the sea, or even as a remote valley (the Valley of No Return where Morgan reigns, in the Arthurian legend) or forest glade. But valley, glade, and island are quite recognizable equivalents. There is a poetic vision of this in the Irish story of *The Voyage of Bran*:

> *There is a distant isle,*
> *all around it sea horses sparkle,*
> *splendid race against the foaming waves,*
> *four feet support it. . . .*
> *Feet of white bronze support it,*
> *shining with beauty throughout the centuries,*
> *fair land through the ages of the world,*
> *where many flowers bloom.*
> *There is an old flowering tree,*

from which birds call out the hours:
it is their harmonious custom
to call out each hour together. . . .
Lamentation and treachery are unknown
in the familiar cultivated land;
there is nothing vulgar or uncouth,
but a sweet music that strikes on the ear.
Neither grief, nor mourning, nor death,
neither illness, nor weakness,
there is the mark of Emain,
rare is a marvel like this one.[26]

And, of course, it is the land of "the joy that lasts forever," it is "a day of endless fair weather," and also a land "where there are thousands of women." Bran, who has reached the marvelous island, does not complain. "They entered a great residence. . . . The food that was placed on each plate did not disappear; it seemed to them that they had been there only a year, and it was several years. No savor was lacking."[27] It is, then, the land of eternal youth, where there is never any scarcity, where death is unknown, where there is no longer aggression but an eternal peace. The word *sidh*, moreover, though understood in the sense of "mound," means "peace" first of all. Time, especially, is abolished. This recalls that text by Plutarch describing the paradisiacal island of Ogygia in the ocean, where Cronus sleeps, in a deep grotto, on a rock that shines like gold. And "it is through sleep that Zeus planned to bind him."[28] The myth revealed by Plutarch takes on its full meaning here. On the one hand Cronus is the god who bestows life and death (he procreates children, but devours them), therefore equivalent to Dagda with his ambiguous cudgel, and his name is linked to the idea of "time"; on the other hand, since the Latin for Cronus is Saturn, originally the god of beginnings and king of the Golden Age, the paradisiacal state of this island is explicitly shown. Time is asleep, that is, abolished. The ideal conditions for the development of a civilization "like that of mythical times" have been reinstated.

It is remarkable that in the world of the *sidh* the famous Indo-European tripartition plays no part. There are no more kings, warriors, or druids. Only the third function, that of fruitfulness, is in effect. And it is often women who rule in this universe. This means that not only is time abolished, but also the traditional distinction between classes. The classless society is finally attained in this ideal world. Similarly, the separation between man and animal no longer exists. We return to the theme of Merlin as Wild Man, controlling the animals to whom he is bound by a new kind of contract, like Saint Blaise at the entrance to his cave; and preaching to them, like Saint Ronan, Saint Hervé, and Saint Francis making his pact with the wolf. Universal brotherhood is restored in its original grandeur; there is no more need to kill animals for food since the Tree of the World, the apple tree, bears delicious fruit all year long. And on the symbolic level, although integrated into the Christian mystique, the meal of the Holy Grail will express the same concept of the "feast of immortality," that feast presided over by Mananann in the universe of the *sidh*.

But how we arrive at this blissful state, in which all the contradictions of terrestrial existence are abrogated? Must we go back in time? Surely not. The myth of future time can be expressed as follows: since the world is round, a man walking forward finds himself really, behind his own back; assuming that he could advance at prodigious speed, he would be able to catch up with himself. That is obviously a utopian view, but it is far from absurd. The secret of eternal youth the *sidh*, otherwise known as the Fountain of Youth, is not found behind but ahead of oneself. All attachment to the past, all desire to return to it must be abandoned in order to move ahead, to follow an evolution that satisfies both body and spirit. Paradise lost is not behind us but before us, in the future.

Especially since Freud's discoveries concerning intrauterine memory, religions have been accused of profiting from this unconscious recollection to project it into the future and make the human race accept the harsh circumstances of its life. That does not explain everything. And it does not take into account human development. The present does not exist, since it is the ideal and abstract meeting of past and future. There are no more than two poles: yesterday and tomorrow. As yesterday can never be recovered, we must content ourselves with tomorrow. It is the meaning of Merlin's confinement in the *nemeton* in any of its forms—*éplumoir*, house of wood, castle of glass, prison of air, or marvelous island projected beyond time and space.

The shamans attained it through ecstasy, as do poets, creators of the most beautiful utopias, and madmen, no longer tied to the contingencies of all-powerful reason. Druids, with their pre-Socratic logic, their "barbarian" mentality, had discovered that great potential of the human spirit: to reach a point where what does not exist is more noble than that which does. For despite all our research, we do not know what matter is, or even if it really exists. The only reality we can affirm is that of our thought, for even in denying it one thinks, thereby affirming it once more. Tangible reality is a formula that means nothing, and the Celts, who sought pure reality behind the deceptive appearances of "truth," were not mistaken. But the spirit of "truth," originating in Greece, poisoned the world. Men have killed each other for millennia for the sake of a "truth" that is merely an appearance, and as such subject to the multiple fluctuations of the moment. Merlin, by means of his *great withdrawal*, achieved by entering into the *nemeton*, shows us the road to follow.

Anyone aspiring to the *nemeton* must act above all on the level of the spirit, the only scientific reality. And as the body is only a dependent of the spirit, and perhaps its contradiction, it will necessarily follow. On the other hand, as a being can be aware of its own existence only in relation to, and in comparison with, another, Merlin's initiative cannot be solitary. He must have Vivian, or Gwendydd, at his side. The dyad prefigures that classless society in which the opposition is no longer ideological or economic, but simply psychoaffective.

For Merlin's confinement symbolizes the rediscovery of an instinctual life. Civilization based on the Roman model, predominant until now, and leading to the advanced industrial technology of today, has discarded humanity's deep instinctive tendencies in favor of reason, however it is defined. Without entering into the argument of those who advocate reason against instinct, it is worth affirming that, in reality, instinct does not differ fundamentally from reason, since reason is nothing more than instinct reflecting upon itself. But the divorce was such as to cause these two functions to seem irreconcilable. As early as the twelfth century the authors of the Arthurian romances, propagating the legend of Merlin, made him an incarnation of instinct.

That is why Merlin assumes the form or wears clothing evocative of an animal. It is why he lives among beasts in the forest, the natural setting most favorable to the privileged exchanges he enjoys with them. To understand the language of animals is, above all, to adopt the thesis advanced by Jean-Jacques Rousseau that the origin of language is psychoaffective. To understand the language of animals is not to regress to childhood, although childhood has much to teach us, but to rediscover our instinctual side, lost by our ancestors when they chose the civilization of writing over oral tradition. For what is written is dead, frozen for eternity. It is no more than a sequence of abstract concepts whose truth is sometimes upheld, sometimes contested, and always suspect. What is spoken is, on the contrary, alive, constantly evolving, in harmony with an individual's deep-seated propensities—his instinct—which is, in the final analysis, reliable because it is capable of stimulating understanding.

In this sense, to understand the language of animals is to open one's eyes and ears (as well as the other sensory organs) to what nature is telling us. And nature is always speaking: it is only that we have lost our comprehension of a language that does not express itself in words or equations but by mysterious signs, those of the sensibility.

If a human being wishes to enter into the *nemeton* to find Merlin and participate in the feast of immortality with him, he must abandon at the outset all the logic with which he has been inculcated since childhood and trust himself to the instinctual life, the only life, ever, to triumph over suffering or death. He must also open his spirit to the messages of trees, animals, minerals. Poets of every age have shown us the importance of this contact with nature. But, being poets, they were not taken seriously; preference was given to the sensible song of scientists, often merely apprentice sorcerers incapable of foreseeing the results of their discoveries.

In this world struggling with its interior conflicts, torn by hate and fanaticism, by racism, violence, and greed, in contempt of the harmonious equilibrium that should reign between people and things—and among humans themselves—it would behoove us not to lose sight of Merlin's example, that his message might reach those who want to rise up out of hell, or escape the Apocalypse.

To listen to animals and speak with them is to discover a new way of relating to others, whoever they may be—a way of relating based not on constraint but on brotherhood. And it is to become aware of the respective exigencies of nature and man, to preserve the delicate balance without which no life is possible on this earth, poised to fall into the universal abyss.

"Everything leads us to believe," wrote André Breton, "that there is a certain point of the spirit from which life and death, the real and the imaginary, the past and the future, the communicable and the incommunicable, the high and the low, cease to be perceived contradictorily." That point is the *nemeton*, the sacred clearing in the heart of the forest where, understanding at last, like Saint Francis of Assisi, the great universal brotherhood, Merlin, enchanter and prophet, sharing the feast of immortality with Vivian in his castle of glass, has reached the summit of the Tree of the World. There, in the ecstasy of the eternal moment, Merlin sings for us.

It is up to us to understand him.

ΩOTES

PREFACE

1. *Brocéliande, ou le Royaume de Merlin*, produced by Jean Kerchbron, FR 3, 1980.

PART 1
THE LITERARY TEXTS

1. Concerning the situation of the Britons of the north, see J. Markale, *King of the Celts: Arthurian Legend and Celtic Tradition* (Rochester, Vt.: Inner Traditions International, 1994), 89–115 and particularly 91–94.

2. On this subject, see Léon Fleuriot, *Les Origines de la Bretagne* (Paris: Payot, 1980), 170–76.

3. The geographical notions are muddled. It is said that Merlin is king of Dyved, southwest of Wales, and one sees him in the forest of Kelyddon with the Britons of the north. In addition, we know that Gwendoleu and Rydderch Hael are chieftains of the Britons of the north, not of the Welsh. It must be noted that the oldest literature of Wales, written in the actual Welsh, is largely built upon frameworks going back to the Britons of the north, since they had preserved more traditions and, after the great Saxon thrust at the end of the sixth century, had taken refuge in Wales where these traditions were combined with those of the Welsh. Moreover, it is not clear who fought whom. Merlin appears to fight in the company of Rydderch and of Peredur, while the poems attributed to him feature his friend Gwendoleu. In the *Vita*, however, Merlin is the brother-in-law of Rydderch. In the passage in which Geoffrey describes him in combat "with" Peredur and Rydderch, the Latin word *cum* is am-

biguous. We do not know if it means "in the company of" or "against."

4. This detail of the fountain will appear again in the legend that evolves; Merlin's favorite abode will be the Fountain of Barenton in the forest of Brocéliande.

5. The same anecdote occurs in the Scottish legend of Lailoken. See chapter 3.

6. According to the Arthurian legend, Cystennin succeeds Arthur after the disaster of Camlann.

7. This episode is rather complex. It contains an entire mythology of the *Cervidae* family; the theme of the vengeance of the first husband (as in the first branch of the Welsh *Mabinogi*, in which Pwyll slays the man who had dared wed his wife Rhiannon, or again in the *Roman de Renard* in which the fox takes revenge on the badger Grimbert who had wed his supposed widow); and the symbol of stag horns as, simultaneously, an image of fecundity, a fearsome weapon (recalling the Paleolithic era), and an ignominious mark of cuckoldry. One must remember also the Gallic god, Cernunnos, with the horns of a stag, and the whole Irish epic cycle of Leinster, in which the heroes are Finn (from his real name, Demne, "the deer"), his wife who sometimes appears in the guise of a doe, his son Oisin (meaning "the fawn"), and his grandson Oscar (meaning "he who loves stags"). The Finn cycle represents a civilization of hunters. It should be noted that in the Middle Ages the stag readily appears in diabolical coloration, save for a passage in the romances of the Round Table in which Lancelot encounters a great white stag with a golden collar who represents Christ.

8. This detail is very curious. Not only do we find ourselves in the presence of the theme of the Wild Man who understands animals and lives with them, like the shaman and probably the Celtic druid (and as Saint Francis will do), but it is astonishing to compare the gray wolf with a character that other versions of the legend offer as Merlin's master, a hermit named Blaise. Now Blaise is nothing but the gallicization of the Welsh word *bleidd* (British *bleiz*) meaning "wolf." There is in addition a complete mythology of the wolf in the British hagiography, notably in regard to Saint Hervé and Saint Ronan.

9. Geoffrey is thinking about the future, for very soon after the *Vita*, he will write the *Prophetiae Merlini*, which will then be inserted in his *Historia Regum Britanniae*. It should be noted that in the versions of the legend in which the hermit Blaise appears, it is to him that Merlin dictates his prophecies and his accounts of battles or events, and it is Blaise who is

considered the author of everything that refers to Merlin. Concerning this, Fleuriot (*Les Origines de la Bretagne*, 236), says: "Geoffrey mentions more than once making use of an ancient British book. There is no reason to think this affirmation false a priori; in any case, we have been able to prove that in the case of the *Prophetiae Merlini* he had recourse to a text in Old British or, more accurately, in a language antedating the separation of British and Cornish; in fact John of Cornwall gives us very brief fragments of this text and an adaptation closer to the original than that of Geoffrey." See *Études celtiques* 14, 43–56.

10. At Saint-Gildas of Rhuys, an ancient and famous abbey that Gildas (Gweltaz) was supposed to have founded, which is probable. Since it has been proven that Taliesin was a historic personage, we now also believe it possible that the Welsh bard visited Gildas on the Rhuys peninsula.

11. In Irish legends, the goddess Morrigan (who plays somewhat the same role) often appears in the form of a crow. In certain episodes of the romances of the Round Table, it is said that King Uryen is the husband of a fairy (Malory plainly calls her Morgan) who can transform herself into a bird and comes to his aid at the head of a flock of crows. Morgan le Fay is the sister of King Arthur. She is the same personage as the Welsh Modron, that is, the Gallic Matrona, otherwise known as the mother goddess.

12. Prytwen in Welsh. In reality, it is Arthur's shield, but in some accounts or poems it becomes Arthur's ship.

13. From the beginning of the eleventh century, the belief that Arthur was not dead, but would return to unite the kingdom of Britain, was widespread in Celtic lands, notably in the peninsula of Cornwall (the historical Arthur's place of origin), according to essential testimony by the monks of Laon visiting this country. The island of Avalon (the word *aval* means "apple") is the counterpart of the island of Ablach in Irish tradition. Obviously it is the Blessed Isle, the Celtic paradise where the fairy women rule. This belief is also found in Greek and Latin authors referring to the Gallic islands inhabited by women seers and sorceresses. For political reasons (the role of the Plantagenets), there was a tendency in the twelfth century to consider Glastonbury Abbey as the island of Avalon. Around 1190, the alleged tombs of Arthur and Guinevere were even discovered there.

14. This proves that he was mad. The little we know of the historic Myrddin is that he went mad after a battle and hid in a forest. But this healing by the fountain's miraculous water recalls the powers attributed

to the water of the Fountain of Barenton in the forest of Paimpont-Brocéliande, Merlin's favorite place. In fact, the water of Barenton also cures madness, as attested by the name of the nearest hamlet, Folle-Pensée, in fact, Fol-Pansit, "that which cures the madman."

15. Here, Geoffrey's source may be certain Welsh poems attributed to Taliesin, unless the poems attributed to Taliesin were inspired by the *Vita Merlini*. In any case, one finds in the poems and in the dissertation the same spirit and the same literary clichés.

16. This is what Geoffrey asserts: "Gautier, archdeacon of Oxford, gave me an ancient book written in the British language [read 'Welsh']. This book, attractively composed to form a seamless narrative, related the deeds of great men, from Brutus, first king of the Britons, to Cadwalladr, son of Cadwallawn. And at the request of Gautier, I made a point of translating it into Latin."

17. In medieval Celtic literature written in Latin, the word *magus* invariably designated a druid. So it seems that unlike Aurelius Ambrosius and Uther Pendragon, who are surrounded by bishops and monks and who represent the pro-Roman side, Vortigern represents Celtic paganism and the anti-Roman faction.

18. The theme of the sacrifice of a child to consolidate the foundations of a fortress or city is known from earliest antiquity. We will refer to it again at length.

19. Erroneous etymology, or a play on words on Kaermerddin, considered to be "the city of Merlin (Myrddin)."

20. The belief in incubi (male demons) and succubi (female demons) who have sexual intercourse with human beings was widespread in the Middle Ages and was very useful for explaining awkward situations and irregular births. In fact, it is based particularly upon erotic dreams and nocturnal pollutions and goes back to the great myth in the *Book of Enoch* of the sexual union of angels with women, whose equivalent is found in Greek mythology (Danaë and the golden shower, Leda and the swan) or in Celtic mythology (the conception of Cuchulainn). The impregnation of the Virgin Mary belongs to the same theory.

21. Here Geoffrey follows the text of the *Historia Brittonum* attributed to Nennius. Its oldest sections date from the end of the sixth century, but in that text the child calls himself "Aurelius Ambrosius"; there is absolutely no mention of Merlin. See chapter 3.

22. At this point Geoffrey inserts a kind of dissertation in which he explains that he has translated Merlin's prophecies "from the Breton language to

Latin" before completing what he has already begun "on the high deeds of the Breton kings." We know from fragments reproduced in other manuscripts that these prophecies of Merlin are in fact translated from the Brythonic.

23. Merlin's behavior is precisely that of the shaman who embarks upon his ecstatic voyage to the otherworld.

24. Evidently the commentaries on these prophecies were extremely numerous. Even Queen Eleanor of Aquitaine and Richard the Lion-Hearted are mentioned.

25. In the *Historia Brittonum*, the author asserts that "the fourth night, the entire citadel was set ablaze by the fire of heaven" (chapter 47). "Others say that Vortigern, a fugitive, wanders from place to place, and that his heart breaks and he dies dishonored. Others yet say that the earth opens and swallows him" (chapter 48). It is clear that there are differing traditions concerning the fate of Vortigern. Now we have learned that Vortigern-Gwrtheyrn is precisely the same person as a certain Gurthiern, who left his name on the island of Groix and who, formerly king in the island of Britain, took refuge in Armorica, where he was supposed to have led a hermit's existence before being recognized as "Saint" Gurthiern and honored as such by the populace. See Markale, *King of the Celts*, 112–13; Markale, *La Tradition celtique en Bretagne armoricaine* (Paris: Payot, 1975), 75–77; and Fleuriot, *Les Origines de la Bretagne*, 171–72 and 278–79.)

26. Tradition generally attributes to Arthur the famous battle of Mount Badon, which marked the halt of Saxon expansion for fifty years (*Annals of Cambria, Historia Brittonum*) around the year 500 (no one is certain of the exact date), but the chronicler Gildas (probably the same person as Saint Gweltaz, abbot of Rhuys) attributes this victory to Aurelius Ambrosius. Fleuriot (175–76 and 247–51) wonders if the legend of Arthur was not born of the glory of Ambrosius.

27. Again the same theme of Merlin by a fountain.

28. We read in the work of the Welsh chronicler of the end of the twelfth century, Gerald of Cambria: "In ancient times in Hibernia [Ireland] there was an admirable collection of stones called Chorea Gigantum [Choir of Giants] because giants had brought them from deepest Africa to Hibernia and erected them on the plain of Kildare as much by magic as by strength" (Gerald , 11.18).

29. This is the first time that Geoffrey tells us of Merlin's magic. Until now he was only a seer.

30. It is the megalithic monument of Stonehenge, near Amesbury, in the great plain of Salisbury in the south of England. This monument dates from the Neolithic era, with the more recent sections from the Bronze Age. Certain of its stones come not from Ireland but from the county of Pembroke in Wales, several hundred kilometers away, which proves that the legend of Merlin transporting the stones is not unwarranted. In the last section of the *Vulgate* of the Round Table, *La Mort du Roi Arthur*, the battle that pits Arthur against Mordret (battle of Salisbury or of Camlann) and during which the old king will be mortally wounded, takes place here. Shortly before the battle, Arthur sees the letters previously written on a rock by Merlin: "On this plain will be fought the mortal battle that will orphan the kingdom of Logres." (Lloegr, in Welsh, really means England.)

31. This is the residence of King Mark in the legend of Tristan and Isolde. It is a stronghold occupied since prehistoric times and contains the forms of a Celtic citadel underneath the ruins of a medieval fortress.

32. At the end of the work there is a single allusion to Merlin concerning his prophecies, particularly the one in which he announces the return of King Arthur. It will be noted, though, that according to Geoffrey there is no contact between Merlin and King Arthur. In the *Historia*, Merlin causes Arthur to be born, and that is all. And in the *Vita*, Merlin merely hears the latest news of Arthur.

33. A more or less legendary personage of British-Armorican origin belonging to a tradition completely alien to the Arthurian tradition, as I demonstrated in *La Tradition celtique en Bretagne armoricaine* (109–32) in restoring the "primary saga of Lancelot," which is based on a German text from the end of the twelfth century that is independent of Chrétien de Troyes and is the adaptation of an Anglo-Norman original, which was itself inspired by an Armorican tale.

34. Also called the *Lancelot in Prose* is the *Vulgate* in Sommer's edition of 1907, which remains the only complete edition according to manuscripts in the British Museum. This *Vulgate* includes *L'Histoire du Saint-Graal*, *L'Histoire de Merlin*, the actual *Lancelot*, *La Quête du Saint-Graal*, and *La Mort du Roi Arthur*. The different parts obviously have different authors, but the whole constitutes a sort of corpus of the Arthurian adventures. No translations exist of the entire work, but there are some adaptations such as those by Jacques Boulenger and Xavier de Langlais.

35. Here we find the extraordinary power possessed by Merlin explained and accounted for. His knowledge is *diabolical*, but because his mother is

good, he will use this knowledge only for good. The figure of the en-chanter-prophet is thus established.

36. This explanation of the fight between the dragons is obviously very different from that given by Geoffrey. Moreover, no mention is made of Aurelius Ambrosius.

37. This is also the theme of the *Vita Merlini*, but in this account Merlin remains in the forest through "wisdom," whereas in the *Vita* it is through "madness."

38. In other texts Ygern survives. In the *Perceval* of Chrétien de Troyes, Gawain meets Arthur's mother. According to Thomas Malory, Arthur has his mother brought to him accompanied by his sister Morgan.

39. In fact the name Excalibur comes from the distortion of an Old British name that is rendered Kaledfoulc'h in Welsh, meaning "hard-edge" or "hard-cut." In the Irish epic tradition there exists a marvelous sword named Caladbolg, which has the same meaning. An inconsistency in *Lancelot in Prose* should be noted: in the primitive version, Excalibur was not the sword embedded in the anvil but a sword given by the famous Lady of the Lake. This explains the scene in *Le Morte d'Arthur* where the old king, wounded, hurls his sword into a lake where a hand seizes it. Thomas Malory's version returned to the primitive tradition.

40. This episode obviously refers to the theme that Boccaccio would later use in writing *Grisélidis*. It seems that the author of *Merlin* wished once again to stress his "wild man" aspect. Moreover, the way in which he describes him is rather significant: "He had a head as big as a calf's, round and protuberant eyes, a mouth that split his face from ear to ear, thick lips always partly open to reveal his teeth, turned-up feet and hands inside out, coarse black hair so long that it reached his belt. . . ." The same rustic appears in the *Yvain* of Chrétien de Troyes, in *Aucassin et Nicolette*, and in numerous Irish narratives, which proves that he comes straight from Celtic mythology. In addition, like the Irish god Dagda, he carries a club.

41. Recollection of fifth century events, notably the battles of the Breton chief Riothame (Aurelius Ambrosius?) against the Romans and the Franks.

42. It is the Fountain of Barenton, a sacred place from earliest antiquity, whose former name Belenton, or Bel-Nemeton, indicates that it was a sanctuary dedicated to the solar god Bélénos (meaning "the brilliant"). The word *nemeton* designates a sacred clearing, a sanctuary in the middle of the forest.

43. Other texts call her Niniane, a Scottish name, or Nimue (Thomas Malory). She is the future "Lady of the Lake," ravisher and teacher of Lancelot of the Lake. The author of *Merlin* claims that the meaning of her name is "naught will I do" in Chaldean. The character of Vivian seems to combine Merlin's sister, (Geoffrey's Ganieda), and the Gwendydd of Welsh texts, particularly the poems attributed to Myrddin-Merlin. See the reference in chapter 4.

44. Since Merlin from the time of his birth appears as a sage, it was clearly necesssary to return to the theme of the "madman of the forest." In this case Merlin does not go mad after a battle but because of his love. But the mythological outline is exactly the same.

45. The authors of the Arthurian epics are always concerned with the need to justify their accounts by referring to an older work written by a witness of the events. In other versions of the legend of Merlin it is his master, the mysterious Blaise, who inscribes the adventures, thanks to which we know them.

46. This tale is published in Barbazan-Méon's book, *Nouveau recueil de contes et fabliaux* (1831).

47. This text, long attributed to Robert de Boron himself, is in reality perfectly apocryphal and dates from about 1250. It appears to be the remainder of an Arthurian epic similar to that of the *Vulgate*, itself attributed (erroneously) to Gautier Map. One could thus suppose a Robert de Boron cycle contrary in numerous details and in its motivation to that of Gautier Map. Huth was the name of the manuscript's owner when it was being edited by Gaston Paris and Jacob Ulrich in 1886.

48. This curious character, who does not appear in the work of Chrétien de Troyes, is found in *The Quest for the Holy Grail* under the name of Barlaans. He has a brother named Balan who is evidently another version of the person. Balin-Balan arose without any doubt from Celtic mythology: he is Bel-Belenos, a solar divinity who can be recognized in the *chansons de geste* with the radiant features and blond hair of the Saracen Balan. The name means "brilliant" and has a connection to the British word for broom (*banadl*, afterwards *banal*, from a Gallic word which became balai in French). He is the hero of a late romance, *Le Roman de Balain*, which resumes this story with many supplementary details.

49. In other words, "of the foreign baldric." According to *The Story of the Holy Grail*, and according to *The Quest*, it is the sword of Solomon, bequeathed to the Fisher King by the heritage of Joseph of Arimathea. This sword has magic powers. Beyond any doubt the origin of this "sword of the

strange clasps" is found in the Celtic accounts of Ireland, the theme of the flaming sword of Nuada in particular.

50. Pellehan is one of the many names of the Fisher King, whom the *Vulgate* calls Pelles, and who is found in the Welsh *Mabinogi* under the name of Pwyll Penn Annwfn.

51. This theme recurs in *The Quest*, where it is Perceval's sister who must give her blood.

52. It is the lance that we see in the procession of the Grail, the one described by Chrétien de Troyes in *Perceval*, which is explained in the other versions as being the lance of Longinus.

53. This is the marvelous castle under the lake where Vivian, who has become the Lady of the Lake, will lead the young Lancelot to bring up and educate him.

54. This episode accounts for Vivian's abduction of the child later on.

55. The author says that all this is told in *Le Conte du Brait*. This text is unfortunately lost. It should be noted, however, that Merlin is not shown as dead in this account. Vivian can rescue him at any time if she so wishes. This "confinement of Merlin" is stranger in the Huth *Merlin* than in Malory's version, which nevertheless follows it closely.

56. This episode resembles certain Irish accounts concerning the enthronement of the king of Tara. The stone of Tara cries out and splits when he who will be the king sits upon it. But here the traditional element, which is Celtic and pagan, is not understood by the Christian author. In fact it is not a matter of a sacrilege or curse but of a true transmission of powers: when he sits on the Perilous Seat, Perceval is not struck down like the audacious men who attempted it before him because he really is the king designated by the gods.

57. In this case as well, the Christian author has understood nothing of the myth expressed in the ritual. It is normal for the old king to be overcome by listlessness because it is Perceval who is the new king.

58. We see the reappearance of this figure, who remains no less mysterious.

59. This is a specifically Celtic trait. Someone comes before the king and asks him for a gift without saying precisely what is meant. The king is obliged to accept if he does not want to be dishonored. Irish narratives are filled with misfortunes arising from this custom. In the Welsh narrative "Culhwch and Olwen" (the oldest Arthurian romance) Arthur is careful to accept, saying: "Anything you wish except my sword, my shield, and my wife."

60. There is an inconsistency, however: normally, young Arthur should be

two years old, but here he is a young man. In *Lancelot* he is crowned at the age of sixteen, which is standard.

61. The belief that Blaise wrote the Arthurian chronicles at Merlin's dictation is very tenacious.

62. This date corresponds to one of the four great Celtic holidays of the year, the festival of Imbolc.

63. In the actual *Lancelot*, and especially in Ulrich von Zatzikhoven's *Lanzelet*, the most archaic version of the legend, the marvelous universe of the Lady of the Lake is described in great detail. It is where Lancelot will be brought up by the Lady of the Lake. See Markale, *La Tradition celtique en Bretagne armoricaine*, 119–20.

64. Thus is the episode of the French *Le Morte d'Arthur* explained, where Arthur is seen ordering the knight Girflet to throw his sword into the lake. A hand seizes the sword and draws it down beneath the water.

65. This is also the only reference we possess with regard to the magic power of the scabbard of the sword Kaledfoulc'h.

66. It is, of course, the "sword of the strange clasps."

67. This seems rather incoherent, as the Lady of the Lake plays an important role later on. But Malory extricates himself by saying that the woman with whom Merlin falls in love is said to be "one of the Ladies of the Lake," which appears logical, since the famous lake of Vivian-Nimue is populated by fairy women.

68. This is the only text in which this character is divided in two.

69. This entire episode comes straight from the Huth *Merlin* and is therefore in the tradition of Robert de Boron. Note, however, that Balin does not perish after the castle's collapse, but later, during one of those stupid encounters that occur so often in the romances of the Round Table in which knights battle and kill each other without being recognized.

70. There is no mention anywhere else in Malory's text that Merlin is the devil's son.

71. The manuscript is from the seventeenth century. The text has been published in *Bulletin of the Board of Celtic Studies* 12, 19–22, and in *Études celtiques* 8, 328 ff.

72. As the general tone of this story is comical, not to say Gallic, one might be tempted to think of it as a joke. In no way is it one. The symbolism of the whale has been exploited in somewhat esoteric traditions. Here, the word *whale* is related to the name of the Gallic solar god Belenos (the Brilliant), and this interpretation can only be reinforced by the sun's role in the "fabrication" of the two personages. Lancelot's blood represents

strength and bravery, Guinevere's nails beauty and sovereignty. One can also speak of a kind of sacred union, since Lancelot and Guinevere represent the perfect couple of lovers.

73. Usually the meaning given for the word Gargamelle is "big throat" or "big mouth." It seems that this is not the case. Like the name Gargantua, the name Gargamelle has links with a Celtic word that recurs in Breton: *gargam*, that is, "lame," literally, "with curved thigh." It is known that lameness is one of the characteristics of certain gods of strength (Tyr in Germanic mythology, Hephaestus in Greek mythology). A folktale of Morbihan introduces a curious person named Gergan who hurls salt at his enemies, as does Pantagruel, Gargantua's son. See Markale, *La Tradition celtique en Bretagne armoricaine*, 25–26.

74. Rabelais interprets the name of Gargantua as a distortion of *que grand tu as (le gosier)*—"how large a throat you have"—as exclaimed by Grandgousier upon the birth of his son. It is known that the name Gargantua is a very ancient one, corresponding to that of a Gallic divinity, a giant by the name of Gargan, found in the toponymy (Livry-Gargan, Mont-Gargan, and Monte-Gargano in Italy) and in the *Historia* of Geoffrey of Monmouth. Gargantua has many points in common with the Irish god Dagda; he is gluttonous like him and is the bearer of a strange bludgeon.

75. It is true that during the early Middle Ages Beauce was the site of an immense forest, the forest of the Carnutes, according to Caesar the most important druidic center in Gaul.

76. The name Belenos occurs again here. Formerly Mont Saint-Michel itself was called Tombelaine, which is natural, as the brightest of the angels, Michael, always replaced a luminous solar divinity.

77. I have shown by my commentaries on these fragments of poems in the critical edition *Autour du Barzaz-Breiz* that I wrote in collaboration with Denise Mégevand (Paris: Payot, 1980) that these so-called popular poems collected by La Villemarqué are fabrications and plagiarisms. This is especially true of the fragments concerning Merlin, which are all more or less imitations of the Arthurian legend and of the Welsh poems attributed to the bard Myrddin.

78. In *Contes populaires de toutes les Bretagne* (Rennes: Ouest-France, 1977) I published a narrative of Upper Britain, *Le Pêcheur de Saint-Cast*, in which Merlin's name is cited as that of a sorcerer who guards a grotto of Menez-Bré, enclosing the water that gives life and the water that brings death. But this allusion to Merlin may be artificial, and in any case has no importance to the development of the action (116–26).

79. It is a ruined dolmen. There are many other "tombs of Merlin" in Great
Britain. It should not be forgotten that the Arthurian legends were located belatedly, and then through the bias of intellectuals, in the forest
of Paimpont. See my work *La Forêt de Brocéliande* (Rennes: Ouest-France,
1976).

Part 2
THE SOURCES

1. See Markale, *King of the Celts.*

Chapter 1: Merlin in History

1. The principal mention of this battle is found in the *Annals of Cambria.*
These *Annals of Cambria*, at least in their basic form, date from the tenth
century and must have been completed toward 954. They provide valuable knowledge of the periods when the Britons of the isle of Britain
were obliged to battle the Saxon invaders. They contain the famous
battle of Mount Badon in which Arthur was victorious, and also the
battle of Camlann, in which he fought against Medrawt (Mordret)—that
is, the battle of Salisbury of the Round Table romances, when the old
king was mortally wounded. Finally, under the date of 573, one reads:
"Battle of Armterid (Arderyd)." The manuscript dates from the twelfth
century, indexed as Harleian 3859, and also contains the *Historia
Brittonum* attributed to Nennius. But there appear to be later additions,
notably after the mention of this battle of Arderyd, where one can read,
in a different handwriting: "*Inter filios Eliffer et Gwendoleu filium Keidiaw, in quo
Gwendoleu cecidit, Merlinus insanus effectus est* [between the sons of Ellifer and
Gwendoleu, son of Keidiaw, in which Gwendoleu died and Merlin became insane]." It must be said that it remains strongly suspect. In addition, the tradition of the Britons of the north, trafficked in by the Welsh,
is known to us only by documents whose historical value is nil, such as
Les Triades de l'Ile de Bretagne. In one of these we are told that the battle of
Arderyd was part of the "three frivolous battles," because it was waged
over a nest of larks. Probably this is a symbolic way of saying that it was
a battle between the Britons themselves for trifling motives. Another
triad states that among the three horses carrying three loads from the
isle of Britain there was one who carried "Gwrci, Peredur, Dunawd, son
of Pabo and Cynfelyn Drwscl, to the funeral pyre of Gwenddoleu at
Arderyd," which would be an indication of Gwenddoleu's death in the

course of that battle. Another triad tells us of the three loyal tribes of the isle: among them was that of Gwenddoleu, son of Keidiaw, "who continued to fight for forty-six days after the death of his chief and did not want to halt the war until he had avenged him." It is clearly a matter of internal warfare among Britons. As for Gwenddoleu, in another triad he is ranked among the three bulls of combat, and we learn from another that he had two brown birds that wore a gold yoke and devoured two Cymry for dinner and two more for supper every day. The latter allusion is purely mythological and refers to an ancient belief common to the Bretons and the Gaels concerning bird-fairies who are supernatural beings and who, depending on the circumstances, come to the aid of some and attack others. The historical King Uryen Rheged and Owein (the Yvain of Chrétien de Troyes) are supposed to have had a "flock of crows," thanks to whom they were always victorious. See Markale, *Women of the Celts* (Rochester, Vt.: Inner Traditions International, 1986), 111–17, regarding the goddess of birds.

2. The Indo-European *qw* persists in the Gaelic languages as it does in Latin, but in the Brythonic languages (Welsh, Cornish, Armorican Breton, and no doubt, Gallic) it becomes *P.* Thus the Welsh *pymp* and the Briton *pemp* (French *cinq*) correspond to the Latin *quinque* and the Gaelic *coic.* The passage from *Cruthni* to *Pretani* is normal. Should we conclude from this that the Picts spoke a Gaelic tongue?

3. See chapter 3 concerning the texts relative to the legend of Merlin.

4. Jarman, *The Legend of Merlin* (Cardiff, 1960).

5. Pronounced *meurzinn.* Moreover, the British equivalent is *merzinn.*

CHAPTER 2: POEMS ATTRIBUTED TO MERLIN

1. This is particularly true of the poems attributed to Llywarch-Hen in the *Red Book.* Certain archaic forms led the Welsh scholar Ifor Williams to move back the date of their composition.

2. These manuscripts were published for the first time by W. F. Skene under the title *Four Ancient Books of Wales,* in 1868 in Edinburgh. Besides the two manuscripts cited, there is also the *Book of Aneurin* (Cardiff manuscript no. 1) from the thirteenth century, which contains the famous *Gododdin* and the entire epic of the Britons of the northeast, and the *Book of Taliesin* (Peniarth, no. 2) from the thirteenth century, containing a considerable variety of poems attributed to Taliesin. Some of these appear to be authentic and others the creation of a neo-bardic school of the end

of the twelfth and beginning of the thirteenth century. In 1956 I published a small anthology of these poems entitled *Les Grands Bardes Gallois* (Paris: Falaize), a work that has since been reissued by J. Picollec.

3. King of Northumbria, the first Saxon king to have attempted the invasion of Wales. The Welshman Cadwallawn II, son of Cadvan, in alliance with the Saxon king Penda of Mercia, drove him back and slew him in 633.

4. The isle of Anglesey, Mona in Latin texts, site of the largest druid college in Great Britain.

5. The Saxons. The Welsh word *Lloegr* designates the country conquered by the Anglo-Saxons and, subsequently, England itself. The word passed into French in the romances of the Round Table as Logres and usually designates the kingdom of Arthur, that is, all of Great Britain.

6. The word *Kymry* in Welsh texts designates the Welsh and, by extension, the Britons. Originally the Britons of the isle of Britain called themselves by the name of Brython and those of the Armorican peninsula the Letavii. The latter term has disappeared in Armorica, giving way to derivations of Brython (Bretonned, Breizh, Brezhonneg) whereas the word caught on in Wales, where the name Llydaw designated Armorican Brittany. It was between the sixth and tenth centuries that the island Britons lost the usage of Brython little by little in favor of Cymro (plural Cymry) from the old *kom-brogos*, "of the same country" or "compatriot." At present Wales in its native language is called Cymru.

7. Messianism always plays havoc with prophecies. It is obvious that this child could be any chief on whom any hope whatsoever is based.

8. Ywerddon is the Welsh name for Ireland. The Gaels of Ireland made numerous incursions into British territory. They even established durable dynasties in Dyvet (south Wales) and to some extent in Gwynedd (the northwest). British mythology and legendry show the effects of Gaelic influence. In the terminology of certain Welsh poems the Gaels are often called Gwyddyl Ffichti, that is, "Gaels-Picts," which leads one to suppose that it refers primarily to the Irish who settled in the northwest of Scotland.

9. The poem appears to have been influenced by a text attributed to Taliesin, "Preiddieu Annwfn" (The Remains of the Abyss) which describes a mysterious expedition of Arthur's in search of a magic cauldron. In this poem, "except for seven, none returns. . . ." This expedition is attributed to Bran Vendigeit in the second branch of the *Mabinogi*, and

there, too, seven people, among them Taliesin, return from Ireland. See the translation of the *Mabinogion* by J. Loth (1913; reprint, Paris: Les Presses d'Aujourd'hui, 1979), 39, as well as the commentaries on this subject by J. Markale in *L'Épopée celtique en Bretagne* (Paris: Payot, 1975), 51–53.

10. Forest in the vicinity of the valley of the Clyde, not far from Dumbarton. The Welsh word comes from the Latin Caledonia, an ancient name for Scotland.

11. One thinks of the *Vita Merlini* where Ganieda and Rodarcus send servants to seize Merlin. But there seems to be more here: if we understand it correctly, the apple tree in which Merlin finds himself (perhaps living in its branches) is *invisible* since Rydderch's nobles do not see it. Now, in the legend cited by the *Lancelot in Prose*, Merlin is a prisoner in the forest of Brocéliande in a castle of invisible air. The coincidence is interesting, for it suggests a knowledge of the continental legend by the Welsh authors of this poem, unless the continental legend had developed from elements of this genre existing in ancient poems.

12. The name Gwendydd seems to have no connection with Ganieda, Vivian, or Nimue. It means "white day."

13. Allusion to a lost episode of the legend of Merlin, unless we are to understand that he killed the son and daughter of Gwassawg at the battle of Arderyd or during the hostilities.

14. Bernicia, one of the Saxon kingdoms.

15. Here are several examples found in *The Red Book of Hergest*: "I am on the mountain. My warrior spirit/no longer drives me. My days are short/now, and my house is in ruins./The wind pierces me. My life is a long penance./The forest again puts on its summer dress,/but I feel weak and weary" (poem 10). "O my crutch, is it not spring?/The cuckoos fly through the air, the sea foam is shining./I am no longer loved by the young woman" (poem 11).

16. Word for word, "the Scot," but the word *scot* in medieval texts is often synonomous with scholar, because the Irish (the Scots) had contributed to the development of continental culture and were considered particularly cultivated scholars.

17. In fact La Villemarqué made use of two popular songs in fabricating this little "saga." The first concerns an event that took place in Melrand (Morbihan)—the murder of a young woman who had rejected the advances of a weaver in 1727. The second really is the story of Yannig

Skolan, of which the great folklorist François-Marie Luzel collected several versions. The name Skolan, despite some alterations, is found in all of these versions. It was sufficient for La Villemarqué to name Skolan in the first song to assure the linking of the two texts. In any case, the song of Yannig Skolan is astonishing. It contains more or less the same words. The wicked fellow Skolan goes home to ask his mother's forgiveness. His mother does not recognize him: "Your horse is black, you are all black yourself; his mane is so rough that it scratches; I smell the odor of burned horns; I have cursed my son Skolan." Skolan confesses that he has come on the devil's horse and will go with him to hell if his mother does not forgive him. She answers: "How could I forgive you? You have done me great harm: you set fire to my bakery, and burned eighteen of my horned beasts." And his mother continues her accusation: "You set fire to seven piles of grain, burned seven churches and seven priests," and above all "you lost my little book, my consolation in this world." It is surprising that La Villemarqué's text, aside from being arranged in terms of the Welsh poem, which he knew, is corroborated by Luzel in other versions. Had there been a direct influence by the Welsh poem on the Armorican song? One is tempted to believe it, so striking are the similarities of names and details. See the text of *Yannig Skolan* and its commentary in Markale and Mégevand, *Autour du Barzaz-Breiz*, 216 ff.

18. See chapter 3 for more on the legend of Suibhné.

19. The Celts began to construct temples only under the Roman occupation. As for the first churches of Ireland, they were inevitably made of wood. There was a kind of reluctance to build a solid edifice for fear of enclosing therein a divinity who by its nature had to be everywhere.

20. A word from the root *nem*, meaning "the projection of a part of the sky on earth," found in the modern Breton *nenv* (sky), the Welsh *nef* (sky), the Irish *niam* (sky), and related to the Latin *nemus* (the sacred wood). *Nemeton* is the "sacred clearing", the "sanctuary." The modern Breton form is found in the name of the forest of Nevet (Finistère). It can be recognized also in the name of Néant (Morbihan), but in a form fixed in the Middle Ages, the region having lost the usage of Breton toward the twelfth century. The image of Merlin officiating in a *nemeton* is the one that stands out in the poems attributed to the bard as well as in the text of the *Vita Merlini*.

21. The word *cyl* means "hidden," "secret." Cylveirdd may signify "lost bards."

22. "The House of Glass." There are many Celtic traditions about a mysterious glass tower in the ocean. One reads in the *Historia Brittonum* that in the course of a voyage the sons of Mile, that is the Gaels, "saw a tower of glass in the middle of the sea, and men on top of the tower. They asked to speak with them, but the others did not answer" (chapter 13). An Irish narrative, "Condla the Handsome," presents an analogous scene, as does an Irish poem of the tenth century, the "Destruction of the Tower of Conan." In Welsh literature Kaer Wydr, the "City of Glass," is mentioned many times. Furthermore, the abbey of Glastonbury, officially recognized at the end of the twelfth century as the Isle of Avalon, had been considered, as a result of an erroneous analysis of the name, the Glass Citadel. And in the *Lancelot* of Chrétien de Troyes, the country to which Meleagant carries Guinevere is the kingdom of Gorre, or Voirre—that is, of Verre (glass). In any case, the tower, the house, or the city of glass is linked to the otherworld.

23. Triad 113, Loth, *Mabinogion*, 301–2.

24. Except in a tradition indicated by Loth (*Mabinogion* 2, 20) concerning the thirteen rarities of the Isle of Britain taken away by Myrddin, son of Morvryn, in *La Maison de Verre*, to Enllin or to Bardsey Island.

25. For example, an eighteenth-century Welsh manuscript that we owe to the antique dealer Lewis Morys contains a fragment that without any doubt has its origin in folklore. It is about the visit of a young man to Myrddin, who lives in the forest with his sister. The young man asks the prophet's advice concerning the woman he is going to marry; Myrddin answers with an exceedingly ambiguous prophecy. See Caerwyn Williams, *Llen a Llafar Mon* (Cyngor Gwlad Mon: Llangfeni, 1963).

26. "Island of Honey," a poetic name found very often in Welsh poems of the Middle Ages.

27. Triad 68, Loth, *Mabinogion*, 2, 274.

28. Triad 101, Loth, *Mabinogion*, 2, 292.

29. This "antiquarian" played an extraordinary role in the evolution of Celticism. He collected numerous oral traditions of his time; he perused manuscripts, many of which have since been lost; but he *reinvented* a particular form of druidism by using many unverifiable sources and giving rein to his imagination. He was unquestionably a forger, but his influence was and is still very great.

CHAPTER 3: THE PARALLEL TEXTS

1. Nennius lived at the end of the ninth century, but studies of the Latin

formulation of this text date it much earlier. And, as one of the manuscripts—that of Chartres—was entitled *Exberta fii Urbagen de libro sancti Germani inventa*, which can be translated "Rediscovered excerpts by the son of Uryen about the book of Saint Germain," one is inclined to attribute the original work's authorship to Rhun, son of Uryen (Urbagen).

2. The *Manuscript of Chartres* was destroyed during World War II, but some photos of it remain as well as the edition of it offered by Ferdinand Lot in the *Revue celtique*. Two other manuscripts seem to be reasonably faithful to the primitive text: the Harleian 3259 from the beginning of the twelfth century, containing the *Annales Cambridge*, and the London Cotton Vesp. D 21 of the twelfth century.

3. *Romania*, 28, 337 ff.

4. F. Lot gives an explanation: Vortigern's magi can only be druids. Now, the druids had disappeared from the island of Britain since the third century of our era. On the other hand, their presence in Ireland is attested to at least until the end of the sixth century. The hypothesis is perfectly plausible though one might prefer to believe in a local tradition of Snowdon. But there had been a very strong Irish influence on Gwynedd, that is, on northwestern Wales.

5. Saint Ronan's curse upon Suibhné recalls the "satires" launched by the druids and the Irish satirical poets against an enemy or against any whom they wished to destroy. It is an ancient pagan ritual of execration found in British hagiography, notably in Saint Gildas's curse on King Konomor in which he called down heaven's fire on his castle. It is the same for King Vortigern, who was cursed by Saint Germain of Auxerre and who allegedly died, with his entire family, in his burning castle. It should not be forgotten that in Irish accounts the saints of Christendom easily took the place formerly allotted to the druids.

6. This is the theme of Penelope, herself an ancient divinity venerated in Ithaca. The woman embodies sovereignty; the king functions only as the virile man who shares her bed. Owing to a kind of impotence that comes from his madness, Suibhné is incapable of assuming the throne in the sense that it is impossible for him to have sexual relations with the queen, incarnation of sovereignty. It is the same in the legend of the Grail, in which the Fisher King, wounded in the thigh (that is, in his sex organs), is unable to reign; his kingdom declines, becoming the Waste Land. In the legend of Arthur, for a time the king implements Guinevere's power; but when Lancelot becomes the queen's lover it is in reality he, no longer Arthur, who assumes responsibility for the

kingdom's stability. One becomes aware of this in the rupture between Lancelot and Arthur: when the kingdom is handed over from one to the other it ends in tragedy. This is the old Celtic idea, so often expressed in Irish, Welsh, and British accounts, ancient or recent, in which power belongs *de jure* to woman and *de facto* to man, and then only if he is capable of assuming it to stabilize all the opposing forces. On this subject see Markale, *Women of the Celts.*

7. There is an identical episode in the *Vita Merlini*, except that Merlin imposes conditions on his wife's freedom. When these conditions are not respected, he takes steps to kill his rival.

8. The yew is a sacred tree in Ireland. It is the druidic tree, the preeminent magic tree. The fact that Suibhné lives in a yew tree must be compared with the poems attributed to Myrddin, in which the mad poet speaks of the invisible apple tree in which he appears to reside. It is the well-known theme of the man who lives like a bird, halfway between earth and sky. The first hermits of the Middle East also lived on top of columns and their behavior shares the same symbolism.

9. It should be remembered that the first Irish monasteries were in fact villages grouped around a sanctuary with inhabitants of both sexes, some celibate, others married, who performed all functions, both intellectual and material.

10. Suibhné dies in fact like the great epic heroes, killed from behind in a cowardly way, as was Siegfried, Achilles, Cuchulainn, and especially like Cuchulainn's enemy, Curoi Mac Dairé. See Markale, *L'Épopée celtique d'Irlande* (Paris: Payot, 1971), 130.

11. In *The Madness of Suibhné* another element is added: the fight between civil and clerical power, which seems to have had some importance in Ireland after its conversion to Christianity. The true story of Saint Columcill bears traces of this. Besides, it is in this way that we discover the problem of the poem Yscolan, attributed to Merlin. This political fight has its counterpart in a rivalry between triumphant Christianity (Ronan) and druidism (Suibhné), a rivalry that does not appear in Merlin's legend, at least in the form in which it has come down to us. A. O. H. Jarman discussed this problem in his article dedicated to the poem "Yscolan," based on the research of Donatien Laurent on the British legend of Skolan, in *Ysgrifau Beirniadol* (1977), 50–78.

12. Cotton Titus manuscript A 19. See *Romania*, 22, 522.

13. In the courtly romance *Meraugis de Portlesguez* by Raoul de Houdenc, as the hero is searching for Gawain he comes to a high rock, where he

finds a dozen witches. He learns that this rock is the *esplumeor Merlin*. This *"éplumoir* Merlin" [see note 6 in chapter 3] is, in the Didot *Perceval*, the dwelling built by Merlin in the middle of the woods in which he resides, invisible to the other Romans.

14. Cotton Titus manuscript A 19, *Romania*, 22, 514. See E. Faral, *La Légende Arthurienne* (Paris: 1929), 2, 348. Note that the three means of death constitute a traditional theme. An Irish legend offers a similar episode: King Diarmaid asks the druids to tell him how he will die. The first druid replies: "By murder, and the night of your death you will wear a shirt made of only one seed of linen and a coat made of the wool of a single sheep." But the second druid says: "You will drown in beer brewed with a single grain." The third druid adds: "You will burn to death." Diarmaid does not believe a word of what they say, but indeed dies in three ways: stricken by means of the shirt and the coat, drowned in a vat of beer, and burned by the Ulates. We see that in the *Vita Merlini* Geoffrey drew upon traditional sources. See S. O'Grady, *Silva Gadelica* (London: 1982), 1, 80.

15. It is a seventeenth-century manuscript, but the anecdotes and allusions relate closely to the subject matter of the poems in the *Book of Taliesin*. If it is not the original legend, it is at least a significant adaptation.

16. This is analogous to the way in which the Irish hero Finn mac Cumail obtained knowledge. He was with a blacksmith who had asked him to cook a magical salmon (symbol of knowledge); Finn touched the salmon, burned himself, and put his finger in his mouth. See "Les Enfances de Finn" in Markale, *L'Épopée celtique d'Irlande*, 146–47.

17. This is a theme frequently encountered in Irish epic literature and also found in the folktales of Armorican Brittany. Thus the account of the *Saga de Koadalan* recounts an episode where the hero, escaping from three sorcerers, transforms himself into various animals. See Markale, *La Tradition celtique en Bretagne armoricaine*, 182–83.

18. In the Armorican tale "Les Treize Grains de Blé Noir," the hero, pursued by the devil, transforms himself into grains of black corn which the devil, changed into a hen, begins to devour. But the thirteenth grain changes into a fox and eats the hen. Markale, *Contes populaires de toutes les Bretagne*.

19. The date is important as it is the festival of Beltaine, one of the four great seasonal holidays of the pagan Celts.

20. The French version can be found in "The Story of Taliesin," in Markale, *L'Épopée celtique en Bretagne*, 94–108.

21. The Irish heroine Etaine, transformed into an insect by magic, is swallowed by the wife of the king of Ireland, who becomes pregnant and gives birth to the new Etaine (Markale, *L'Épopée celtique d'Irlande*, 48). And there are many other examples. There is no doubt that in extremely ancient times the ingestion of sperm by women was believed to be fecundating, which explains the sacred role of fellation in certain religious traditions, especially among Native Americans and also Indians. The matter of fecundating fellation must be examined in relation to the theme of the Virgin Mary.

22. An unknown character. R. S. Loomis suggests it may be Gawain, Arthur's nephew.

23. Pwyll (the Fisher King Pellès of the *Quest for the Grail*) and his son Pryderi are the heroes of the first branch of the Welsh *Mabinogi*. Pryderi reappears in the third and fourth branches. He is the son of the mother goddess Rhiannon, that is, the Welsh-Roman Epona, and perhaps the prototype of Vivienne.

24. Note here the Irish word *sidh*, designating the megalithic monuments, those "fairy mounds" where the gods and heroes of ancient times lived in a marvelous universe.

25. It is the cauldron of inspiration and rebirth analogous to that of Keridwen. In the second branch of the *Mabinogi* Bran launches his expedition to Ireland in order to recover this cauldron. It is the same for Arthur in the tale of *Culhwch and Olwen*, earliest of the Arthurian accounts. The Cimbres, a very celticized Germanic nation, had a sacred cauldron, "their most precious and dearest possession," which they gave to the emperor Augustus as a sign of friendship (Strabo, 7.2). We know that it was in the territory formerly occupied by the Cimbres that the famous Gundestrup cauldron was found, one of the most interesting monuments of Celtic art. The inexhaustible bowl of Rydderch, one of the treasures of the island of Britain, could also be cited. These marvelous cauldrons or vases appear to have later been Christianized, before reappearing in the form of the Holy Grail. The nine maidens who heat the cauldron recall the witches of European folk traditions, as well as the nine priestesses of the isle of Sein, spoken of by Pomponius Mela (3.6), who are called Gallicènes and have the power to loose or subdue tempests, transform animals, heal incurable diseases, and prophesy. We recognize Morgan and her nine sisters on the isle of Avalon. It should also be noted that Pwyll was supposed to own a miraculous cauldron. In the

Irish poem "La Forteresse des Ombres" (that I published in *Les Cahiers du Sud*, 335, 16–17), this cauldron is described: "There was a cauldron in this fortress. /It streamed with gold and silver /what a splendid discovery. . . . /This cauldron was given to us /by the king's daughter." This king's daughter perhaps prefigures the virgin who carries the Grail, she who, from Lancelot's trials, will give birth to Galahad. But the Irish poem refers to the crafty struggle between Cuchulainn and Curoi Mac Dairé. Both of them take part in the expedition intent to seize the cauldron. The young girl, who is Blathnait, is taken away by Curoi though it is Cuchulainn who is in love with her. Later Cuchulainn kills Curoi by treachery and with Blaithnit's complicity. In "Culhwch and Olwen" Arthur must seize the cauldron of Diwrnach the Gael, analogous, perhaps, to that of the Irish god Dagda, a cauldron one never left without feeling sated. In the Welsh text of *Peredur* (archaic version of *Perceval*) there is also a cauldron that revives the dead, a role Bran's cauldron may play. There is such an intermingling of mythological themes in this poem that it is impossible to separate them.

6. According to the second branch of the *Mabinogi*, Bran's expedition to Ireland ends in disaster. Only seven people, Taliesin among them, are able to return to the Isle of Britain. See Loth, *Mabinogion* (1979) 25–42, and Markale, *L'Épopée celtique en Bretagne*, 42–53. The French version of "The Remains of the Abyss" can be found in Markale, *Les Grands Bardes gallois*, 76–77.

7. According to the earliest sources, Arthur's principal companions were Kay and Bedwyr. See "Culhwch and Olwen" in Loth, *Mabinogion*, 99–145. See also Markale, *L'Épopée celtique en Bretagne*, 137–52, and with reference to Arthur's companions, Markale, *King of the Celts*, 164–66.

8. He becomes Girflet, son of Do, companion to King Arthur in the French romances, the last knight of the Round Table to see Arthur alive.

9. "La Chaire de Keridwen," one of the poems attributed to Taliesin, refers to this anecdote: "The cleverest man I ever heard of was Gwyddion, son of Don, with tremendous powers . . . who stole the pigs from the south, for he had the greatest knowledge. With cut and bent chains he made remarkable chargers and saddles from the dirt of the yard." *Book of Taliesin*, poem 16.

10. This is typically a refusal of maternity. Arianrod is a rather strange goddess in the Celtic pantheon. Her name means "wheel of silver." But she appears to have some connections with Vivian and with Gwendydd.

31. In this way she acknowledges her maternity and implicitly, her brother Gwyddyon's paternity. Incest is clear here, as it is latent between Myrddin and Gwendydd.

32. That is, Little one of the sure hand.

33. In the strangest of the poems attributed to Taliesin, the "Cad Goddeu," which in fact contains fragments of several older poems, there is a reference to this episode: "When I came to life, my creator fashioned me from the fruit of fruits, from the fruit of the primordial god, from the primroses and the flowers of the hillside, from the flowers of trees and bushes, from the earth and its terrestrial course, I was fashioned from the flowers of the nettle, from the water of the ninth wave. I was marked by Math before becoming immortal [or "immortelle"], I was marked by Gwyddyon, the great purifier of the British . . ." (*Book of Taliesin*, poem 8).

34. See the account of the fourth branch of the *Mabinogi* in Loth, *Mabinogion*, 59–81. See also Markale, *L'Épopée celtique en Bretagne*, 59–76, and for more concerning Blodeuwedd, the chapter entitled "The Rebellion of the Flower-Daughter" in Markale, *Women of the Celts*, 147–72.

35. I published the complete French version of "Cad Goddeu" in *The Celts: Uncovering the Mythic and Historic Origins of Western Culture* (Rochester, Vt.: Inner Traditions International, 1993), 237–43, with all of the appropriate commentaries.

36. It is found also in the account of the death of the Irish hero Cuchulainn (Markale, *L'Épopée celtique d'Irlande*, 133) and in Shakespeare's *Macbeth*. See Markale, *The Celts*.

37. One cannot help thinking of the Gallic people of the Viducasses who left their name to the town of Vieux (Calvados), a name that means "combatants of the wood." The word *gwydd* (and its variations) comes from the same root as the English "wood." Note that the name of the Germanic god Wotan-Odin also springs from this root, as does, curiously enough, the Latin *videre* (to see). When one knows that the word "druid" comes from an ancient *dru-wid*, meaning "very visionary" or "very learned" (compare the Breton *gwizek*, "learned"), one must be impressed by the number of coincidences surrounding Merlin: the woods, the druidism, the clairvoyance, and the knowledge seem to meet in the *éplumoir*, the prison of air where he lives, remaining invisible to common mortals, yet seeing the whole world.

38. This very charming tale can be found in Markale, *Contes populaires de toute la France* (Paris: Stock, 1980), 214–17.

39. This tale and the commentaries to which it gave rise can be found in Markale, *La Tradition celtique en Bretagne armoricaine*, 219–23.

40. This is an anecdote very widely known in the British oral tradition. Korrigans (or *ozegaññed*) are a kind of goblin, neither good nor bad, possessing subterranean riches and magical powers. They often dance on the heath but cannot finish a song. It is up to the passerby to finish it. If he does, he is rewarded with gifts; If not, he is punished.

41. The complete text of this tale is found in Markale, *La Tradition celtique en Bretagne armoricaine*, 230–35.

42. This text can be found in Markale, *Contes populaires de toutes les Bretagne*, 264–69.

43. The Tuatha Dé Danann, or "the People of the Goddess Dana," are the ancient gods of Ireland, preeminent in the Gaelic pantheon in which we find Dagda, Ogma, Lug, Nuada, Morrigane, and many others. Mananann mac Lir ("Son of the Waves") is their king from the time when, defeated by the Gaels, they were banished to the islands and the subterranean world of the *sidhs*, or the megalithic mounds. A pact between the Tuatha and the Gaels stipulates that the surface of Ireland belongs to the Gaels and the subterranean world to the Tuatha. But the Tuatha often burst onto the surface and launch expeditions against humans who, not to be outdone, often enter the subterranean world to raid the supernatural flocks, steal magic objects, and seize great treasures. It is said that Mananann presides over a "banquet of immortality" in the abode of the blacksmith-god Gobniu. Be that as it may, Mananann is the eponymous hero of the Isle of Man in the Irish Sea and is found in the Welsh tradition, especially in the second and third branches of the *Mabinogi* and in the poems attributed to Taliesin under the slightly modified name of Manawydan ab Llyr, brother of the heroine Branwen and the hero Bran Vendigeit. Manawydan marries the goddess Rhiannon, Pwyll's widow and mother of Pryderi. In another version of the legend Mongan claims to be the reincarnation of the hero Finn mac Cumail, chief of the Fiana and father of Oisin (Ossian).

44. The phrase is Christian but refers to the Celtic paradise, the Blessed Isle where no one is afflicted with sorrow, sickness, or death, and where the fruit is always ripe. It is the isle of Emain Ablach, the Island of Apple Trees, equivalent to the Insula Pomorum of Geoffrey, that is, Avalon.

45. Mongan and the king of Leinster had sworn "perfect friendship," by virtue of which neither could refuse the other anything. The king had

given a magnificent flock to Mongan in the understanding that he in turn would claim a present from him later on.

46. Here we find the same theme as that of the *Vita Merlini*, in which Merlin changes Uther Pendragon's appearance to give him access to the bed of the duke of Cornwall's wife. The episode also parallels several in the legend of Tristan, in which, disguised as a madman, beggar, or leper he enters Mark's castle and spends the night with the beautiful Iseult.

47. *The Book of Fermoy*. See Kuno Meyer, *The Voyage of Bran*. The legend of Mongan has many links with that of King Arthur. See Markale, *King of the Celts*.

Part 3
THE DIVINE COUPLE

1. On this subject, see the chapter "Iseult, or the lady of the Orchard" in Markale, *Women of the Celts*.

2. I have given this title to the first chapter of my work *The Celts*, 21–36. See also Markale, *La Tradition celtique en Bretagne armoricaine*, 60–108, the conjectural reconstruction of the entire legend of the city of Ys from ancient texts and folktales.

3. See *The Celts*, 94–102.

4. It also has been suggested that the two words *mor* (sea), and *dyn* (man), are the roots of Myrddin-Merddin. He would then be a "man of the sea."

5. The word *artu-* in Welsh has the sense of "bear" (*arth* in Welsh, *arz* in Breton). A second root, *matu-*, signifying "ours," is found in the name Math, son of Mathonwy, who is similar to Arthur in many respects. See Markale, *King of the Celts*, 179–81.

6. This would explain, in part, Merlin's mysterious *éplumoir* mentioned in the Didot *Perceval* and in Raoul de Houdenc's romance, *Meraugis de Portzlegvez, éplumoir* having as its principal meaning "place of shedding" [of coat, hair, antlers, etc.].

Chapter 4: Vivian or Gwendydd?

1. In fact, the forest of Brocéliande was the great forest that covered the entire center of the Breton peninsula from the Arrée Mountains to the Meu River. There remain only some wooded mountains like the forest of Quénécan and the forests of Loudéac, Camors, Floranges, Lanvaux, Lanouée, Molac, and that of Paimpont, the most important in terms of

area. I explained in my small work *La Forêt de Brocéliande,* how this portion
of the ancient forest was considered, for essentially political reasons, the
theater of the exploits of Arthur's companions, whereas the Arthurian
legend is absolutely insular.

2. Unless Rhiannon comes from an ancient Rig-Annon where we find the
Anaon (the *trépasés* [the dead] in Breton), in which case she would be a
goddess of the otherworld, goddess of the deceased. Rhiannon is the
same person as the Gallo-Roman Epona, the mare goddess familiar from
ancient Irish or Welsh mythological texts. See Markale, *Women of the Celts,*
particularly the chapter "The Great Queen."

3. Furious because she has been forced to marry against her will, Rivanone
leaves her husband on her wedding night and curses the son she has just
conceived. The son will be blind and will become the famous Saint
Hervé. Here Rivanone more closely resembles Arianrod, who refuses
maternity and curses her son Lleu, than Rhiannon who, unjustly de-
prived of her son, spends her time searching and waiting for him. See
the *Mabinogi* of Pwyll in Loth, *Mabinogion,* 23.

4. *Histoire de Merlin,* Sommer edition, 209. To be fair, it should be noted that
in the edition of *Merlin* printed in Paris in 1528 this phrase appears:
"Nymanne est ung nom de Caldee qui est a dire en françois rien nen feroye." Now
the two syllables *rien nen* are those that most closely resemble the Welsh
name *Rhiannon,* read as if it were French. Chance, coincidence? In any
event, in the minds of the scribes the name Vivian or Niniane had nothing to do with French, since they felt compelled to explain it by means
of a foreign language, in this case Chaldean.

5. At this time Apollo defeated the serpent Python (telluric feminine symbol) and took his place at Delphi, introducing the masculine solar cult
to a populace that had apparently followed cults and beliefs linked to
gynecocracy. It should not be forgotten that in the Celtic languages
(as well as in the Germanic, and Hebrew) the sun is always feminine
and the moon masculine. In the story of Tristan he is the moon while
Iseult the Blonde represents an ancient solar divinity. Moreover, the
Irish archetype of Iseult, Grainé, bears a name that comes from *greine,* or
"sun."

6. *Speculum* 20, 426 ff.

7. It is the account of the courtship of Etaine. The heroine, daughter of a
king of Ireland, after a courtship by the hero Oengus, is given in marriage to Mider, a kind of god of the otherworld. But Mider's first wife

transforms Etaine into an insect which, once collected by Oengus, is swallowed by a woman who gives birth to the new Etaine. She weds King Eochaid, but Mider manages to get her back. See Markale, *L'Épopée celtique d'Irlande*, 43–55. Be-Finn is the name given by Mider to Etaine when he appears to her at night and invites her to follow him to his enchanted land.

8. G. Dottin, *L'Épopée irlandaise* (Paris: Presses d'Aujourd'hui, 1980), 75–90.

9. In the country, the adjective precedes the noun in place names. The "good spring" is Bonnefont. According to excavations there, the site, which is very isolated and in the middle of the woods, seems to have been soley a sanctuary surrounded by dwellings. It is neither a camp nor a fortress. In addition, the landscape and the location of the clearing (the famous Gallic *nemeton*) overwhelmingly recall the site of the Foundation of Barenton about which we will speak again. Mention should be made of a very important cult of the holy queen, who is simply the Christianized form of the Celtic mother goddess, in this region.

Chapter 5: Sacred Incest

1. Gawain was supplanted in the continental versions by Lancelot of the Lake, who indeed assumes the place reserved for the nephew, a sign that the archaic theme was no longer understood by the writers. It should also not be forgotten that Mordret usurps power by pretending that Arthur is dead. Now Mordret is also one of the sons of Arthur's sister, but is in addition his own incestuous son, from which the gravity of the usurpation derives.

2. There is no such thing as an Indo-European race, no matter what those who are nostalgic for the Third Reich, or certain intellectuals who do not even understand the enormities they propound, may think. Indo-Europeans are people, of diverse origins, *who speak an Indo-European language*, and that is all. It is a linguistic, not a racial or an even ethnic classification, since the civilization of the countries called Indo-European varies according to the importance of the civilization of the native inhabitants who were subdued by speakers of an Indo-European language. The Indo-European entirety includes the following linguistic groups: Indo-Iranian, Slav, Hellenic, Italic (Latin being only one of numerous Italic languages), Germano-Scandinavian (including Anglo-Saxon, which became English), and Celtic (originally Goedelic and Brythonic, later the Gaelic of Ireland, the Gaelic of Man, the Gaelic of Scotland, Welsh

(Cymraeg), Cornish, and Armorican-Breton (Brezhonneg). But Celtophones, like all other inhabitants of Europe, belong to ethnic branches that are sometimes very different.

3. Loth, *Mabinogion*, 209–10.

4. See "The Childhood of Finn" and "The Education of Cuchulainn," in Markale, *L'Épopée celtique d'Irlande*, 141–42; 88–95.

5. In fact, the Gaelic Morrigu (genitive Morrigan) can be translated as "queen of the *chauchemards*," or simply as "great queen," whereas Morgan comes from an ancient *mori-gena*, meaning "born of the sea" (in Gaelic that would be Muirgen). It is, moreover, the name of the famous monk Morgan, who hellenized his name to Pelagius, by which he is universally known and which has this precise meaning. But there are many elements common to Morrigane and Morgan, such as the art of changing themselves into birds, and the blazing sexuality by which they set into motion the human potential for action.

6. Reading the great Christian mystic texts makes one aware of this: sensuality dominates widely, but is of course sublimated, transcended to its uttermost limits.

7. The madman in ancient societies—and even now in many societies called primitive—has always been considered to be inspired by the gods. He was listened to attentively and had his place among the other members of the community. There was absolutely no question of locking him up. The celebrated office of the "king's fool," of which there are so many examples, even later (but by then it had become a purely honorific office, the fool being no more than the jester given the task of entertaining or amusing), comes from the idea that the madman knows and says what others are incapable of understanding. He reveals the future and is permitted the worst insolence toward the king. He is a kind of translator of the unconscious, and the role he plays in the life of kings is one of reflection and stability.

8. The details are important: the girl represents fire, while the boy represents water. In the act of love it is the woman (the sun) who is set ablaze and who desperately searches for moisture (the moon) to soothe her burning. It is the exact meaning of *The Quest for the Grail* in which the sterile and dessicated kingdom represents woman (the girl who carries the Grail) waiting for the young man who will make her fertile, and so restore prosperity to the kingom without a king since the Fisher King, wounded in the thigh—that is in his sexual parts—became impotent.

9. Whenever a prohibition is violated the fault devolves on the parents because of their negligence or their incompetence.

10. Mint is considered an aphrodisiac. This is the theme of the philtre of Tristan and Iseult, driving force of the plot and principal cause of the transgression of the interdiction.

11. The contents of the philtre are always absorbed by mistake or clumsiness. If it is drunk by Tristan and Iseult, it is because of an alleged error on the part of the attendant Brengwain. If the Irish hero Finn achieves knowledge, it is because he sucks his finger, burned by the salmon of knowledge that he is cooking and that was not meant for him. The same is true of Gwyon Bach, the future Taliesin: the three drops that fall on him and transform his psyche were not intended for him.

12. In this way they return to primordial life, the life of the human species in the age of its aquatic ancestors. They also return to the intrauterine state, a paradisiacal state. It is in this sense that we speak of "seventh heaven."

13. Orgasm is tantamount to death, well known since the work of Freud, reexamined and revised by psychologists and doctors. The union of brother and sister is so perfect that it is sufficient unto itself: they have no need to begin again because they have achieved the supreme goal, the total fusion of two beings separated for a moment (let us not forget that sex signifies separation, division), the phantasmal restoration of the primitive dyad or, if one prefers, of the primordial androgyne, corresponding to the episode of Adam's rib in the Bible.

14. It can be seen that the legend of Tristan and Iseult springs form a universal myth, and that the detail of the tree that unites the two graves of the lovers (sometimes it is a bramble) is not an invention of a medieval poet. It is actually the essence of the tree from which the famous philtre was made.

15. B. Malinowski, *La Vie sexuelle des sauvages du nord-ouest de la Mélanésie* (Paris: Payot) 389–98.

16. Markale, *L'Épopée celtique d'Irlande*, 76–78.

17. Markale, *La Tradition celtique en Bretagne armoricaine*, 109–32.

18. If, as we are told, there is only one God in three persons, the Holy Spirit is of the same nature as the Son. Therefore Jesus, in the capacity of progenitor, engenders himself in the breast of the Virgin. He is both husband and son. There is nothing shocking in taking note of this, and no theologian can deny these facts.

19. Another version gives the name of Ethné, but Ethné is just another name

for Boinn and Brigit. It is the same word as Étaine, heroine of a narrative whose mythological origins go very far back in time.

20. Oengus means "unique choice" and Mac Oc means "young son." Mac Oc represents a rejuvenated and renewed Dagda, newly incarnate, as Taliesin reembodies Gwyon Bach, and Horus, Osiris.

21. Oengus obtains the loan of the domain of Brug na Boyne for the duration of a day and a night. Symbolically, this period of time equals eternity.

22. The version of *L'Histoire d'Étaine;* Markale, *L'Épopée celtique d'Irlande,* 43–44. A third version states that Mananann advises Oengus to act in this way.

CHAPTER 6: THE GOD CONFINED

1. Dottin, *L'Épopée irlandaise,* 23–24.

2. Loth, *Mabinogion,* 30, 38, 221–22.

3. In fact, Glastonbury is a Saxon word (Glastingabiry) meaning "establishment of Glast"; the confusion was made possible by a faulty division of the name, so that it was seen as the English word *glass.* Guillaume de Malmesbury in his *De Antiquitate Glastoniensis ecclesiae* repeats some legends about the Abbey and asserts that, at the time of the Britons, the place was called Ynisgwtrin, or "Isle of Glass." Glastonbury, a true island in the midst of marshland and an ideal site for this type of legend, is in Somerset, in a region that was formerly very densely populated by Britons, on the road that goes from Cornwall-Devon to Wales by way of the low valley of the Severn. It is not far from the famous Plain of Salisbury where Stonehenge stands and from Cadbury, which is without doubt the Arthurian Kamaaloth. But it goes without saying that the work of Guillaume de Malmesbury was ordered by the Plantagenets. In 1184 the Abbey of Glastonbury had been almost entirely destroyed by fire, and it is Henry II who largely financed its reconstruction. To establish the reputation of their abbey and please Henry II, who had political motives for proving the truth of the Arthurian legend, the monks made a point of developing a belief in Arthur and the Isle of Avalon. And so, in 1190, the tombs of Arthur and Guinevere were found in the abbey. See Markale, *King of the Celts,* 73–80.

4. This myth has been taken over by science-fiction writers. It is not unusual to find in certain stories descriptions of strange cities lost in the midst of ice and snow, with a dome made of glass—or Plexiglas— protecting them from the outside atmosphere. In some cases this isle of glass is projected into space, like the "castle in the air" of popular oral

tradition. In the daily life of our times the myth is revived in subterranean "forums" and other covered commercial centers where a city
labyrinth, with its flora, and even its atmosphere and light, have been
artificially reconstructed in a setting that gives human beings a feeling of
security, and shelters them from the aggressivity of modern cities.

PART 4
THE MAN OF THE FOREST

1. In Welsh, a play on words exists between *gutrin*, or *wydr*, "verre" [glass]
   and *goed* or *gwyd* (from the old Celtic *vidu*) meaning "bois" [wood], but it
   is much less pronounced than in the French-language texts.

CHAPTER 7: THE SACRED CLEARING

1. This is the reason why at Entremont, a hill that dominates Aix-en-
   Provence, there is a whole city in ruins, built in the indigenous way, with
   a sanctuary. But the city, capital of the Salyens, was destroyed by the
   Romans in 122 B.C. and never used again. Its Mediterranean influence is
   evident.
2. The *Pharsalia*, 452 ff.
3. The *Pharsalia*, 339 ff.
4. Mistletoe is rarely found on oaks, and only on one particular variety;
   this adds to the value of oak mistletoe and its gathering.
5. See earlier references concerning the legends parallel to Merlin's, especially that of Gwyddyon.
6. *Dissertations*, 3, 8.
7. See earlier references to Gwyddyon. The text of the poem is in
   Markale, *The Celts*, 238–43.
8. M. Eliade, *Le Chamanisme* (Paris: 1968), 109–10.
9. Ibid., 220.
10. C. Gaignebet, *Le Carnaval* (Paris: 1974), 68.
11. See earlier material concerning the "divine couple," particularly the
    study of Vivian. See also *Ogam* 10, 371–80.
12. Eliade, *Le Chamanisme*, 127.
13. The *Pharsalia*, 3, 399–425.

CHAPTER 8: THE SANCTUARY AND THE SPRING

1. *Yvain*, verses 410 ff.
2. Loth, *Mabinogion*, 170.

3. In oral folktales the hero always meets the woman he is to marry in forms other than the definitive aspect with which he will fall in love. They are generally horrible old women, or monsters, or even animals such as does or sows. See "La Chasse au Blanc Porc" in Markale, *La Tradition celtique en Bretagne armoricaine*, 52–59, and the chapter entitled "Our Lady of the Night" in Markale, *Women of the Celts*, 85–117.

4. This chapel appears also in the account of Chrétien de Troyes, proof that the poet from Champagne had knowledge of events relative to Éon and the priory of Moinet. It is said that when the chapel was razed its stones were used in the construction of the beautiful church of Saint-Léry (Morbihan), a village located not far from Barenton.

5. Except for the Vita Merlini, the Historia, and the Welsh poems, all the essential texts of the legend are subsequent to the affair of Éon de l'Étoile. It would be surprising not to find in the character of Merlin the enchanter, as seen by the authors of the French romances, more or less faithful echoes of the heretical monk, especially in his role of magician. For in the early texts Merlin is primarily a prophet; he becomes a magician only in the French texts (with the exception of certain wonders accomplished by him in the Historia). And this is all the more true since Merlin is not a figure from the oral folk tradition of Brocéliande. Like most Arthurian legends, his legend was located in the forest of Brocéliande arbitrarily by scholars and poets, and for decidedly political reasons— first in the eleventh century by one of the lords of the forest, Raoul de Gaël, companion of William the Conqueror, then at the end of the twelfth century by the Plantagenet, Henry II, who wanted the support of the myth of Arthur to establish his authority over Great and Little Britain.

6. The establishment must have been destroyed in the second century of our era. Excavations indicate traces of a raging fire. There are Roman cannonballs, but no fortification has been discovered, no sign of defense. It would seem that the sanctuary had been savagely attacked. A local legend, difficult to explain in depth, speaks of a church that was alledgedly destroyed while people were assembled there. Obviously, the word "church" in oral folk tradition can denote the idea of any sanctuary. As this type of legend is tenacious, it is possible that it does not take into account an actual situation: the destruction of a druidic sanctuary by "enemies" who could just as well have been Romans as romanized Gauls. (This legend was reported by M. Roger Mathieu, a native of the Fontboine area, who for several years has been attempting to research all

the elements concerning this strange site.)

7. A local legend relates that originally the springs flowed at Rougères. The waters had great curative properties, but the fairies (that is, the mother divinity) had forbidden their defilement—they had particularly prohibited women from washing their underclothes in the spring (the eternal terror of menstrual blood). Since one woman was caught violating the taboo, the fairies dried up the waters of Rougères and caused them to flow at Vichy, where springs are still to be found. See Markale, *Contes populaires de toute la France*, vol. 1, 155–57.

8. The Latin word meaning high, *altus*, also means low. It is simply a matter of verticality. Everything occurs as if the world were deployed around a central axis (the mast of the world or the Cosmic Tree), so that the concept of depth or height is only a point of view. In an Armorican Breton folktale, the hero falls into a well and soon finds himself in a castle that floats in the air (Markale, *La Tradition celtique en Bretagne armoricaine*, 178–79). We know the formula of the *Tabula Smaragdina* (Emerald Tablet), a veritable résumé of esoteric science, which states: "That which is above is like that which is below." Under the circumstances, in the *nemeton* the Tree represents the junction of heaven with earth in its most subterranean aspects, for the roots descend to the infernal world. But to this has been added the spring, representing "what comes from the world below," that is, humidity, water, the possibility of life and therefore of fertility. For a land can be fertilized only with what is provided by death. This is the justification for the presence of springs and fountains in the majority of religious traditions concerning the Virgin: it is not unusual to find a well or a fountain underneath a sanctuary dedicated to the Virgin Mary, or in its immediate vicinity. In any case, it is proof that the Christian sanctuary was simply superimposed on a pagan one.

9. This is notably the case at Sainte-Anne d'Auray (Morbihan). It is true that the miraculous state of "Saint" Anne and the "miraculous" circumstances of its discovery by Nicolazic in the seventeeth century have more to do with genuine paganism than with Christianity. A serious rehabilitation by the Catholic clergy was necessary in order for the sanctuary to be one of the high places of Christianity.

10. The young women must say: "Fountain, smile upon me" when they throw in the pin. If the fountain remains motionless they will not marry. If the fountain "smiles," that is, if it bubbles, they will surely be married within the year. The fountain's bubbles are nitrogen bubbles, from which comes its reputation as the fountain whose water "boils, though it is

colder than marble" (Chrétien de Troyes).

11. There are also legends with regard to the "holes of hell" in various marshes. It is known that marshes are special places for exchanges between life and death, and therefore, traditionally, between the world of the living and the world of the dead or of the gods. This is true of the famous Yeun Ellez in the mountains of Arrée (Finistère) where numerous legends circulate concerning a passage to the otherworld. See Markale, *Huelgoat* (Rennes: Éditions Ouest-France, 1980), 27.

12. Dottin, *L'Épopée irlandaise*, 23–24.

13. "It is . . . regrettable that ancient authors, and especially so many modern ones, have combined in the same vague concept, tainted with primitivism, the *immortality of the soul* and what they called *metempsychosis*, even confusing *transmigration, metamorphosis*, and *reincarnation* under this label. . . . We must interpret the word metempsychosis in its strict sense: the passage of psychic elements from one body to another. We have no option but to establish at once that metempsychosis was not part of the Celtic world" (Françoise Le Roux and Christian-J. Guyonvarch', *Les Druides* [1978], 259). The same authors, speaking of the famous "Cad Goddeu," the poem on which the partisans of metempsychosis among the Celts rely, allude to the opinion rendered in the first edition of their book, the only serious work on the subject of the druids: "We ourselves were formerly on the side of metempsychosis" (260). The druidic doctrine is, in fact, so shrouded in mist that it is sometimes difficult to interpret the few fragments that have survived. But it does not change the fact that this doctrine is basically a meditation on the relationship between man and nature.

CHAPTER 9: THE RUSTIC AND THE MADMAN

1. *Yvain*, v. 287 ff.

2. Loth, *Mabinogion*, 169.

3. Markale, *L'Épopée celtique d'Irlande*, 114.

4. This is a detail often cited with reference to Cuchulainn in numerous Irish narratives.

5. Trans. Boulenger, 29.

6. If one takes a look at the history of allegedly civilized people, it is frightening to observe how many paranoiacs of all varieties have dominated one part of the world and caused the destruction of another. Alexander the Great, Julius Caesar, Napoleon, Hitler, and Stalin, to mention only the most striking, were bloodthirsty paranoiacs, which

does not stop posterity from erecting statues of them. One must believe that humanity loves its executioners, and in that case Freud was correct when he elucidated the sadomasochistic component in interpersonal relations. Of course one excludes the extreme cases such as Nero or Caligula, even Heliogabalus, but Clovis is still considered a hero and benefactor of humanity, at least in France (which did not exist at the time). This is because that the paranoiac seems to behave normally in daily life, whereas the schizophrenic takes things the wrong way and so considerably upsets acquired habits.

7. Some social groups in "developing" countries still know how to make this distinction, fortunately for them. But when these former colonial countries brutally integrate Western civilization, paranoiacs commit ravages there: the example of Uganda under the thumb of Idi Amin Dada is typical.

$\mathcal{P}$ART 5
THE GREAT WITHDRAWAL

CHAPTER 10: HEIR OF THE DRUIDS

1. Dottin, *L'Épopée irlandaise*, 17.
2. Dottin, *L'Épopée irlandaise*, 35–46.
3. W. Brandt, ed. Seghers, fifteenth-century classics.
4. *Polybius*, 24.5.
5. *Historia naturalis*, 4.27.
6. The tale is very long. I have published an abridged version of it in volume 2 of my *Contes populaires de toute la France* devoted to the Occitan region. The Basque version, which I did not retain in volume 2 of these *Contes*, is entitled "Montagne Noire" [Black Mountain].
7. Markale, *La Tradition celtique en Bretagne armoricaine*, 186–91.
8. There is a variation on this theme in a tale from Upper Brittany (a Francophone country) entitled "The Maid in White." It is a kind of much-abridged version of "The Green Mountain," but the episode of the maiden dismembered in the cauldron is respected. See Markale, *Contes populaires de toutes les Bretagne*, 36–47.
9. Other folktales concern the devil's wife, or even his "mistress-servant." This is true of another type of story, the "Three Hairs of the Devil" which the young hero must bring back in order to affirm his identity, and thanks to which he can eliminate the devil and marry his wife. The

version from Upper Brittany emphasizes the help given him by the devil's wife (Markale, *La Tradition celtique en Bretagne armoricaine*, 197–200). The version from Champagne assigns this role to the servant, who sleeps in the devil's bed (Markale, *Contes populaires de toute la France*, vol. 1, 91–102).

10. An oral tale of Upper Brittany, "The Thirteen Grains of Black Corn," describes a somewhat simple young man who has been the devil's servant and knows the art of transforming things and of transforming himself (Markale, *Contes populaires de toutes les Bretagnes*, 23–36). A tale from Lower Brittany "The Saga of Koadalan," presents somewhat the same situation, but it is because of a fairy-mare that the hero acquires the powers of an enchanter. He also succeeds in transforming himself (Markale, *La Tradition celtique en Bretagne armoricaine*, 169–85).

11. A peculiar Norman tale relates how a young man became a dog because at the seminary he had read a book to which he did not have the right of access. See Markale, *Contes populaires de toute la France*, vol. 1, 169–73. The belief in werewolves is also of the same order. A tale from the Vendée takes note of a man who became a "werewolf" during a church service (ibid., 266–71).

12. Markale, *L'Épopée celtique en Bretagne*, 96–97.

13. Ibid, 59–76. In the end Gwyddyon transforms the flower-daughter Blodeuwedd into an owl to punish her for the murder of his son Lleu.

14. Ibid., 210–15.

15. Méla, 3, 6.

16. Markale, *L'Épopée celtique d'Irlande*, 46–48.

17. *Celticum* 18, 324–25.

18. Loth, *Mabinogion*, 222–23.

19. This fantasy finds expression in legends like the one of the ring of Gyges as well as in the daily routine in which magic no longer plays a part. Indeed, two-way mirrors and internal television circuits widely used in modern civilization are made so that one can see (and even spy upon) without being seen.

20. *Oratio*, 49.

21. *De bello Gallico*, 7, 33. Royalty no longer existed among the Gauls in Caesar's time. The chieftains were elected magistrates, but the importance of the priestly class was no less strong because of it.

22. This text is found in the famous manuscript entitled the *Livre Jaune* of Lecan, col. 310, *Revue celtique* 23, 396 ff.

23. We are reminded of Don Quixote tilting at windmills. It should not be

forgotten that Cervantes was brought up on ancient popular traditions, and that it was never his intention to ridicule the character of Don Quixote. The latter's madness is in fact related to Merlin's, for it is a sacred madness, a kind of confinement in a separate world.

24. In "The Death of Cuchulainn" the hero is invited by a witch to eat roasted dog. One of his prohibitions consists of never refusing an invitation to dinner. But by accepting, he violates another major taboo: not to eat dog, the animal whose name he bears (Cu-Chulainn, "the Dog of Culann"). From then on he violates all the other interdictions and must of necessity die (Markale, *L'Épopée celtique d'Irlande*, 131–37). After Diarmaid, hero of another Irish narrative, has run away with Grainné, wife of Finn, the old king pursues and finds them. To make Diarmaid come out of his cave, Finn obliges him to accept an invitation to the hunt, which he cannot refuse. But Diarmaid thereby violates the ban on killing wild boar, and it leads to his death (ibid., 162–64). In "The Destruction of the House of Da Derga" the king of Ireland, Conair the Great, violates a taboo: he is immediately obliged to transgress all the others, and in the end he dies (ibid., 171–84).

CHAPTER 11: THE MASTER OF WORLDS, OR NATURE RECONCILED

1. Every carnivalesque celebration emphasizes the breath, sometimes in an apparently derisory way, in a kind of inversion. For all carnival feasts include the ingestion of flatulent foods, as if to insist on the importance of the breath "down below," equivalent to the breath above. Belief in the departure of souls through the anus was very widespread during ancient and medieval times. It is repeated in all of the works of Rabelais; the character of Gargantua, a carnival hero if ever there was one, is the living symbol of it. The role of blacksmiths in all these traditions should also be cited, for they are not only masters of fire but also masters of breath, thanks to their bellows. And fire cannot exist without breath. So we come again to alchemy, where Spirit or breath appears as the fifth element, the fourth element existing only because breath gives life to the first three, for fire is merely the transformation of other elements.

2. Traces of this belief are found in a passage from Titus Livius regarding a Roman expedition to Cisalpine Gaul. When the consul Postumius led his army into a forest, all of its trees fell on the Romans, who all perished in this catastrophe. It is difficult to imagine all the trees of the forest being sawed through in advance and falling all together on the Romans.

We must be dealing with the same mythical theme as in the Battle of the Trees.

3. Loth, *Mabinogion*, 73–74.

4. Markale, *Contes populaires de toutes les Bretagne*, 30.

5. *Tale of Etaine*, see *Celticum* 15, 321.

6. Markale, *L'Épopée celtique d'Irlande*, 192–95.

7. Ibid., 135; Dottin, *L'Épopée irlandaise*, 153–55.

8. As in the story of Condlé le Beau: a fairy who has fallen in love with the king's son brings him an apple, and from that moment the young man is overcome with an illness of languor until such time as the fairy comes back for him. In "The Voyage of Bran" it is a branch from an apple tree that a fairy brings to Bran to make him decide to leave. Dottin, *L'Épopée irlandaise*, 37.

9. Eliade, *Le Chamanisme*, 146.

10. *Yvain*, v. 334 ff.

11. Loth, *Mabinogion*, 169–70.

12. In the Musée de Cluny, Paris.

13. A silver cauldron decorated with numerous representations of mythological personages, in the museum of Copenhagen. It probably dates from the second century A.D. and does not reflect any Roman influence.

14. Gaignebet, *Le Carnaval*, 136.

15. We have evidence of this in "The Siege of Druim Damhgaire." The famous druid Mog Ruith has brought to him his "hide of a bull" and a headdress in the form of a bird. By means of these, he can fly away. Markale, *L'Épopée celtique d'Irlande*, 193.

16. It is also said that when he was in prison a woman sacrificed her pig for him and brought him the animal's head and feet, with a loaf of bread and a candle. Blaise blessed the woman and promised her an abundance of benefits and light for the entire year. It is obviously a fertility rite connected with Candlemas.

17. Eliade, *Le Chamanisme*, 92–93.

18. Dottin, *L'Épopée irlandaise*, 30.

19. One can read this story, *"Le Taureau bleu,"* in Markale, *Contes populaires de toutes les Bretagne*, 143–49. Characterized by a restrained beauty and great mythological and philosophical import, this tale can be considered one of the masterpieces of popular literature. There is also a Burgundian version of the story, "La Petite Annette," in Markale, *Contes populaires de toute la France*, vol. 1, 125–31.

20. Eliade, *Le Chamanisme*, 93.

21. A typical example is the Camp of Artus in the forest of Huelgoat (Finistère). An impregnable fortress, the camp was used only during periods of war, notably in 56 B.C. at the moment of the Armorican revolt against Caesar, as a gathering place for neighboring populations. But one finds no trace of urbanization as such. Urbanization is more overt in the Mediterranean area, in Entremont, for example, above Aix-en-Provence.

22. *Historia Regum Britanniae*, 5.

23. Strabo, 4.4.

24. Dottin, *L'Épopée irlandaise*, 31.

25. On this subject, see the last part of my book *King of the Celts*, which attempts to make the same point concerning the historical and philosophical premises of this topic.

26. Dottin, *L'Épopée irlandaise*, 37–41.

27. *Sur l'autre face de la Lune*, 26.

28. Ibid., 46.

INDEX

Abelard, 90

Alain, 24

Alchemy, 145–146, 170, 216(n1)

Ambrosius Aurelianus (Embreis Guletic, Emrys Gwledig), 8, 10–11, 55, 57–58, 78
   and battle of Mount Badon, 184(n26)
   See also Myrddin Emrys

Aneurin, 37, 40, 43, 46

Animals
   druidism and, 161–165
   Merlin and, 177–178
   in mythology/folklore, 163, 167–169, 191–192(n1), 217(n19)
   See also Nature

Anna, 11. *See also* Morgan le Fay

Annals of Cambria, 39, 42, 191–192(n1)

Antor (Hector), 15, 26

"Apple Trees, The," 44, 46–49

Arcluyd, kingdom of, 38–39

Arderyd, battle of, 37, 39–40, 41, 43
   Annals of Cambria on, 191–192(n1)
   and Merlin's poems, 45–46, 93

Argyll, kingdom of, 38

Arianrod, 68, 88, 201(n30), 205(n3)
   and incest, 95, 202(n31)

Armes Prydein, 53

Armorican Brittany
   folklore/myth from, 51, 70–72, 76–77, 146, 194–195(n17)

Merlin and history of, viii–ix, 82–83
   names for, 193(n6)
   See also Brocéliande, forest of

Art, son of King Conn, 108

Arthur, King
   battle of Mount Badon, 184(n26)
   battle of Salisbury, 185(n30)
   connection with Taliesin, 65–66
   crowning of, 188–189(n60)
   in "Culhwch and Olwen," 200–201(n25)
   in Didot *Perceval*, 25
   etymology of "Arthur," 78, 204(n5)
   Guinevere and power of, 197–198(n6)
   in *Historia Regum Britanniae*, 11
   historical figure of, 36
   and historical Merlin, 45
   in Huth *Merlin*, 21
   and incest, 94
   in *Lancelot in Prose*, 15–16, 19
   in *Le Morte d'Arthur*, 26–29
   and Merlin, 154, 185(n32)
   in *The Real Gargantua*, 32, 33
   return of, 182(n13)
   in *Vita Merlini*, 5

Arthurian/Round Table legends
   early literary texts, 6, 25–26
   entrance of Merlin into, 12
   political use of, viii–ix, 7, 211(n5)

Attis, 99

Aucassin and Nicolette, 133